ECOTOURISTS
SAVE THE WORLD

ECOTOURISTS
SAVE THE WORLD

The Environmental Volunteer's Guide to
More Than 300 International Adventures to Conserve,
Preserve, and Rehabilitate Wildlife and Habitats

Pamela K. Brodowsky
and the National Wildlife Federation

A PERIGEE BOOK

A PERIGEE BOOK
Published by the Penguin Group
Penguin Group (USA) Inc.
375 Hudson Street, New York, New York 10014, USA
Penguin Group (Canada), 90 Eglinton Avenue East, Suite 700, Toronto, Ontario M4P 2Y3, Canada
(a division of Pearson Penguin Canada Inc.)
Penguin Books Ltd., 80 Strand, London WC2R 0RL, England
Penguin Group Ireland, 25 St. Stephen's Green, Dublin 2, Ireland (a division of Penguin Books Ltd.)
Penguin Group (Australia), 250 Camberwell Road, Camberwell, Victoria 3124, Australia
(a division of Pearson Australia Group Pty. Ltd.)
Penguin Books India Pvt. Ltd., 11 Community Centre, Panchsheel Park, New Delhi—110 017, India
Penguin Group (NZ), 67 Apollo Drive, Rosedale, North Shore 0632, New Zealand
(a division of Pearson New Zealand Ltd.)
Penguin Books (South Africa) (Pty.) Ltd., 24 Sturdee Avenue, Rosebank, Johannesburg 2196, South Africa
Penguin Books Ltd., Registered Offices: 80 Strand, London WC2R 0RL, England

While the author has made every effort to provide accurate telephone numbers and Internet addresses at the time of publication, neither the publisher nor the author assumes any responsibility for errors, or for changes that occur after publication. Further, the publisher does not have any control over and does not assume any responsibility for author or third-party websites or their content.

First edition: April 2010

Library of Congress Cataloging-in-Publication Data

Brodowsky, Pamela K.
  Ecotourists save the world : the environmental volunteer's guide to more than 300 international adventures to conserve, preserve, and rehabilitate wildlife and habitats / Pamela K. Brodowsky and the National Wildlife Federation.
    p. cm.
  Includes index.
  ISBN 978-0-399-53576-5
  1. Ecotourism—Guidebooks.   2. Voluntarism—Guidebooks.   3. Environmentalism—Guidebooks.
4. Nature conservation—Guidebooks.   I. National Wildlife Federation.   II. Title.
  G156.5.E26B76 2010
  363.7'0574—dc22   2009044860

PRINTED IN THE UNITED STATES OF AMERICA
10 9 8 7 6 5 4 3 2 1

Outdoor recreational activities are by their very nature potentially hazardous. All participants in such activities must assume the responsibility for their own actions and safety. If you have any health problems or medical conditions, consult with your physician before undertaking any outdoor activities. The information contained in this guide book cannot replace sound judgment and good decision making, which can help reduce risk exposure, nor does the scope of this book allow for disclosure of all the potential hazards and risks involved in such activities. Learn as much as possible about the outdoor recreational activities in which you participate, prepare for the unexpected, and be cautious. The reward will be a safer and more enjoyable experience.

Most Perigee books are available at special quantity discounts for bulk purchases for sales promotions, premiums, fund-raising, or educational use. Special books, or book excerpts, can also be created to fit specific needs. For details, write: Special Markets, Penguin Group (USA) Inc., 375 Hudson Street, New York, New York 10014.

A sincere thank-you to all who donate their time and energy to our world's wildlife and the habitats in which they live.

ACKNOWLEDGMENTS

With our deepest gratitude we would like to thank the entire group at Perigee for their contributions, time, and efforts, which have clearly made this book possible. A very special thank-you goes to our publisher John Duff; associate editor Jeanette Shaw; editorial intern Brian Sweeney; senior designer Tiffany Estreicher; copyeditor Candace Levy; and associate art director Benjamin Gibson for the cover design.

CONTENTS

INTRODUCTION

Did you know . . . one in three amphibians, nearly half of all turtles and tortoises, one in four mammals, one in five sharks and rays, and one in eight bird species are now considered at risk of extinction? Habitat destruction, exploitation, pollution, and climate change are taking their toll on our world's species and the places that they inhabit.

On a lighter note, it's not too late. There is still time to save the majority of species if conservation organizations and eco-concerned individuals pull together and commit to lending a hand to wildlife and habitats in need.

Ecotourists Save the World is a book for every conservation-minded citizen, eco-adventurer, or wildlife enthusiast—an international travel guide to more than 300 volunteer opportunities that work to make a difference in the lives of our world's wildlife and help preserve the habitats in which they live.

From assisting scientists with a study of the affects of climate change and habitat loss of the mammals of Nova Scotia to hand-feeding orphaned lion cubs in a rescue sanctuary in Africa, tracking the wild elephant herds in Asia, and restoring the lost rain forests of Costa Rica, there is a hands-on experience for everyone willing to give back. *Ecotourists Save the World* pays particular attention to opportunities that can make a difference for our species, our planet, and ultimately future generations.

THINGS YOU SHOULD KNOW

This guide is arranged generally by continent. In some instances—for example, Australia—we have included territories that, while not technically part of that continent, fit quite naturally into the geographical region. The listings for each continent are then arranged alphabetically by site name or, as in larger territories such as the United States, arranged alphabetically first by state and second by site name. In addition to the project description, each listing contains information on the point of contact, location, volunteer category, cost, dates and duration, how to apply, and field notes.

CONTACT. Gives direct contact information, such as address, telephone numbers, website, and email addresses.

LOCATION. In most instances, lists the specific location of the volunteer position. In cases in which the volunteer position is remote, lists the rendezvous point at which you will meet with your volunteer team and project coordinator.

CATEGORY. States the specific volunteer category, such as conservation, preservation, or rehabilitation.

COST. Provides an approximate estimate of what it costs to participate in the volunteer opportunity for the selected program length. This section also includes provisions made by the sponsor for such things as housing and training.

DATES & DURATION. Provides specific time frames for open positions.

TO APPLY. Supplies information on the best way to initiate contact for application to open positions.

FIELD NOTES. Provides useful information regarding the volunteer position, including whether the project is suitable for families, groups, and/or solo travelers; any age restrictions; special skills or other requirements needed to participate; cautions or warnings for safety and comfort; and, in some instances, recommendations for local sites to visit and activities to enjoy while in service.

NOTES FOR AMERICANS TRAVELING ABROAD

The US government encourages travelers to register with the Department of State. This is a precautionary measure taken in the event of an emergency in the United States or in the country you are visiting so that you can be contacted if needed. Registration is a free service and is easily accomplished online at https://travel registration.state.gov.

Many countries have restrictions on what may be imported. It is best to check with the embassies of your destination countries concerning their lists of prohibited items. A listing of foreign embassies and consulates is available online at http://state.gov/s/cpr/rls/dpl/32122.htm.

General guidance on required entrance vaccinations and other health-related precautions in regard to visiting foreign countries can be found at the Centers for Disease Control and Prevention's website, www.cdc.gov/travel/default.aspx.

All international travel now requires a passport. For information on applying for a US passport, visit www.travel.state.gov/passport/passport_1738.html, or pick up an application form at your local post office or library.

NORTH AMERICA

United States, Canada, Mexico, Bahamas,

US Virgin Islands

ALASKA MARITIME NATIONAL WILDLIFE REFUGE

ALASKA, USA

Home to an incredible diversity of sea-birds, including the tufted puffin, the cackling goose, and the whiskered auklet, the Alaska Maritime National Wildlife Refuge also offers visitors the chance to see an amazing, endangered mammal in the wild—the Steller sea lion. Volunteers help park staff survey the local fish and other wildlife, conduct tours, educate school groups and visitors, and maintain the refuge's hiking trails. Lucky partici-pants may even help with special projects, working to remove invasive plant species from park grounds or banding birds.

CONTACT: Alaska Maritime National Wildlife Refuge, 95 Sterling Hwy, Suite 1 MS 505, Homer, AK 99603; Tel: 9072356546; Fax: 9072357783; Web: alaskamaritime .fws.gov; Email: alaskamaritime@fws.gov.

LOCATION: Homer, AK.

CATEGORY: Conservation.

COST: Free in exchange for service. Vol-unteers receive a small stipend, and RV pads with full hookups are provided.

DATES & DURATION: Spring through sum-mer; 12–24 weeks; April to July or June to September. To qualify, participants must commit to a 32-hour workweek.

TO APPLY: Applications can be obtained by contacting the refuge office (see Con-tact) or by visiting the US Fish and Wild-life Service at www.fws.gov/volunteers.

FIELD NOTES: Both full- and part-time positions are available. Families, groups, and solo travelers are welcome. Partici-pants should be aware that volunteer duties may change to meet the reserve's current needs and goals.

ALASKA PENINSULA NATIONAL WILDLIFE REFUGE

ALASKA, USA

From its high mountain peaks to rocky coastlines, the Alaska Peninsula National Wildlife Refuge is a prime habitat for more than 200 diverse species, including brown bears, wolves, caribou, and tundra swans. While enjoying the area's abundant wildlife, volunteers can opt to assist the staff in a hands-on bird-banding program, help educate refuge visitors, and conduct species inventories.

CONTACT: Alaska Peninsula National Wildlife Refuge, PO Box 277 MS545, King Salmon, AK 99613; Tel: 9072463339; Fax: 9072466696; Web: alaskapeninsula.fws .gov; Email: akpeninsula@fws.gov.

LOCATION: King Salmon, AK.

CATEGORY: Conservation.

COST: Free in exchange for service. Bunkhouse and field camp accommodations are provided.

DATES & DURATION: Summer; 12–24 weeks. To qualify, volunteers must commit to a 40-hour workweek.

TO APPLY: Applications can be obtained by contacting the refuge office (see Contact) or by visiting the US Fish and Wildlife Service at www.fws.gov/volunteers.

FIELD NOTES: Both full- and part-time positions are available. Families, groups, and solo travelers are welcome. Participants should be aware that volunteer duties may change to meet the reserve's current needs and goals.

ARCTIC NATIONAL WILDLIFE REFUGE

ALASKA, USA

Luckily for now, the Arctic National Wildlife Refuge remains an unspoiled wilderness, where visitors can catch a glimpse of its many incredible animals, such as the gray wolf, the arctic fox, the grizzly bear, and the lynx. During the winter, visitors might even spot polar bears at the reserve's northern border; in the summertime, when the ice has melted, visitors may see the majestic humpback whale complete its seasonal migration. Volunteers at the refuge help the staff survey this incredible wildlife. Participants work to conduct species inventories of birds, mammals, and fish.

CONTACT: Arctic National Wildlife Refuge, 101 12th Ave, Room 236, Fairbanks, AK 99701; Tel: 9074560250; Fax: 9074560428; Web: arctic.fws.gov; Email: arctic_refuge@fws.gov.

LOCATION: Fairbanks, AK.

CATEGORY: Conservation.

COST: Free in exchange for service. Bunkhouse and trailer accommodations are provided.

DATES & DURATION: Summer; 2–12 weeks. To qualify, volunteers must commit to a 40-hour workweek.

TO APPLY: Applications can be obtained by contacting the refuge office (see Contact) or by visiting the US Fish and Wildlife Service at www.fws.gov/volunteers.

FIELD NOTES: Positions in this refuge are suitable for experienced outdoorsmen only. Available volunteer programs are based on the refuge's particular needs at the time of service. The bunkhouse can accommodate up to 10 people.

INNOKO NATIONAL WILDLIFE REFUGE

ALASKA, USA

Established in 1980 to protect water-fowl, peregrine falcons, black bears, and other animals, the Innoko National Wildlife Refuge plays a crucial part in the preservation of this area's wildlife. Volunteers of all ages conduct biological surveys and help staff with their field research. During the summer, participants can focus on the neotropical birds that populate the refuge.

CONTACT: Innoko National Wildlife Refuge, 40 Tonzona Ave, Box 69 MS 549, McGrath, AK 99627-0069; Tel: 9075243251; Fax: 9075243141; Web: innoko.fws.gov; Email: innoko@fws.gov.

LOCATION: McGrath, AK.

CATEGORY: Conservation.

COST: Free in exchange for service. Field headquarters provides walled tents as accommodations.

DATES & DURATION: Summer; 2–12 weeks. To qualify, volunteers must commit to a 40-hour workweek.

TO APPLY: Applications can be obtained by contacting the refuge office (see Contact) or by visiting the US Fish and Wildlife Service at www.fws.gov/volunteers.

FIELD NOTES: Positions here are suitable for families, groups, and solo travelers. Living conditions are basic, and volunteers work and live as a group. White-fronted-goose banding programs and waterfowl surveys are conducted annually during the summer months. Interested parties should apply in advance.

KANUTI NATIONAL WILDLIFE REFUGE

ALASKA, USA

Situated at the edge of the Arctic Circle, Kanuti National Wildlife Refuge encompasses over 1 million acres of unspoiled wilderness, providing a home for over 130 migratory and resident bird species. Surrounded by wetlands and boreal forests, visitors find themselves in the company of wolves, moose, caribous, and lynxes. Participants work to help researchers track and survey the refuge's amazing wildlife. Kanuti is a remote wilderness where temperatures can fluctuate drastically at any time of year. Volunteers should be well prepared for any conditions that may arise.

CONTACT: Kanuti National Wildlife Refuge, 101 12th Ave, MS 555, Room 262, Fairbanks, AK 99701; Tel: 9074560329; Fax: 9074560428; Web: kanuti.fws.gov; Email: kanuti_refuge@fws.gov.

LOCATION: Fairbanks, AK.

CATEGORY: Conservation.

COST: Free in exchange for service. Bunkhouse accommodations are provided.

DATES & DURATION: Summer; unlimited.

To qualify, volunteers must commit to a 20- or 40-hour workweek.

TO APPLY: Applications can be obtained by contacting the refuge office (see Contact) or by visiting the US Fish and Wildlife Service at www.fws.gov/volunteers.

FIELD NOTES: All ages are welcome. Participants should be aware that volunteer duties may change to meet the reserve's current needs and goals. Volunteers should be aware that refuge waters may contain *Giardia*, so fresh drinking water or a filtration system may be needed. Positions are suitable for families, groups, and solo travelers.

KENAI NATIONAL WILDLIFE REFUGE

ALASKA, USA

Established as the Kenai National Moose Range but renamed in 1980, the Kenai National Wildlife Refuge was originally created to protect the giant Kenai moose. Today, the refuge supports an incredible diversity of wildlife, including caribous, Dall sheep, mountain goats, black and brown bears, and wolves. Participants can work as campground hosts, welcoming campers and providing information about the refuge and its activities, or can volunteer for the Student Conservation Assistant Program, in which participants help with visitor services, and backcountry and biology programs.

CONTACT: Kenai National Wildlife Refuge, Ski Hill Rd, PO Box 2139,

MS 519, Soldotna, AK 99669-2139; Tel: 9072627021; Fax: 9072623599; Web: kenai.fws.gov; Email: kenai@fws.gov.

LOCATION: Soldotna, AK.

CATEGORY: Conservation.

COST: Free in exchange for service. *Student Conservation Assistant Program:* 12–16 weeks of work; each volunteer receives a round-trip travel grant to the refuge, a weekly subsistence allowance, and free housing. *Campground Host Program:* Hosts must commit to a minimum of 16 weeks in exchange for free camping (tents or RVs are not provided) and a monthly subsistence allowance.

DATES & DURATION: Summer; 12–16 weeks.

TO APPLY: Applications can be obtained by contacting the refuge office (see Contact) or by visiting the US Fish and Wildlife Service at www.fws.gov/volunteers.

FIELD NOTES: Volunteers also participate in environmental education programs, campground and refuge cleanup duties, and trail maintenance. Positions are suitable for families, groups, and solo travelers.

KODIAK NATIONAL WILDLIFE REFUGE

ALASKA, USA

Inaccessible by road, the remote Kodiak National Wildlife Refuge is home to over 250 species of birds, a diverse array of fish, and incredible mammals, such as its famous Kodiak brown bear population. Volunteers help run visitor services by greeting visitors and assisting with educational programs. Summer camp volunteers can choose from two positions: the Kodiak Summer Science Camp or the Salmon Camp Counselor program. Positions are also available in remote field camp programs assisting with visitor services and biological studies.

CONTACT: Kodiak National Wildlife Refuge, 1390 Buskin River Rd, MS 559, Kodiak, AK 99615; Tel: 9074872600; Fax: 9074872144; Web: kodiak.fws.gov; Email: kodiak@fws.gov.

LOCATION: Kodiak, AK.

CATEGORY: Conservation.

COST: Free in exchange for service. Field camp accommodations are provided.

DATES & DURATION: Summer; 16 weeks.

TO APPLY: Applications can be obtained by contacting the refuge office (see Contact) or by visiting the US Fish and Wildlife Service at www.fws.gov/volunteers.

FIELD NOTES: Living conditions are basic and in the open wilderness. Positions are suitable for adults traveling solo or in groups.

KOYUKUK NATIONAL WILDLIFE REFUGE

ALASKA, USA

At Alaska's Koyukuk National Wildlife Refuge, more than 100,000 ducklings hatch in a single nesting season, and wolves, lynxes, grizzlies, and large herds of caribou can be found year-round. Volunteers are welcome to participate in bird-banding projects, species inventories, and programs designed to improve and maintain wildlife habitats. Participants may also help survey the local moose, waterfowl, and wolf populations.

CONTACT: Koyukuk National Wildlife Refuge, 101 Front St, PO Box 287, MS 525, Galena, AK 99741-0287; Tel: 9076561231; Fax: 9076561708; Web: koyukuk.fws.gov; Email: r7kynwr@fws.gov.

LOCATION: Galena, AK.

CATEGORY: Conservation.

COST: Free in exchange for service. Bunkhouse accommodations are provided.

DATES & DURATION: Summer; varies.

TO APPLY: Applications can be obtained by contacting the refuge office (see Contact) or by visiting the US Fish and Wildlife Service at www.fws.gov/volunteers.

FIELD NOTES: Positions are suitable for families, groups, and solo travelers.

SELAWIK NATIONAL WILDLIFE REFUGE

ALASKA, USA

Selawik National Wildlife Refuge houses an incredible array of species within its boreal forest, wetland, and meadow environments. Wolves, arctic and red foxes, lynxes, and wolverines are just a few of the many animals that reside within its amazing wilderness. Volunteers assist with wildlife and waterfowl surveys.

CONTACT: Selawik National Wildlife Refuge, 160 2nd Ave, MS 565, Kotzebue, AK 99752; Tel: 9074423799; Fax: 9074423124; Web: selawik.fws.gov; Email: selawik@fws.gov.

LOCATION: Kotzebue, AK.

CATEGORY: Conservation.

COST: Free in exchange for service. Apartment and cabin housing are provided.

DATES & DURATION: Summer; varies.

TO APPLY: Applications can be obtained by contacting the refuge office (see Contact) or by visiting the US Fish and Wildlife Service at www.fws.gov/volunteers.

FIELD NOTES: Positions are suitable for families, groups, and solo travelers.

TOGIAK NATIONAL WILDLIFE REFUGE

ALASKA, USA

With its pristine lakes, flowing rivers, and towering mountains, Togiak National Wildlife Refuge offers visitors a chance to see a wide range of wildlife, including moose, caribou, Pacific walrus, Steller sea lion, and of course salmon. Participants help local conservationists with various research programs, including fish-, bird-, and mammal-focused surveys. From March through April, volunteers may participate in annual owl inventories, and in May, participants begin to monitor the arrival of spring migratory bird species.

CONTACT: Togiak National Wildlife Refuge, PO Box 270, MS 569, Dillingham, AK 99627-0069; Tel: 9078421063; Fax: 9078425402; Web: togiak.fws.gov; Email: togiak@fws.gov.

LOCATION: Dillingham, AK.

CATEGORY: Conservation.

COST: Free in exchange for service. Bunkhouse accommodations are provided.

DATES & DURATION: Summer; varies. To qualify, volunteers must commit to a 40-hour workweek.

TO APPLY: Applications can be obtained by contacting the refuge office (see Contact) or by visiting the US Fish and Wildlife Service at www.fws.gov/volunteers.

FIELD NOTES: Positions are suitable for families, groups, and solo travelers. Participants should be aware that volunteer duties may change to meet the reserve's current needs and goals.

YUKON DELTA NATIONAL WILDLIFE REFUGE

ALASKA, USA

Bordering the Bering Sea, Alaska's Yukon Delta National Wildlife Refuge not only is home to one of the largest populations of waterfowl in the world but also hosts 44 species of fish, brown and black bears, caribous, moose, wolves, and even killer whales! Volunteers help researchers document this incredible wildlife, restore damaged habitats, and maintain the refuge's facilities. Participants may also help with special projects, such as the banding of birds so that their movements, survival rates, and behavioral traits can be determined.

CONTACT: Yukon Delta National Wildlife Refuge, 807 Chief Eddie Hoffman Rd, PO Box 346, MS 535, Bethel, AK 99559; Tel: 9075433151; Fax: 9075434413; Web: yukondelta.fws.gov; Email: yukondelta_refuge@fws.gov.

LOCATION: Bethel, AK.

CATEGORY: Conservation.

COST: Free in exchange for service. Bunkhouse accommodations are provided.

DATES & DURATION: Summer; varies. To qualify, volunteers must commit to a 40-hour workweek.

TO APPLY: Applications can be obtained by contacting the refuge office (see Contact) or by visiting the US Fish and Wildlife Service at www.fws.gov/volunteers.

FIELD NOTES: Both full- and part-time positions are available. This project is suitable for families, groups, and solo travelers.

YUKON FLATS NATIONAL WILDLIFE REFUGE

ALASKA, USA

Working at the Yukon Flats National Wildlife Refuge, visitors can encounter a remarkable range of amazing creatures, including more than 150 types of birds (2 million ducks arrive each year), caribou, Dall sheep, moose, wolves, black bears, and grizzlies! Volunteers help study waterfowl, survey local plant life, and design and run environmental education programs.

CONTACT: Yukon Flats National Wildlife Refuge, 101 12th Ave, Room 264, MS 575, Fairbanks, AK 99701; Tel: 9074560440; Fax: 9074560447; Web: yukonflats.fws .gov; Email: yukonflats_refuge@fws.gov.

LOCATION: Fairbanks, AK.

CATEGORY: Conservation.

COST: Free in exchange for service. Field camp accommodations are provided.

DATES & DURATION: Summer; varies.

TO APPLY: Applications can be obtained by contacting the refuge office (see Contact) or by visiting the US Fish and Wildlife Service at www.fws.gov/volunteers.

FIELD NOTES: Volunteers work in both the field and the office. Full- and part-time positions are available. Positions are suitable for families, groups, and solo travelers.

ALCHESAY-WILLIAMS CREEK NATIONAL FISH HATCHERY

ARIZONA, USA

Located on the Ft. Apache Indian Reservation, Alchesay-Williams Creek National Fish Hatchery was primarily created to breed trout. The hatchery has had much success raising the golden-colored Apache trout, a species once listed as endangered but now upgraded to threatened. Here, volunteers participate in a variety of projects, including feeding the resident fish, cleaning tanks and raceways, conducting sample counts, and maintaining the facility and grounds.

CONTACT: Alchesay-Williams Creek National Fish Hatchery, PO Box 2430, Pinetop, AZ 85935; Tel: 9283384901; Fax: 9283384977; Web: www.fws.gov/southwest/fisheries/AWCNFH.html; Email: phil_hines@fws.gov.

LOCATION: Whiteriver, AZ.

CATEGORY: Conservation.

COST: Free in exchange for service. Cabin accommodations are provided.

DATES & DURATION: Varies; unlimited.

TO APPLY: Applications can be obtained by contacting the hatchery office (see Contact) or by visiting the US Fish and Wildlife Service at www.fws.gov/volunteers.

FIELD NOTES: Participants must be at least 18 years of age. The hatchery produces rainbow, brook, and brown trout for various Indian reservations throughout the Southwest. Position is suitable for adults traveling solo.

BILL WILLIAMS RIVER NATIONAL WILDLIFE REFUGE

ARIZONA, USA

During the spring breeding season, Bill Williams River National Wildlife Refuge is home to a variety of neotropical migratory birds, including the yellow warbler, vermillion flycatcher, and summer tanager. Volunteers help research these birds and maintain the park's facilities. Participants may also work on park construction and maintenance projects, including the building of structures and landscaping.

CONTACT: Bill Williams River National Wildlife Refuge, 60911 Hwy 95, Parker, AZ 85344; Tel: 9286674144; Fax: 9286673402; Web: www.fws.gov/southwest/refuges/Arizona/billwill.html; Email: leslie_denney@fws.gov.

LOCATION: Parker, AZ.

CATEGORY: Conservation.

COST: Free in exchange for service. Full RV hookups are provided.

DATES & DURATION: Year-round; varies.

TO APPLY: Applications can be obtained by contacting the refuge office (see Contact) or by visiting the US Fish and Wildlife Service at www.fws.gov/volunteers.

FIELD NOTES: Volunteers must make their camping arrangements at least two months in advance. Positions are suitable for families, groups, and solo travelers.

BUENOS AIRES NATIONAL WILDLIFE REFUGE

ARIZONA, USA

Established in 1985, Buenos Aires National Wildlife Refuge was originally created as a safe haven for the masked bobwhite quail but is now home to 325 different bird species, 53 types of reptiles and amphibians, and 58 kinds of mammals (including pronghorns, mule deer, and mountain lions). Volunteers help maintain this amazing reserve, working on trails, cleaning campsites, and repairing fences. Participants may also work on park construction projects as needed.

CONTACT: Buenos Aires National Wildlife Refuge, PO Box 109, Sasabe, AZ 85633; Tel: 5208234251; Web: www.fws .gov/southwest/refuges/Arizona/ buenosaires.

LOCATION: Sasabe, AZ.

CATEGORY: Conservation.

COST: Free in exchange for service. Full RV hookups are provided.

DATES & DURATION: Year-round; 16 weeks. To qualify, volunteers must stay for 3 months and work 4 days per week, 8 hours per day.

TO APPLY: Applications can be obtained by contacting the refuge office (see Contact) or by visiting the US Fish and Wildlife Service at www.fws.gov/volunteers.

FIELD NOTES: Positions fill fast during the winter months, so volunteers wishing to participate in the program should apply 4–6 months in advance. Positions are suitable for families, groups, and solo travelers.

CABEZA PRIETA NATIONAL WILDLIFE REFUGE

ARIZONA, USA

Home to the endangered Sonoran pronghorn, the Cabeza Prieta National Wildlife Refuge offers visitors the chance to see some amazing reptiles in the wild, including the dangerous Western diamondback rattlesnake. Volunteers help with the park's various ecological study projects, such as wildlife surveys and monitoring programs. Participants may also help maintain the reserve's facilities or work as a refuge interpreter, teaching leave-no-trace techniques to school groups and visitors while leading nature hikes.

CONTACT: Cabeza Prieta National Wildlife Refuge, 1611 North 2nd St, Ajo, AZ 85321; Tel: 5203876483; Fax: 5203875359; Web: www.fws.gov/southwest/refuges/Arizona/cabeza.html; Email: fw2_rw_cabezaprieta@fws.gov.

LOCATION: Ajo, AZ.

CATEGORY: Conservation.

COST: Free in exchange for service. Bunkhouses and full RV hookups are provided.

DATES & DURATION: October through May; varies. To qualify, volunteers must commit to a 40-hour workweek.

TO APPLY: Applications can be obtained by contacting the refuge office (see Contact) or by visiting the US Fish and Wildlife Service at www.fws.gov/volunteers.

FIELD NOTES: Volunteers who wish to participate in fieldwork assignments need a 4-wheel-drive vehicle. Both full- and part-time positions are available. Positions are suitable for families, groups, and solo travelers.

CIBOLA NATIONAL WILDLIFE REFUGE

ARIZONA, USA

Established in 1964, the Cibola National Wildlife Refuge now provides a home for 288 different types of bird, including many songbirds. Visitors can also expect to see bobcats, desert mule deer, and coyotes roaming the refuge grounds. At this site, volunteers help with research projects, run environmental education programs, design conversation awareness campaigns, and work on park construction projects as needed.

CONTACT: Cibola National Wildlife Refuge, 66600 Cibola Lake Rd, RR 2, Box 1, Cibola, AZ 85328; Tel: 9288573253; Fax: 9288573420; Web: www.fws.gov/southwest/refuges/arizona/cibola.html; Email: r2rw_ci@fws.gov.

LOCATION: Cibola, AZ.

CATEGORY: Conservation.

COST: Free in exchange for service. Full RV hookups and other housing options are provided.

DATES & DURATION: Year-round; varies.

TO APPLY: Applications can be obtained by contacting the refuge office (see Contact) or by visiting the US Fish and Wildlife Service at www.fws.gov/volunteers.

FIELD NOTES: Positions are suitable for families, groups, and solo travelers.

IMPERIAL NATIONAL WILDLIFE REFUGE

ARIZONA, USA

Imperial National Wildlife Refuge hosts a remarkable array of wild creatures, including desert bighorn sheep, mule deer, black-tailed jackrabbits, and even Western whiptail lizards. Participants help with biological research programs, environmental education, visitors center assistance, and maintenance duties.

CONTACT: Imperial National Wildlife Refuge, PO Box 72217, Yuma, AZ 85365; Tel: 9287833371; Fax: 9287830652; Web: www.fws.gov/southwest/refuges/arizona/imperial.html; Email: fw2_rw_imperial@fws.gov.

LOCATION: Yuma, AZ.

CATEGORY: Conservation.

COST: Free in exchange for service. Full RV hookups are provided.

DATES & DURATION: Year-round; varies.

TO APPLY: Applications can be obtained by contacting the refuge office (see Contact) or by visiting the US Fish and Wildlife Service at www.fws.gov/volunteers.

FIELD NOTES: Because the refuge is located in a desert climate, volunteers should take appropriate precautions. Sunblock and drinking water should be readily accessible at all times. Hats and lightweight neutral colored clothing should be worn. Both full- and part-time positions are available. Projects are suitable for families, groups, and solo travelers.

TURPENTINE CREEK WILDLIFE CENTER

ARKANSAS, USA

Home to lions, tigers, leopards, and other animals, Arkansas's Turpentine Creek Wildlife Center provides a safe environment to animals that have been rescued, abused, or abandoned. Interns and volunteers help care for over 100 exotic cats currently in residence. Participants prepare meals, feed the cats, clean their enclosures, monitor their health, and control any pest problems that may arise.

CONTACT: Turpentine Creek Wildlife Center, 239 Turpentine Creek Ln, Eureka Springs, AR 72632; Tel: 4792535841; Web: www.turpentinecreek.org; Email: tigers@turpentinecreek.org.

LOCATION: Eureka Springs, AR.

CATEGORY: Conservation.

COST: Free in exchange for service. Housing and a small weekly stipend for food are provided for interns.

DATES & DURATION: Year-round; unlimited. Volunteers are needed year-round, but internships begin on February 1.

TO APPLY: Email emily@turpentine creek.org or write to the office (see Contact).

FIELD NOTES: Direct contact with the animals may be minimal. Volunteers must be at least 12 years of age. Training is provided. The work is often very demanding. Positions are suitable for families with older children, groups, and solo travelers.

HAVASU NATIONAL WILDLIFE REFUGE

CALIFORNIA, USA

Known as one of the premiere birding sites on the lower Colorado River, Havasu National Wildlife Refuge offers visitors the chance to spot the endangered Yuma clapper rail, southwestern willow flycatcher, peregrine falcon, and southern bald eagle. Volunteers assist park staff with wildlife surveys and counts, general refuge maintenance, and habitat-modification projects that work to aid the refuge's growing wildlife population.

CONTACT: Havasu National Wildlife Refuge, PO Box 3009, Needles, CA 92363; Tel: 7603263853; Fax: 7603265745; Web: www.fws.gov/southwest/refuges/arizona/havasu; Email: carol_berry@fws.gov.

LOCATION: Needles, CA.

CATEGORY: Conservation.

COST: Free in exchange for service. Full RV hookups or trailer accommodations are provided.

DATES & DURATION: Summer; varies.

TO APPLY: Applications can be obtained by contacting the refuge office (see Contact) or by visiting the US Fish and Wildlife Service at www.fws.gov/volunteers.

FIELD NOTES: Positions are suitable for families, groups, and solo travelers.

HUMBOLDT BAY NATIONAL WILDLIFE REFUGE

CALIFORNIA, USA

Located on the coast of northwestern California, Humboldt Bay National Wildlife Refuge offers visitors the chance to see incredible birds, such as the threatened western snowy plover and the marbled murrelet, in their natural habitat—the tidal flats, mud flats, salt marshes, and freshwater wetlands that make up this breathtaking 3,000-acre reserve. Volunteers assist park staff with a variety of projects and programs, from office work to interpretive and environmental education to wildlife management and general refuge maintenance.

CONTACT: Humboldt Bay National Wildlife Refuge, 1020 Ranch Rd, Loleta, CA 95551; Tel: 7077335406; Web: www.fws .gov/humboldtbay; Email: humboldtbay@ fws.gov.

LOCATION: Loleta, CA.

CATEGORY: Conservation.

COST: Free in exchange for service.

DATES & DURATION: Varies; unlimited.

TO APPLY: Applications can be obtained by contacting the refuge office (see Contact) or by visiting the US Fish and Wildlife Service at www.fws.gov/volunteers.

FIELD NOTES: Positions are suitable for families, groups, and solo travelers. Participants should be aware that volunteer duties may change to meet the reserve's current needs and goals.

KERN NATIONAL WILDLIFE REFUGE

CALIFORNIA, USA

Established in 1960, the Kern National Wildlife Refuge was formed to provide a wintering area for migratory waterfowl, such as the white-faced ibis, greater white-fronted goose, and tundra swan, as well as for year-round residents, such as the greater egret and bufflehead. Birding is optimal from October through March, when migrating and wintering species are at their peak numbers. Volunteers help survey the refuge's bird species, assist with general refuge maintenance, and participate in habitat restoration projects.

CONTACT: Kern National Wildlife Refuge Complex, PO Box 670, Delano, CA 93216-0670; Tel: 661725 2767; Web: www.fws.gov/kern/refuges/kern; Email: dave_hardt@fws.gov.

LOCATION: Delano, CA.

CATEGORY: Conservation.

COST: Free in exchange for service. Trailer accommodations are provided.

DATES & DURATION: Varies; unlimited.

TO APPLY: Applications can be obtained by contacting the refuge office (see Contact) or by visiting the US Fish and Wildlife Service at www.fws.gov/volunteers.

FIELD NOTES: Positions are suitable for families, groups, and solo travelers. Participants should be aware that volunteer duties may change to meet the reserve's current needs and goals.

MAPPING CHANGE IN CALIFORNIA'S MOUNTAINS

CALIFORNIA, USA

Only 100 miles from Los Angeles, the recently designated San Jacinto and Santa Rosa Mountains National Monument is the perfect place to study the effects of global warming on the environment. Hiking through this desert wilderness, volunteers for Mapping Change in California's Mountains collect plant samples and log data to help scientists better understand the effects of climate change on this amazing local ecosystem.

CONTACT: Earthwatch Institute, 3 Clock Tower Pl, Suite 100, Box 75, Maynard, MA 01754; Tel: 9784610081 or 8007760188; Fax: 9784612332; Web: www.earthwatch.org/exped/russellr.html; Email: expeditions@earthwatch.org.

LOCATION: Ontario, CA.

CATEGORY: Conservation.

COST: US$2,500 for 8 days. Fee includes accommodations, meals, ground transfers, training, and support.

DATES & DURATION: Determined by participant interest; varies.

TO APPLY: Applications can be obtained by contacting the office (see Contact).

FIELD NOTES: Volunteers should be moderately fit and expect long days of hiking in hot temperatures over rocky and steep terrain. Participants must also carry all of their own gear. Positions are suitable for adult groups and solo travelers.

MARINE MAMMAL CENTER

CALIFORNIA, USA

Located within sight of San Francisco's Golden Gate Bridge, the Marine Mammal Center offers refuge to injured, sick, and orphaned marine mammals, including Steller sea lions and elephant seals. Volunteers feed the animals, clean their enclosures, and administer necessary medications to rehabilitate these amazing creatures. Participants may even get to assist staff with a rescue!

CONTACT: Marine Mammal Center, Marin Headlands, GGRNA, Sausalito, CA 94965. Tel: 4152897235 or 4159794357; Fax: 4152897333; Web: www .marinemammalcenter.org; Email: volunteer@tmmc.org.

LOCATION: Sausalito, CA.

CATEGORY: Conservation.

COST: Free in exchange for service. Volunteers must provide their own housing, food, and transportation.

DATES & DURATION: Year-round; volunteers are needed most during the busiest months, March through August; long-term positions are available.

TO APPLY: Applications can be obtained by contacting the office (see Contact).

FIELD NOTES: Upon arrival, volunteers must attend a training and orientation session and complete a liability waiver. Minimum age requirement of 18. Participants must have an up-to-date tetanus shot. Volunteers must be comfortable working with wild animals. Positions are suitable for adult groups and solo travelers.

MODOC NATIONAL WILDLIFE REFUGE

CALIFORNIA, USA

With mountainous terrain, gorgeous meadows, and pristine freshwater lakes and ponds, Modoc National Wildlife Refuge provides a diverse range of habitats for over 250 types of birds. Participants help create an inventory of the park's wildlife. During the summer months, volunteers assist with the refuge biological program, conducting species inventories and assisting with bird-banding projects.

CONTACT: Modoc National Wildlife Refuge, PO Box 1610, Alturas, CA 96101; Tel: 5302333572; Fax: 5302334143; Web: www.fws.gov/modoc; Email: modoc@fws.gov.

LOCATION: Alturas, CA.

CATEGORY: Conservation.

COST: Free in exchange for service. Mobile-home accommodations are provided.

DATES & DURATION: Year-round; unlimited.

TO APPLY: Applications can be obtained by contacting the refuge office (see Contact) or by visiting the US Fish and Wildlife Service at www.fws.gov/volunteers.

FIELD NOTES: Positions are suitable for families, groups, and solo travelers. Children of all ages are welcome.

SACRAMENTO NATIONAL WILDLIFE REFUGE

CALIFORNIA, USA

Home to over 300 types of birds and mammals, the Sacramento National Wildlife Refuge provides visitors the chance to see amazing creatures, such as the otter and dabbling duck, in their natural environment. The refuge encompasses marshes, ponds, riparian areas, and water-grass habitats. Volunteers help with plant studies and airboat surveys, and assist naturalists with presentations, trail maintenance, and tree plantings. Participants may also be called on to assist with bird-banding projects when deemed appropriate by the refuge.

CONTACT: Sacramento National Wildlife Refuge, 752 County Rd, 99 W, Willows, CA 95988; Tel: 5309342801; Fax: 5309347814; Web: www.fws.gov/ sacramentovalleyrefuges; Email: sacramentovalleyrefuges@fws.gov.

LOCATION: Willows, CA.

CATEGORY: Conservation.

COST: Free in exchange for service. Accommodation is provided.

DATES & DURATION: Year-round; unlimited.

TO APPLY: Applications can be obtained by contacting the refuge office (see Contact) or by visiting the US Fish and Wildlife Service at www.fws.gov/volunteers.

FIELD NOTES: Both full- and part-time positions are available. Families, groups, and solo travelers are welcome. Participants should be aware that volunteer duties may change to meet the reserve's current needs and goals.

SHARKS AND RAYS OF MONTEREY PROGRAM

CALIFORNIA, USA

Working on the gorgeous Monterey Bay, volunteers at the Shark and Rays of Monterey Program study the population dynamics of seven species of these amazing creatures. During open-water capture studies, participants assist with the bating, capture, and tagging of sharks and rays. Surveys are conducted 5 to 7 days per week for approximately 7 hours per day. All volunteers need to participate daily.

CONTACT: Earthwatch Institute, 3 Clock Tower Pl, Suite 100, Box 75, Maynard, MA 01754; Tel: 9784610081 or 8007760188; Fax: 9784612332; Web: www.earthwatch .org/exped/vansommeran.html; Email: expeditions@earthwatch.org.

LOCATION: Monterey, CA.

CATEGORY: Conservation.

COST: US$2,650 for 10 days. Fee includes accommodations, meals, ground transfers, training, and support.

DATES & DURATION: Determined by participant interest; 10 days.

TO APPLY: Applications are accepted online and by fax or mail. Contact the office (see Contact).

FIELD NOTES: The program accepts a maximum of six volunteers at any one time. Participants must be at least 18 years of age. Volunteers must be in good physical condition and be able to swim. Positions are suitable for adult groups and solo travelers.

TULE LAKE NATIONAL WILDLIFE REFUGE

CALIFORNIA, USA

Founded in 1928, Tule Lake National Wildlife Refuge provides a home for a variety of species, including the American bald eagle, which can be spotted during the winter months. Year-round, visitors can catch a glimpse of some incredible mammals, including the black bear, elk, mountain lion, and red and gray fox. Volunteers help survey the local bird populations and assist with habitat modification and restoration projects to ensure that these animals will continue to have a home.

CONTACT: Tule Lake National Wildlife Refuge, 4009 Hill Rd, Tule Lake, CA 96134; Tel: 5306672231; Web: www.fws .gov/klamathbasinrefuges/tulelake/ tulelake.html; Email: david_chapine@ fws.gov.

LOCATION: Tule Lake, CA.

CATEGORY: Conservation.

COST: Free in exchange for service. Mobile-home and other accommodations are provided.

DATES & DURATION: Year-round; varies.

TO APPLY: Applications can be obtained by contacting the refuge office (see Contact) or by visiting the US Fish and Wildlife Service at www.fws.gov/volunteers.

FIELD NOTES: Positions are suitable for families, groups, and solo travelers.

ARAPAHO NATIONAL WILDLIFE REFUGE

COLORADO, USA

Established to provide a secure habitat for waterfowl to nest and raise their young, Arapaho National Wildlife Refuge bustles in April and May, when more than 5,000 ducks arrive to nest and hatch their eggs. Canada geese arrive in June, and the waterfowl season peaks in late September and early October, when the refuge plays host to at least 8,000 birds. Volunteers assist park staff with bird surveys, habitat modification and restoration projects, and refuge upkeep and maintenance.

CONTACT: Arapaho National Wildlife Refuge, 953JC Rd #32, Walden, CO 80480; Tel: 9707238202; Web: www.fws.gov/arapaho/index.html; Email: arapaho@fws.gov.

LOCATION: Walden, CO.

CATEGORY: Conservation.

COST: Free in exchange for service. Full RV hookups and housing are provided.

DATES & DURATION: Summer; unlimited.

TO APPLY: Applications can be obtained by contacting the refuge office (see Contact) or by visiting the US Fish and Wildlife Service at www.fws.gov/volunteers.

FIELD NOTES: Positions are suitable for families, groups, and solo travelers. Participants should be aware that volunteer duties may change to meet the reserve's current needs and goals.

HOTCHKISS NATIONAL FISH HATCHERY

COLORADO, USA

Established in 1967, Hotchkiss National Fish Hatchery rears rainbow trout for stocking in Colorado and New Mexico reservoirs and federal water developments. Volunteers participate in a variety of projects, including feeding and care of the resident fish, and public outreach activities.

CONTACT: Hotchkiss National Fish Hatchery, 8342 Hatchery Rd, Hotchkiss, CO 81419; Tel: 9708723170; Web: www .fws.gov/hotchkiss; Email: hotchkiss@ fws.gov.

LOCATION: Hotchkiss, CO.

CATEGORY: Conservation.

COST: Free in exchange for service. Housing is provided.

DATES & DURATION: Varies; unlimited. To qualify, volunteers must commit to a 40-hour workweek.

TO APPLY: Applications can be obtained by contacting the hatchery office (see Contact) or by visiting the US Fish and Wildlife Service at www.fws.gov/ volunteers.

FIELD NOTES: More than 7,500 people visit Hotchkiss each year. Volunteers may be asked to lead tours. Participants must be at least 18 years of age. Positions are suitable for adult groups and solo travelers.

PRIME HOOK NATIONAL WILDLIFE REFUGE

DELAWARE, USA

Located on the Atlantic flyway, the 10,000-acre Prime Hook National Wildlife Refuge offers a home for a variety of birds, mammals, fish, reptiles, and insects, including more than 100,000 snow geese and 80,000 ducks that arrive during the fall migration. Volunteers help survey the local bird and horseshoe crab populations, monitor bluebird nests, and maintain the park's trails. Participants may also work at the visitors center and help with refuge tours, annual festivals, and other events.

CONTACT: Prime Hook National Wildlife Refuge, 11978 Turkle Pond Rd, Milton, DE 19968; Tel: 3026848419; Web: www.fws.gov/northeast/primehook; Email: fw5rw_phnwr@fws.gov.

LOCATION: Milton, DE.

CATEGORY: Conservation.

COST: Free in exchange for service. Full RV hookups are provided.

DATES & DURATION: Year-round; unlimited.

TO APPLY: Applications can be obtained by contacting the refuge office (see Contact) or by visiting the US Fish and Wildlife Service at www.fws.gov/volunteers.

FIELD NOTES: Participants may be called on to conduct biweekly bird surveys of marsh habitats and to conduct volunteer patrols of the refuge grounds. Positions are suitable for families, groups, and solo travelers.

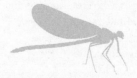

BIG CAT RESCUE

FLORIDA, USA

A haven for over 100 abused and abandoned big cats, including tigers, lions, leopards, cougars, bobcats, and lynxes, the Big Cat Rescue is always in need of help. Volunteers and interns assist with preparing meals and feeding resident wildlife, cleaning enclosures, and maintaining the grounds. Before interacting with the cats, volunteers and interns must complete a series of training programs. The rescue program offers two options: Keeper Training, which focuses on animal husbandry, and Administrative Training, for tour guiding and guest relations.

CONTACT: Big Cat Rescue, 12802 Easy St, Tampa, FL 33625; Tel: 8134265948; Web: www.bigcatrescue.org; Email: training@bigcatresuce.org.

LOCATION: Tampa, FL.

CATEGORY: Conservation.

COST: A service fee of US$75 covers the cost of the required uniform T-shirt, training manual, and walkie-talkie. Housing is provided for interns, who are responsible for their own food and transportation expenses. Volunteers must provide their own housing and food.

DATES & DURATION: Year-round; unlimited. Interns must commit to 3 months; volunteers, to a minimum of 16 hours per month.

TO APPLY: Applications can be obtained by contacting the program office (see Contact). The internship program is available throughout the year; apply 4–6 months before you wish to begin.

FIELD NOTES: Participants must be at least 18 years of age. Volunteers and interns must participate in a training and orientation program before the start of service. Positions are suitable for adult groups and solo travelers.

CEDAR KEYS NATIONAL WILDLIFE REFUGE

FLORIDA, USA

Cedar Keys National Wildlife Refuge, which is made up of 12 islands, is one of the largest colonial bird nesting sites in north Florida. Brown pelican, white ibis, eagle, osprey, and great blue heron also nest on refuge grounds. Volunteers help conduct bird and wildlife surveys. Spring is an active time in the refuge: bird migration begins in March, peak numbers of songbirds appear in April, and hatchlings are seen in May.

CONTACT: Cedar Keys National Wildlife Refuge, 16450 NE 31st Pl, Chiefland, FL 32626; Tel: 3524930238; Web: www.fws .gov/cedarkeys; Email: lowersuwannee@ fws.gov.

LOCATION: Chiefland, FL.

CATEGORY: Conservation.

COST: Free in exchange for service. Full RV hookups are provided.

DATES & DURATION: Year-round; unlimited.

TO APPLY: Applications can be obtained by contacting the refuge office (see Contact) or by visiting the US Fish and Wildlife Service at www.fws.gov/ volunteers.

FIELD NOTES: The refuge is home to a variety of biting insects. Tick repellent is advised to be worn year-round on refuge grounds. Volunteers looking for something to do in their free time can opt to explore the Suwannee River or the Gulf of Mexico by boat. Rentals are available nearby. Both full- and part-time positions are available. Families, groups, and solo travelers are all welcome. Participants should be aware that volunteer duties may change to meet the reserve's current needs and goals.

CHASSAHOWITZKA NATIONAL WILDLIFE REFUGE

FLORIDA, USA

Established in 1941, Chassahowitzka National Wildlife Refuge provides a home for over 250 types of birds, 50 different kinds of reptiles and amphibians, and 25 types of mammals—including the endangered West Indian manatee. Volunteers help with wildlife surveys and educational programs. Participants also help maintain the refuge's manatee sanctuary.

CONTACT: Chassahowitzka National Wildlife Refuge, 1502 SE Kings Bay Dr, Crystal River, FL 34429; Tel: 3525632088; Fax: 3527957961; Web: www.fws.gov/chassahowitzka; Email: chassahowitzka@fws.gov.

LOCATION: Crystal River, FL.

CATEGORY: Conservation.

COST: Free in exchange for service. Full RV hookups and other housing options are provided.

DATES & DURATION: Year-round; unlimited.

TO APPLY: Applications can be obtained by contacting the refuge office (see Contact) or by visiting the US Fish and Wildlife Service at www.fws.gov/volunteers.

FIELD NOTES: Both full- and part-time positions are available. Positions are suitable for families, groups, and solo travelers.

CRYSTAL RIVER NATIONAL WILDLIFE REFUGE

FLORIDA, USA

At the Crystal River National Wildlife Refuge, volunteers can help save the endangered and majestic West Indian manatee! To that end, participants help park staff educate the public about manatee sanctuary locations and boat-speed regulations. Volunteers also help survey the park's wildlife and restore local habitats.

CONTACT: Crystal River National Wildlife Refuge, 1502 SE Kings Bay Dr, Crystal River, FL 34429; Tel: 3525632088; Fax: 3527957961; Web: www.fws.gov/crystal river; Email: chassahowitzka@fws.gov.

LOCATION: Crystal River, FL.

CATEGORY: Conservation.

COST: Free in exchange for service. Full RV hookups and apartments are provided.

DATES & DURATION: Year-round; unlimited.

TO APPLY: Applications can be obtained by contacting the refuge office (see Contact) or by visiting the US Fish and Wildlife Service at www.fws.gov/volunteers.

FIELD NOTES: Biting insects are abundant on refuge grounds. Repellent should be worn at all times. Positions are suitable for families, groups, and solo travelers.

EGMONT KEY NATIONAL WILDLIFE REFUGE

FLORIDA, USA

Founded in 1974, Egmont Key National Wildlife Refuge provides a home for a variety of endangered and threatened species, such as the red-cockaded woodpecker. Volunteers help researchers survey the local wildlife, maintain the refuge, and educate visitors about the importance of conservation.

CONTACT: Egmont Key National Wildlife Refuge, 1502 SE Kings Bay Dr, Crystal River, FL 34429; Tel: 3525632088; Fax: 3527957961; Web: www.fws.gov/egmontkey; Email: chassahowitzka@fws.gov.

LOCATION: Crystal River, FL.

CATEGORY: Conservation.

COST: Free in exchange for service. Full RV hookups and other accommodations are provided.

DATES & DURATION: Year-round; unlimited.

TO APPLY: Applications can be obtained by contacting the refuge office (see Contact) or by visiting the US Fish and Wildlife Service at www.fws.gov/volunteers.

FIELD NOTES: Positions are suitable for families, groups, and solo travelers.

FLORIDA PANTHER NATIONAL WILDLIFE REFUGE

FLORIDA, USA

At more than 26,000 acres, the Florida Panther National Wildlife Refuge is home to over 700 types of plants and some amazing animals, including black bears, bobcats, foxes, coyotes, alligators, and, of course, Florida panthers. Volunteers help with interpretive services, invasive plant species removal, and educational environmental awareness programs. Participants may also lead tours and hikes and give presentations on the importance of conservation to local schoolchildren.

CONTACT: Florida Panther National Wildlife Refuge, 3860 Tollgate Blvd, Suite 300, Naples, FL 34114; Tel: 2393538442; Fax: 2393538640; Web: www.fws.gov/floridapanther; Email: floridapanther@fws.gov.

LOCATION: Naples, FL.

CATEGORY: Conservation.

COST: Free in exchange for service. Trailer accommodations are provided.

DATES & DURATION: Year-round; unlimited.

TO APPLY: Applications can be obtained by contacting the refuge office (see Contact) or by visiting the US Fish and Wildlife Service at www.fws.gov/volunteers.

FIELD NOTES: Both full- and part-time positions are available. Positions are suitable for families, groups, and solo travelers.

LAKE WOODRUFF NATIONAL WILDLIFE REFUGE

FLORIDA, USA

The 21,000-plus acres of Lake Woodruff National Wildlife Refuge include cypress swamps, upland regions, lakes, canals, and streams, and provide a breeding ground for the endangered manatee. The refuge hosts more than 215 bird species, including neotropical songbirds, migratory waterfowl, shore and wading birds, and raptors. Other threatened or endangered species—the Eastern indigo snake, American alligator, wood stork, and snail kite—can also be found here. Volunteers help survey the local wildlife, maintain refuge grounds, and aid staff in habitat restoration projects.

CONTACT: Lake Woodruff National Wildlife Refuge, 2045 Mud Lake Rd, De Leon Springs, FL 31230; Tel: 3869854673; Fax: 3869850926; Web: www.fws.gov/lakewoodruff; Email: lakewoodruff@fws.gov.

LOCATION: De Leon Springs, FL.

CATEGORY: Conservation.

COST: Free in exchange for service. Full RV hookups are provided. Internet access and laundry facilities are available on-site.

DATES & DURATION: Year-round; unlimited.

TO APPLY: Applications can be obtained by contacting the refuge office (see Contact) or by visiting the US Fish and Wildlife Service at www.fws.gov/volunteers.

FIELD NOTES: The refuge marshlands host a variety of biting insects; proper precautions should be taken. Positions are suitable for families, groups, and solo travelers. Participants should be aware that volunteer duties may change to meet the reserve's current needs and goals.

LOWER SUWANNEE NATIONAL WILDLIFE REFUGE

FLORIDA, USA

Home to swallow-tailed kites, bald eagles, and West Indian manatees, the 53,000-acre Lower Suwannee National Wildlife Refuge offers visitors the chance to see incredible wildlife in action. Volunteers help with wildlife surveys, maintain the refuge, and restore damaged habitats. Participants may also be called on to assist staff in any special events held on refuge grounds.

CONTACT: Lower Suwannee National Wildlife Refuge, 16450 NE 31st Pl, Chiefland, FL 32626; Tel: 3524930238; Fax: 3524931935; Web: www.fws.gov/lowersuwannee; Email: lowersuwannee@fws.gov.

LOCATION: Chiefland, FL.

CATEGORY: Conservation.

COST: Free in exchange for service. Full RV hookups are provided.

DATES & DURATION: Year-round; varies.

TO APPLY: Applications can be obtained by contacting the refuge office (see Contact) or by visiting the US Fish and Wildlife Service at www.fws.gov/volunteers.

FIELD NOTES: Note that the refuge is popular with volunteers, so apply early. Families, groups, and solo travelers are all welcome. Participants should be aware that volunteer duties may change to meet the reserve's current needs and goals.

MERRITT ISLAND NATIONAL WILDLIFE REFUGE

FLORIDA, USA

From its freshwater impoundments to its saltwater estuaries, the Merritt Island National Wildlife Refuge, located on the same island as NASA's John F. Kennedy Space Center, provides a home to over 500 different types of animals, including the West Indian manatee, green turtle, and Atlantic hawksbill. Volunteers help with environmental education campaigns, interpretive services, wildlife surveys, trail and refuge maintenance, gardening, and other visitor services.

CONTACT: Merritt Island National Wildlife Refuge, PO Box 2683, Titusville, FL 32781; Tel: 3218610667; Web: www.fws.gov/merrittisland/index.html; Email: merrittisland@fws.gov.

LOCATION: Titusville, FL.

CATEGORY: Conservation.

COST: Free in exchange for service. Full RV hookups are provided. Laundry facilities and Internet access are available on-site.

DATES & DURATION: Year-round; unlimited.

TO APPLY: Applications can be obtained by contacting the refuge office (see Contact) or by visiting the US Fish and Wildlife Service at www.fws.gov/volunteers.

FIELD NOTES: Since the refuge borders the John F. Kennedy Space Center, it receives over 600,000 visitors a year. Volunteers should, therefore, apply early to secure a spot. Positions are suitable for families, groups, and solo travelers.

ST. MARKS NATIONAL WILDLIFE REFUGE

FLORIDA, USA

Within its coastal marshes, islands, and tidal creeks, St. Marks National Wildlife Refuge hosts a number of endangered species, including the red-cockaded woodpecker; wood stork; West Indian manatee; and loggerhead, leatherback, and Atlantic green turtles. Participants help with visitor services, environmental education programs, wildlife monitoring, trail maintenance, and resource management.

CONTACT: St. Marks National Wildlife Refuge, PO Box 6504, Titusville, FL 32752; Tel: 3218610667; Web: www.fws.gov/saintmarks; Email: merrittisland@fws.gov.

LOCATION: Titusville, FL.

CATEGORY: Conservation.

COST: Free in exchange for service. Full RV hookups are provided. Volunteers must commit to a 32-hour workweek for a minimum of 30 days.

DATES & DURATION: Year-round; unlimited.

TO APPLY: Applications can be obtained by contacting the refuge office (see Contact) or by visiting the US Fish and Wildlife Service at www.fws.gov/volunteers.

FIELD NOTES: Resident volunteer programs usually run from September through May. Positions are suitable for families, groups, and solo travelers.

WILD ANIMAL SANCTUARY PROGRAM

FLORIDA, USA

Home to tigers, cougars, capuchin monkeys, tamarins, and lemurs, the Wild Animal Sanctuary Program in Zolfo Springs, Florida, offers volunteers the chance to work hands-on with some incredible creatures. Participants help feed and clean the animals, prepare their meals, construct and clean enclosures, and maintain the center's facilities.

CONTACT: Eco Volunteer Organization c/o The Great Canadian Travel Company Ltd, 158 Fort St, Winnipeg, MB, Canada R3C 1C9; Tel: 2049490199 or 8006613830; Web: www.ecovolunteer.org; Email: ecovolunteer@gctc-mst.com.

LOCATION: Zolfo Springs, FL.

CATEGORY: Conservation.

COST: US$295–$199 per week for 1–12 weeks. Fee includes accommodations, meals, airport pickup and drop-offs, ground transfers, training, and support.

DATES & DURATION: Year-round; 1–12 weeks.

TO APPLY: Applications are accepted online and by fax or mail. Contact the office (see Contact).

FIELD NOTES: Minimum age requirement of 21. Applicants must be in good physical condition, be up-to-date on inoculations, and have proof of medical insurance. Positions are suitable for adult groups and solo travelers.

KILAUEA POINT NATIONAL WILDLIFE REFUGE

HAWAII, USA

Now home to many different types of birds, the Kilauea Point National Wildlife Refuge was originally established as a safe place for the Laysan albatross and Hawaiian goose to nest and rear their young. Due to the reserve's success, travelers to the refuge can now spot those magnificent birds as well as many other species. Aquatic mammals, such as the majestic humpback whale and the spinner dolphin, are sometimes seen from the refuge. Volunteers help replant and maintain native coastal plants, and work on public educational campaigns that focus on wildlife conservation. Participants may also lead tours.

CONTACT: Kilauea Point National Wildlife Refuge, State Hwy 56 and Lighthouse Rd, Kilauea, HI 96754-1128; Tel: 8088281413; Web: www.fws.gov/kilaueapoint; Email: shannon_smith@fws.gov.

LOCATION: Kilauea, HI.

CATEGORY: Conservation.

COST: Free in exchange for service. Accommodation is provided.

DATES & DURATION: Year-round; unlimited.

TO APPLY: Applications can be obtained by contacting the refuge office (see Contact) or by visiting the US Fish and Wildlife Service at www.fws.gov/volunteers.

FIELD NOTES: This project is suitable for families, groups, and solo travelers.

MIDWAY ATOLL NATIONAL WILDLIFE REFUGE

HAWAII, USA

At Hawaii's gorgeous Midway Atoll National Wildlife Refuge, visitors can catch a glimpse of some incredible animals, including 18 species of birds, spinner dolphins, green turtles, and the endangered monk seal. Volunteers help restore local habitats, plant native flora, remove invasive and non-native plant species, and monitor seabirds. Other duties include keeping the beaches clean.

CONTACT: Midway Atoll National Wildlife Refuge, Box 50167, Honolulu, HI 96754-1128; Tel: 8086748237; Web: www.fws.gov/midway/index.html; Email: matt_d_brown@fws.gov.

LOCATION: Honolulu, HI.

CATEGORY: Conservation.

COST: Free in exchange for service. Apartments are provided.

DATES & DURATION: Year-round; unlimited.

TO APPLY: Applications can be obtained by contacting the refuge office (see Contact) or by visiting the US Fish and Wildlife Service at www.fws.gov/volunteers.

FIELD NOTES: Positions are suitable for solo travelers and couples. Note that volunteer positions fill quickly; apply well in advance.

CAMAS NATIONAL WILDLIFE REFUGE

IDAHO, USA

Camas National Wildlife Refuge was established to provide a safe and protected haven to a selection of migratory bird species, including songbirds. The refuge is also home to several waterfowl species, such as the trumpeter swan, snowy egret, great blue heron, and white-faced ibis. Volunteers help with wildlife and bird inventories, bird-banding projects, and grounds maintenance.

CONTACT: Camas National Wildlife Refuge, 2150 East 2350 N Hamer, ID 83425; Tel: 2086625423; Web: www.fws.gov/camasnwr; Email: Contact form on website.

LOCATION: Hamer, ID.

CATEGORY: Conservation.

COST: Free in exchange for service. Full RV hookups are provided; laundry facilities are available on-site.

DATES & DURATION: Year-round; unlimited.

TO APPLY: Applications can be obtained by contacting the refuge office (see Contact) or by visiting the US Fish and Wildlife Service at www.fws.gov/volunteers.

FIELD NOTES: The collection of natural objects, such as plants, animals, antlers, and Indian artifacts, is prohibited. Hunting is permitted in designated areas. Both full- and part-time positions are available. Families, groups, and solo travelers are all welcome. Participants should be aware that volunteer duties may change to meet the reserve's current needs and goals.

DEER FLAT NATIONAL WILDLIFE REFUGE

IDAHO, USA

From its islands to its riparian forests, Idaho's Deer Flat National Wildlife Refuge plays host to large populations of Canada geese; bald eagles; ospreys; and a variety of ducks, including mallards, northern pintails, green-winged teals, and wood ducks. Volunteers help survey goose nests, remove invasive plant species, and work at the visitors center. Participants may also be called on to assist staff with the annual fall duck-banding program.

CONTACT: Deer Flat National Wildlife Refuge, 13751 Upper Embankment Rd, Nampa, ID 83686; Tel: 2084679278; Fax: 2084671019; Web: www.fws.gov/deerflat; Email: deerflat@fws.gov.

LOCATION: Nampa, ID.

CATEGORY: Conservation.

COST: Free in exchange for service. Housing is provided.

DATES & DURATION: Year-round; unlimited.

TO APPLY: Applications can be obtained by contacting the refuge office (see Contact) or by visiting the US Fish and Wildlife Service at www.fws.gov/volunteers.

FIELD NOTES: While volunteers of all ages are welcome, participants under the age of 18 must be accompanied by a parent or have written permission. Training and equipment are provided. Both full- and part-time spots are available and are filled based on availability. Positions are suitable for families, groups, and solo travelers.

KOOSKIA NATIONAL FISH HATCHERY

IDAHO, USA

Established in 1961, Kooskia National Fish Hatchery works with the primary objective of rearing spring Chinook salmon. Volunteers participate in a variety of projects, including feeding resident fish, cleaning tanks and raceways, conducting sample counts, maintaining the facility, landscaping, and participating in public outreach activities.

CONTACT: Kooskia National Fish Hatchery, Route 1, Box 98A, Kooskia, ID 83539; Tel: 2089264591; Web: www.fws.gov/kooskia; Email: Contact form on website.

LOCATION: Kooskia, ID.

CATEGORY: Conservation.

COST: Free in exchange for service. Full RV hookups and trailer housing is provided.

DATES & DURATION: April through September; unlimited.

TO APPLY: Applications can be obtained by contacting the hatchery office (see Contact) or by visiting the US Fish and Wildlife Service at www.fws.gov/volunteers.

FIELD NOTES: Applicants must be at least 18 years of age. Couples are encouraged to apply, but positions are suitable for families, groups, and solo travelers.

KOOTENAI NATIONAL WILDLIFE REFUGE

IDAHO, USA

Home to 22 types of fish, 13 types of reptiles and amphibians, 45 types of mammals, and 223 species of birds, the Kootenai National Wildlife Refuge is bustling with wildlife. Visitors can spot moose, elk, mountain lions, bobcats, and black bears on park grounds. Volunteers help with wildlife surveys and grounds maintenance and with ensuring that the refuge remains a pristine environment for its amazing inhabitants. Participants may also help design education programs about the importance of conservation.

CONTACT: Kootenai National Wildlife Refuge, 287 Westside Rd, Bonners Ferry, ID 83805; Tel: 2082673888; Fax: 2082675570; Web: www.fws.gov/kootenai; Email: Contact form on website.

LOCATION: Bonners Ferry, ID.

CATEGORY: Conservation.

COST: Free in exchange for service. Full RV hookups and apartment housing are provided.

DATES & DURATION: Varies; unlimited.

TO APPLY: Applications can be obtained by contacting the refuge office (see Contact) or by visiting the US Fish and Wildlife Service at www.fws.gov/volunteers.

FIELD NOTES: Positions are suitable for families, groups, and solo travelers. Participants should be aware that volunteer duties may change to meet the reserve's current needs and goals.

MUSCATATUCK NATIONAL WILDLIFE REFUGE

INDIANA, USA

Established in 1966, Indiana's Muscatatuck National Wildlife Refuge provides a habitat for native waterfowl and other wildlife, such as wood ducks, Canada geese, blue herons, great egrets, and migrating warblers. The rare cooperbelly water snake also makes its home in this wetland habitat. Volunteers participate in interpretive services and school-group tours, staff the visitors center and bookstore, help with landscaping and tree planting, and work on refuge and trail maintenance.

CONTACT: Muscatatuck National Wildlife Refuge, 12985 East US Hwy 50, Seymour, IN 47274; Tel: 8125224352; Web: midwest.fws.gov/muscatatuck; Email: muscatatuck@fws.gov.

LOCATION: Seymour, IN.

CATEGORY: Conservation.

COST: Free in exchange for service. Full RV hookups are provided; laundry facilities are available on-site.

DATES & DURATION: Year-round; unlimited.

TO APPLY: Applications can be obtained by contacting the refuge office (see Contact) or by visiting the US Fish and Wildlife Service at www.fws.gov/volunteers.

FIELD NOTES: Both full- and part-time positions are available. Families, groups, and solo travelers are all welcome. Participants should be aware that volunteer duties may change to meet the reserve's current needs and goals.

WOLF PARK

INDIANA, USA

Wolf Park, founded in 1972, offers visitors the chance to learn about and get up close and personal with wolves. Volunteers help feed and care for the wolves and other mammals, such as bison and foxes. From May to November, participants also help with park tours and public relations.

CONTACT: Wolf Park, 4004 East 800 North, Battle Ground, IN 47920; Tel: 7655672265; Fax: 7655674299; Web: www.wolfpark.org; Email: wolfpark@wolfpark.org.

LOCATION: Battle Ground, IN.

CATEGORY: Conservation.

COST: Free in exchange for service. Accommodations and transportation are provided.

DATES & DURATION: Year-round; long- and short-term assignments are available.

TO APPLY: Contact Dana Drenzek at dana@wolfpark.org or contact the office (see Contact).

FIELD NOTES: Volunteers are expected to work a minimum of two shifts per month. Training is provided. All volunteers are required to complete an application and a liability release form. Participants must be 18 years of age or older to enter the wolves' enclosures. To minimize scratching, volunteers should wear long pants and long-sleeved shirts and are not allowed to wear jewelry. Positions are best suited for adults traveling solo or in small groups.

DESOTO NATIONAL WILDLIFE REFUGE

IOWA, USA

A stopover point for migrating ducks and geese, Iowa's DeSoto National Wildlife Refuge offers visitors the opportunity to see some incredible waterfowl, especially in the fall. Working with researchers, participants help with wildlife surveys and nest-box monitoring. Participants should also expect to work on maintaining the reserve's idyllic walking trails.

CONTACT: DeSoto National Wildlife Refuge, 1434 316th Ln, Missouri Valley, IA 51555; Tel: 7126424121; Fax: 7126422877; Web: www.fws.gov/midwest/desoto; Email: larry_klimek@fws.gov.

LOCATION: Missouri Valley, IA.

CATEGORY: Conservation.

COST: Free in exchange for service. Full RV hookups are provided.

DATES & DURATION: Varies; depends on project.

TO APPLY: Applications can be obtained by contacting the refuge office (see Contact) or by visiting the US Fish and Wildlife Service at www.fws.gov/volunteers.

FIELD NOTES: Fishing, boating, and hunting are permitted on refuge grounds in designated areas. Projects are suitable for solo travelers and couples.

NEAL SMITH NATIONAL WILDLIFE REFUGE

IOWA, USA

Every year, 200,000 visitors enjoy biking and birding on the 8,000 acres of rolling tallgrass prairies and oak savannas of Iowa's Neal Smith National Wildlife Refuge. Volunteers help collect native seeds for replanting in an effort to recreate the pre-1800s prairie ecosystem. Participants also work to maintain the park's hiking trails and assist with general refuge maintenance projects.

CONTACT: Neal Smith National Wildlife Refuge, PO Box 399, Prairie City, IA 50228; Tel: 5159943459; Web: www.fws.gov/midwest/nealsmith; Email: nealsmith@fws.gov.

LOCATION: Prairie City, IA.

CATEGORY: Conservation.

COST: Free in exchange for service. Housing is provided.

DATES & DURATION: Varies; depends on project.

TO APPLY: Applications can be obtained by contacting the refuge office (see Contact) or by visiting the US Fish and Wildlife Service at www.fws.gov/volunteers.

FIELD NOTES: Training is provided onsite. Positions are suitable for families, groups, and solo travelers.

FLINT HILLS NATIONAL WILDLIFE REFUGE

KANSAS, USA

Located in Kansas's Neosho River Valley, Flint Hills National Wildlife Refuge provides a home for native waterfowl, such as mallards, blue-winged teals, and snow geese, and other wildlife, such as white-tailed deer and bobcats. Volunteers help with biodiversity surveys, refuge facility maintenance, and interpretive and visitor services.

CONTACT: Flint Hills National Wildlife Refuge, PO Box 128, Hartford, KS 66854; Tel: 6203925553; Web: www.fws.gov/flinthills; Email: flinthills@fws.gov.

LOCATION: Hartford, KS.

CATEGORY: Conservation.

COST: Free in exchange for service. Trailer accommodations are provided.

DATES & DURATION: Varies; depends on project.

TO APPLY: Applications can be obtained by contacting the refuge office (see Contact) or by visiting the US Fish and Wildlife Service at www.fws.gov/volunteers.

FIELD NOTES: Boating, fishing, and picnicking are permitted on refuge grounds. Wild food gathering and hunting are permitted in designated areas only. Both full- and part-time positions are available. Families, groups, and solo travelers are all welcome. Participants should be aware that volunteer duties may change to meet the reserve's current needs and goals.

QUIVIRA NATIONAL WILDLIFE REFUGE

KANSAS, USA

Cranes, cuckoos, falcons, and swans are among the 300 species of birds found within Kansas's Quivira National Wildlife Refuge. Black-tailed prairie dogs, red foxes, and even river otters also make their home in the refuge. Working with the refuge staff, volunteers help survey the local bird populations and clean up the park's walking trails. Participants may also be called on to assist staff with educational programs and special events.

CONTACT: Quivira National Wildlife Refuge, 1434 NE 80th St, Stafford, KS 67578; Tel: 6204862392; Web: www.fws.gov/quivira; Email: quivira@fws.gov.

LOCATION: Stafford, KS.

CATEGORY: Conservation.

COST: Free in exchange for service. Bunkhouse accommodations are provided.

DATES & DURATION: Year-round; unlimited.

TO APPLY: Applications can be obtained by contacting the refuge office (see Contact) or by visiting the US Fish and Wildlife Service at www.fws.gov/volunteers.

FIELD NOTES: Both full- and part-time positions are available. Positions are suitable for families, groups, and solo travelers.

ATCHAFALAYA NATIONAL WILDLIFE REFUGE

LOUISIANA, USA

At 15,000 acres, Louisiana's Atchafalaya National Wildlife Refuge offers visitors the chance to see black bears, American alligators, white-tailed deer, and even wild turkeys. Volunteers help with wildlife surveys and general maintenance. Participants may also be called on to assist the refuge staff with scientific research and interpretive or demonstration activities.

CONTACT: Atchafalaya National Wildlife Refuge, US Fish and Wildlife Service, Southeast Louisiana Refuges, Bayou Lacombe Centre, 61389 Hwy 434, Lacombe, LA 70445; Tel: 9858822000; Fax: 9858829133; Web: www.fws.gov/atchafalaya; Email: atchafalaya@fws.gov.

LOCATION: Lacombe, LA.

CATEGORY: Conservation.

COST: Free in exchange for service. Full RV hookups and other housing options are provided.

DATES & DURATION: Year-round; unlimited. To qualify, volunteers must commit to a 32-hour workweek.

TO APPLY: Applications can be obtained by contacting the refuge office (see Contact) or by visiting the US Fish and Wildlife Service at www.fws.gov/volunteers.

FIELD NOTES: Training is provided onsite. Participants should be aware that volunteer duties may change to meet the reserve's current needs and goals. Positions are suitable for families, groups, and solo travelers.

BAYOU SAUVAGE NATIONAL WILDLIFE REFUGE

LOUISIANA, USA

Louisiana's Bayou Sauvage National Wildlife Refuge is home to wading and shore birds, marsh rabbits, white pelicans, alligators, and the endangered brown pelican. At the site, volunteers help with habitat restoration projects and wildlife surveys. Participants also maintain the refuge and its facilities.

CONTACT: Bayou Sauvage National Wildlife Refuge, US Fish and Wildlife Service, Southeast Louisiana Refuges, Bayou Lacombe Centre, 61389 Hwy 434, Lacombe, LA 70445; Tel: 9858822000; Fax: 9858829133; Web: www.fws.gov/bayousauvage; Email: bayousauvage@fws.gov.

LOCATION: Lacombe, LA.

CATEGORY: Conservation.

COST: Free in exchange for service. Full RV hookups are provided. To qualify, volunteers must commit to a 32-hour workweek.

DATES & DURATION: Year-round; unlimited.

TO APPLY: Applications can be obtained by contacting the refuge office (see Contact) or by visiting the US Fish and Wildlife Service at www.fws.gov/volunteers.

FIELD NOTES: Participants may be asked to assist with tree and marsh planning efforts. Training is provided on-site. Positions are suitable for families, groups, and solo travelers.

BAYOU TECHE NATIONAL WILDLIFE REFUGE

LOUISIANA, USA

Originally established as a safe haven for the threatened Louisiana black bear, Bayou Teche National Wildlife Refuge now plays host to a variety of animals, including American alligators and bald eagles. Volunteers are needed for nest box and interpretive display construction and installation. Participants work on grounds and garden maintenance, litter control, and habitat restoration projects. Volunteers may also be asked to assist refuge staff with environmental education and visitors center operations.

CONTACT: Bayou Teche and Mandalay National Wildlife Refuges, US Fish and Wildlife Service, Southeast Louisiana Refuges, 3599 Bayou Black Dr, Houma, LA 70360; Tel: 9858531078; Fax: 9858531079; Web: www.fws.gov/bayouteche; Email: bayouteche@fws.gov.

LOCATION: Houma, LA.

CATEGORY: Conservation.

COST: Free in exchange for service. Full RV hookups and other housing options are provided; laundry facilities are available on-site.

DATES & DURATION: Year-round; unlimited. To qualify, individuals must commit to a 32-hour workweek; couples, to a 24-hour workweek per person.

TO APPLY: Applications can be obtained by contacting the refuge office (see Contact) or by visiting the US Fish and Wildlife Service at www.fws.gov/volunteers.

FIELD NOTES: Volunteers may be asked to assist staff with wildlife monitoring and surveying duties and special events. Families, groups, and solo travelers are all welcome. Participants should be aware that volunteer duties may change to meet the reserve's current needs and goals.

BIG BRANCH MARSH NATIONAL WILDLIFE REFUGE

LOUISIANA, USA

From its pinewood flats to its saltwater marshlands, Louisiana's Big Branch Marsh National Wildlife Refuge is home to many threatened and endangered species, including the red-cockaded woodpecker, brown pelican, Louisiana black bear, and gopher tortoise. Volunteers help restore wildlife habitats and monitor species' safety at the reserve. Participants may also help design educational programs focusing on the importance of conservation.

CONTACT: Big Branch Marsh National Wildlife Refuge, US Fish and Wildlife Service, Southeast Louisiana Refuges, Bayou Lacombe Centre, 61389 Hwy 434, Lacombe, LA 70445; Tel: 9858822000; Fax: 9858829133; Web: www.fws.gov/bigbranchmarsh; Email: bigbranchmarsh @fws.gov.

LOCATION: Lacombe, LA.

CATEGORY: Conservation.

COST: Free in exchange for service. Full RV hookups and other housing options are provided; laundry facilities are available on-site.

DATES & DURATION: Year-round; unlimited. To qualify, individuals must commit to a 32-hour workweek; couples, to a 24-hour workweek per person.

TO APPLY: Applications can be obtained by contacting the refuge office (see Contact) or by visiting the US Fish and Wildlife Service at www.fws.gov/volunteers.

FIELD NOTES: Biting insects are plentiful on refuge grounds, so insect repellent should be worn at all times. Positions are suitable for families, groups, and solo travelers.

BLACK BAYOU LAKE NATIONAL WILDLIFE REFUGE

LOUISIANA, USA

At 4,600 acres, Louisiana's Black Bayou Lake National Wildlife Refuge provides a home for many migratory waterfowl, neotropical songbirds, and other resident wildlife, such as the broadbanded water snake, red-eared slider, wood duck, and coyote. Participants work on outdoor conservation programs, assist with refuge maintenance, work in the visitors center and nature shop, and help with educational programs.

CONTACT: Black Bayou Lake National Wildlife Refuge, North Louisiana Refuge Complex, 11372 Hwy 143, Farmerville, LA 71363-0201; Tel: 3183871114; Fax: 3183872628; Web: www.fws.gov/northlouisiana/blackbayoulake; Email: brett_hortman@fws.gov.

LOCATION: Farmerville, LA.

CATEGORY: Conservation.

COST: Free in exchange for service. Full RV hookups are provided; other housing can be arranged.

DATES & DURATION: Year-round; unlimited. To qualify, volunteers must commit to 1 month of service and a 24-hour workweek.

TO APPLY: Applications can be obtained by contacting the refuge office (see Contact) or by visiting the US Fish and Wildlife Service at www.fws.gov/volunteers.

FIELD NOTES: Training is provided onsite. Positions are suitable for families, groups, and solo travelers. The reserve needs help 7 days a week.

BOGUE CHITTO NATIONAL WILDLIFE REFUGE

LOUISIANA, USA

Louisiana's Bogue Chitto National Wildlife Refuge is home to many threatened and endangered species, including the ringed-sawback turtle, American alligator, gopher tortoise, inflated heel-splitter mussel, and gulf sturgeon. Volunteers help restore these marvelous creatures' habitats and assist with the general upkeep of the refuge. Participants may also help researchers conduct biodiversity surveys.

CONTACT: Bogue Chitto National Wildlife Refuge, US Fish and Wildlife Service, Southeast Louisiana Refuges, Bayou Lacombe Centre, 61389 Hwy 434, Lacombe, LA 70445; Tel: 9858822000; Fax: 9858829133; Web: www.fws.gov/boguechitto; Email: boguechitto@fws.gov.

LOCATION: Lacombe, LA.

CATEGORY: Conservation.

COST: Free in exchange for service. Full RV hookups and other housing options are provided; laundry facilities are available on-site.

DATES & DURATION: Year-round; unlimited. To qualify, individuals must commit to a 32-hour workweek; couples, to a 24-hour workweek per person.

TO APPLY: Applications can be obtained by contacting the refuge office (see Contact) or by visiting the US Fish and Wildlife Service at www.fws.gov/volunteers.

FIELD NOTES: Volunteers receive orientation and training upon arrival. Families, couples, and solo travelers are all welcome.

BRETON NATIONAL WILDLIFE REFUGE

LOUISIANA, USA

Established in 1904, Breton National Wildlife Refuge provides a home for nesting and wading seabirds and wintering shorebirds. Other waterfowl include the laughing gull, Caspian and Sandwich tern, and endangered brown pelican. Volunteers help with wildlife surveys and refuge maintenance. Participants are also welcome to assist refuge staff in annual bird-banding projects and special events.

CONTACT: Breton National Wildlife Refuge, US Fish and Wildlife Service, Southeast Louisiana Refuges, Bayou Lacombe Centre, 61389 Hwy 434, Lacombe, LA 70445; Tel: 9858822000; Fax: 9858829133; Web: www.fws.gov/breton; Email: breton@fws.gov.

LOCATION: Lacombe, LA.

CATEGORY: Conservation.

COST: Free in exchange for service. Full RV hookups and other housing options are provided; laundry facilities are available on-site.

DATES & DURATION: Year-round; unlimited. To qualify, individuals must commit to a 32-hour workweek; couples, to a 24-hour workweek per person.

TO APPLY: Applications can be obtained by contacting the refuge office (see Contact) or by visiting the US Fish and Wildlife Service at www.fws.gov/volunteers.

FIELD NOTES: Training is provided upon arrival. Positions are suitable for families, groups, and solo travelers.

LACASSINE NATIONAL WILDLIFE REFUGE

LOUISIANA, USA

At Louisiana's Lacassine National Wildlife Refuge, visitors can spot some incredible waterfowl, such as the ibis, roseate spoonbill, egret, and bald eagle. The refuge is also home to the Louisiana black bear. Volunteers help park staff restore animal habitats and conduct wildlife surveys. Participants may also work on environmental education programs.

CONTACT: Lacassine National Wildlife Refuge, 2089 Nature Rd, Lake Arthur, LA 70549; Tel: 3377745923; Web: www.fws.gov/swlarefugecomplex/lacassine; Email: lacassine@fws.gov.

LOCATION: Lake Arthur, LA.

CATEGORY: Conservation.

COST: Free in exchange for service. Refuge housing and a small stipend are provided.

DATES & DURATION: Year-round; unlimited.

TO APPLY: Applications can be obtained by contacting the refuge office (see Contact) or by visiting the US Fish and Wildlife Service at www.fws.gov/volunteers.

FIELD NOTES: Hours and assignments are flexible. Both full- and part-time positions are available. Positions are suitable for families, groups, and solo travelers.

SABINE NATIONAL WILDLIFE REFUGE

LOUISIANA, USA

Each year, thousands of wintering waterfowl traveling along the Mississippi and Central flyways stop at Louisiana's Sabine National Wildlife Refuge to enjoy the reserve's protected wetlands. In 2005, the refuge was heavily affected by Hurricane Rita. Damage to the canals and marshes are considered severe. Habitat restoration projects are under way, and volunteers are needed to help return these grounds to their natural state. The refuge is currently closed to the public.

CONTACT: Sabine National Wildlife Refuge, 3000 Holly Beach Hwy, Hackberry, LA 70645; Tel: 3377623816; Web: www.fws.gov/swlarefugecomplex/sabine; Email: sabine@fws.gov.

LOCATION: Hackberry, LA.

CATEGORY: Conservation.

COST: Free in exchange for service. Full RV hookups and other housing arrangements are provided.

DATES & DURATION: Year-round; unlimited.

TO APPLY: Applications can be obtained by contacting the refuge office (see Contact) or by visiting the US Fish and Wildlife Service at www.fws.gov/volunteers.

FIELD NOTES: Training is provided onsite. Both full- and part-time positions are available. Positions are suitable for families, groups, and solo travelers.

TENSAS RIVER NATIONAL WILDLIFE REFUGE

LOUISIANA, USA

Home to over 400 species of mammals, birds, reptiles, and fish, Louisiana's Tensas River National Wildlife Refuge gives visitors the chance to spot one of the area's most threatened animals—the Louisiana black bear. Volunteers help conduct wildlife surveys and assist with refuge maintenance and habitat restoration. During spring and fall, volunteers may also help with educational camps for school groups and other organizations.

CONTACT: Tensas River National Wildlife Refuge, 2312 Quebec Rd, Tallulah, LA 71282; Tel: 3185742664; Fax: 3185741624; Web: www.fws.gov/tensasriver; Email: tensasriver@fws.gov.

LOCATION: Tallulah, LA.

CATEGORY: Conservation.

COST: Free in exchange for service. Trailer accommodations are provided.

DATES & DURATION: Year-round; unlimited.

TO APPLY: Applications can be obtained by contacting the refuge office (see Contact) or by visiting the US Fish and Wildlife Service at www.fws.gov/volunteers.

FIELD NOTES: Participants should be aware that volunteer duties may change to meet the reserve's current needs and goals. Positions are suitable for families, groups, and solo travelers.

MOOSEHORN NATIONAL WILDLIFE REFUGE

MAINE, USA

Maine's Moosehorn National Wildlife Refuge is located on the Atlantic flyway, making it an ideal spot for bird-watching. The refuge is also home to deer, grouse, and bear. Volunteers help researchers with wildlife surveys and work on any habitat modification and restoration projects. Volunteers may be asked to lead tours; provide information and interpretive services; take part in special events; and help with seasonal projects, such as bird banding.

CONTACT: Moosehorn National Wildlife Refuge, RR 1, Box 202, Suite 1, Charlotte Rd, Baring, ME 04694; Tel: 2074547161; Fax: 2074542550; Web: www.fws.gov/northeast/moosehorn; Email: fw5rw_mhnwr@fws.gov.

LOCATION: Baring, ME.

CATEGORY: Conservation.

COST: Free in exchange for service. A small stipend and dormitory housing and rustic-style barracks are provided.

DATES & DURATION: Summer; unlimited. To qualify, volunteers must commit to a 40-hour workweek.

TO APPLY: Applications can be obtained by contacting the refuge office (see Contact) or by visiting the US Fish and Wildlife Service at www.fws.gov/volunteers.

FIELD NOTES: Volunteers under 18 years of age must have parental consent. Both full- and part-time spots are available. Positions are suitable for families, groups, and solo travelers.

RACHEL CARSON NATIONAL WILDLIFE REFUGE

MAINE, USA

Spring at the Rachel Carson National Wildlife Refuge definitely isn't silent! In fact, the refuge is bustling with all sorts of animals, including piping plovers, peregrine falcons, bald eagles, moose, black bears, bobcats, and gray foxes. At the refuge, volunteers help the staff survey local wildlife and work on habitat restoration. Volunteers may also be asked to lead tours and nature walks and talk with visitors about the importance of protecting the environment for future generations.

CONTACT: Rachel Carson National Wildlife Refuge, 321 Port Rd, Wells, ME 04090; Tel: 2076469226; Fax: 2076466554; Web: www.fws.gov/northeast/rachelcarson; Email: rachelcarson@fws.gov.

LOCATION: Wells, ME.

CATEGORY: Conservation.

COST: Free in exchange for service.

Rustic-style accommodations are provided.

DATES & DURATION: Summer; unlimited.

TO APPLY: Applications can be obtained by contacting the refuge office (see Contact) or by visiting the US Fish and Wildlife Service at www.fws.gov/volunteers.

FIELD NOTES: Both full- and part-time positions are available. Positions are suitable for families, groups, and solo travelers.

SUNKHAZE MEADOWS NATIONAL WILDLIFE REFUGE

MAINE, USA

With the second largest peat-land ecosystem in Maine, Sunkhaze Meadows National Wildlife Refuge provides a home for a variety of different species, such as the rough-legged hawk, northern saw-whet owl, and American black duck. Volunteers help with wildlife surveys, hiking trail maintenance, and habitat restoration. Participants are needed to lead nature hikes and canoe trips through the refuge, and naturalists are welcome to share their passion for wildlife tracking with refuge visitors.

CONTACT: Sunkhaze Meadows National Wildlife Refuge, PO Box 495, 16 Rockport Park Centre, Rockport, ME 04856; Tel: 2072366970, Ext. 11; Fax: 2072366972;

Web: www.fws.gov/northeast/me/sunk hazemeadows; Email: michael_langlois@ fws.gov or info@sunkhaze.org.

LOCATION: Milford, ME.

CATEGORY: Conservation.

COST: Free in exchange for service. Cabin accommodations are provided.

DATES & DURATION: Summer; unlimited.

TO APPLY: Applications can be obtained by contacting the refuge office (see Contact) or by visiting the US Fish and Wildlife Service at www.fws.gov/volunteers.

FIELD NOTES: Biting flies and mosquitoes are abundant during the summer months; repellent should be worn at all times. Training is provided on-site upon arrival. Positions are suitable for families, groups, and solo travelers.

JORDAN RIVER NATIONAL FISH HATCHERY

MICHIGAN, USA

Jordan River National Fish Hatchery specializes in the rearing of lake trout. The hatchery produces and releases nearly 2 million yearlings annually. Volunteers assist staff with stocking and feeding fish, cleaning tanks and raceways, taking samples, maintaining the facility, and doing landscaping. Participants may also be called on to assist with ongoing public outreach activities.

CONTACT: Jordan River National Fish Hatchery, 6623 Turner Rd, Elmira, MI 49730; Tel: 2315842461; Fax: 2315842462; Web: www.fws.gov/midwest/jordanriver; Email: jordanriver@fws.gov.

LOCATION: Elmira, MI.

CATEGORY: Conservation.

COST: Free in exchange for service. Housing for eight to ten volunteers at a time is provided.

DATES & DURATION: Varies; unlimited.

TO APPLY: Applications can be obtained by contacting the hatchery office (see Contact) or by visiting the US Fish and Wildlife Service at www.fws.gov/volunteers.

FIELD NOTES: The hatchery offers two types of internships; more information is available at the website. Positions are suitable for adults traveling solo or by group.

AGASSIZ NATIONAL WILDLIFE REFUGE

MINNESOTA, USA

At over 61,000 acres, Minnesota's Agassiz National Wildlife Refuge offers safe haven for an assortment of waterfowl and migratory birds, 21 types of amphibians and reptiles, and 49 species of mammals (including the moose, gray wolf, red fox, and coyote). Volunteers help with wildlife surveys and laboratory research. Participants also remove invasive plant species, maintain the grounds and trails, and stock fish.

CONTACT: Agassiz National Wildlife Refuge, 22996 290th St NE, Middle River, MN 56737; Tel: 2184494115; Fax: 2184493241; Web: www.fws.gov/midwest/agassiz; Email: agassiz@fws.gov.

LOCATION: Middle River, MN.

CATEGORY: Conservation.

COST: Free in exchange for service. Bunkhouse accommodations are provided.

DATES & DURATION: Summer; unlimited.

TO APPLY: Applications can be obtained by contacting the refuge office (see Contact) or by visiting the US Fish and Wildlife Service at www.fws.gov/volunteers.

FIELD NOTES: Training is provided onsite. Volunteers of all ages are welcome, but those under the age of 18 must have written parental permission. Positions are suitable for families, groups, and solo travelers.

AMERICAN BEAR ASSOCIATION: VINCE SHUTE WILDLIFE SANCTUARY

MINNESOTA, USA

At the American Bear Association's Vince Shute Wildlife Sanctuary, volunteers have the chance to work hands-on with the black bear, an amazing creature. Nestled in the Minnesota woods, the 300-acre reserve also provides a home for the white-tailed deer, bald eagle, timber wolf, bobcat, and lynx. Participants help prepare meals for the bears, clean their feeding areas, and plant vegetation to maintain the sanctuary grounds. Volunteers and interns are needed for long- and short-term assignments.

CONTACT: American Bear Association, PO Box 77, Orr, MN 55771; Tel: 2187570172; Web: www.americanbear .org/volunteers.htm; Email: bears@ rangenet.com

LOCATION: Orr, MN.

CATEGORY: Conservation.

COST: Free in exchange for service. Accommodations and meals are provided; long-term volunteers receive first choice of accommodations.

DATES & DURATION: May through September; unlimited.

TO APPLY: Applications can be obtained by contacting the office (see Contact).

FIELD NOTES: All volunteers must sign a

liability waiver and read and comply with the volunteer handbook. Participants should be physically fit and be able to lift a 50-pound seed bag. Positions are suitable for adult groups and solo travelers.

CRANE MEADOWS NATIONAL WILDLIFE REFUGE

MINNESOTA, USA

Established in 1992, Crane Meadows National Wildlife Refuge plays host to one of Minnesota's largest remaining populations of the greater sandhill crane. Volunteers are needed for a variety of projects, such as trail maintenance, habitat restoration, and wildflower gardening. Participants may be asked to patrol for any signs of habitat destruction or vandalism, and assist with a variety of other maintenance duties.

CONTACT: Crane Meadows National Wildlife Refuge, 19502 Iris Rd, Little Falls MN 56345; Tel: 3206321575; Web: www.fws.gov/midwest/cranemeadows; Email: cranemeadows@fws.gov.

LOCATION: Little Falls, MN.

CATEGORY: Conservation.

COST: Free in exchange for service. Housing is provided.

DATES & DURATION: Summer; unlimited.

TO APPLY: Applications can be obtained by contacting the refuge office (see Contact) or by visiting the US Fish and Wildlife Service at www.fws.gov/volunteers.

FIELD NOTES: Volunteers are required to

attend an orientation and training session before the start of their service commitment. Projects may vary depending on current needs. Positions are suitable for families, groups, and solo travelers.

DETROIT LAKES WETLAND MANAGEMENT DISTRICT

MINNESOTA, USA

Established in 1968, Detroit Lakes Wetland Management District remains a critical waterfowl and bird migration area to almost 300 species. Volunteers are involved with facility maintenance, landscaping, and public outreach activities. Participants may also be called on to assist with clerical work, visitor services, and gardening.

CONTACT: Detroit Lakes Wetland Management District, 26624 North Tower Rd, Detroit Lakes, MN 56501; Tel: 2188474431; Web: www.fws.gov/midwest/detroitlakes; Email: scott_kahan@fws.gov.

LOCATION: Detroit Lakes, MN.

CATEGORY: Conservation.

COST: Free in exchange for service. Housing is provided for up to six volunteers.

DATES & DURATION: Varies; unlimited.

TO APPLY: Applications can be obtained by contacting the office (see Contact) or by visiting the US Fish and Wildlife Service at www.fws.gov/volunteers.

FIELD NOTES: Participants must be at least 18 years of age. Some volunteer positions require a driver's license. Positions are suitable for adult groups and solo travelers.

RICE LAKE NATIONAL WILDLIFE REFUGE

MINNESOTA, USA

Rice Lake National Wildlife Refuge, at 4,500 acres, is famous for its extensive rice beds—an important food source for the area's 227 species of migratory and resident waterfowl, including an extremely large population of ring-necked ducks. Working at this amazing site, volunteers help maintain the park's scenic trails and help researchers survey the local wildlife. Participants also monitor nests and assist with general refuge maintenance.

CONTACT: Rice Lake National Wildlife Refuge, 36298 State Hwy 65, McGregor, MN 55760; Tel: 2187682402; Web: www .fws.gov/midwest/ricelake; Email: ricelake@fws.gov.

LOCATION: McGregor, MN.

CATEGORY: Conservation.

COST: Free in exchange for service. Housing is provided.

DATES & DURATION: Summer; unlimited.

TO APPLY: Applications can be obtained by contacting the refuge office (see Contact) or by visiting the US Fish and Wildlife Service at www.fws.gov/volunteers.

FIELD NOTES: Training is provided upon arrival. Positions are suitable for families, groups, and solo travelers.

HILLSIDE NATIONAL WILDLIFE REFUGE

MISSISSIPPI, USA

Known for its large concentration of wintering waterfowl, Hillside National Wildlife Refuge provides an important nesting habitat for over 200 species of neotropical migratory birds, such as warblers, tanagers, and vireos. Volunteers help with wildlife surveys, wood-duck banding, and restoration of habitats. Participants also lead visitor tours and assist with the general maintenance.

CONTACT: Hillside National Wildlife Refuge, 1562 Providence Rd, Cruger, MS 38924; Tel: 6622354989; Fax: 6622355303; Web: www.fws.gov/hillside; Email: yazoo@fws.gov.

LOCATION: Cruger, MS.

CATEGORY: Conservation.

COST: Free in exchange for service. Trailer accommodations are provided.

DATES & DURATION: Summer; unlimited.

TO APPLY: Applications can be obtained by contacting the refuge office (see Contact) or by visiting the US Fish and Wildlife Service at www.fws.gov/volunteers.

FIELD NOTES: Organized group participation is welcomed and encouraged. Both full- and part-time positions are available. Families, groups, and solo travelers are all welcome. Participants should be aware that volunteer duties may change to meet the reserve's current needs and goals.

MISSISSIPPI SANDHILL CRANE NATIONAL WILDLIFE REFUGE

MISSISSIPPI, USA

Originally established to offer a safe haven for the endangered crane, Mississippi Sandhill Crane National Wildlife Refuge now plays host to a variety of amazing birds, including the pied-billed grebe, green heron, and indigo bunting. Volunteers help survey the local bird and amphibian populations and monitor the reserve's magnificent cranes. Participants may also be asked to work in the visitors center, provide talks to school groups, and help maintain the refuge's walking trails.

CONTACT: Mississippi Sandhill Crane National Wildlife Refuge, 7200 Crane Ln, Gautier, MS 39553; Tel: 2284975407; Web: www.fws.gov/mississippisandhillcrane; Email: mississippisandhillcrane@fws.gov.

LOCATION: Gautier, MS.

CATEGORY: Conservation.

COST: Free in exchange for service.

DATES & DURATION: Summer; unlimited.

TO APPLY: Applications can be obtained by contacting the refuge office (see Contact) or by visiting the US Fish and Wildlife Service at www.fws.gov/volunteers.

FIELD NOTES: All ages are welcome. Positions are suitable for families, groups, and solo travelers.

BOWDOIN NATIONAL WILDLIFE REFUGE

MONTANA, USA

Montana's Bowdoin National Wildlife Refuge is home to some incredible shorebirds, waterfowl, and native western mammals. Visitors have the chance to spot bald eagles, piping plovers, white-tailed deer, and even pronghorn antelope. Volunteers help survey wildlife, maintain hiking trails, and do office work. Volunteers may also be called on to assist with native prairie habitat restoration and construction projects.

CONTACT: Bowdoin National Wildlife Refuge, 194 Bowdoin Auto Tour Rd, Malta, MT 59538; Tel: 4066542863; Fax: 4066542866; Web: www.fws.gov/bowdoin; Email: bowdoin@fws.gov.

LOCATION: Malta, MT.

CATEGORY: Conservation.

COST: Free in exchange for service. Housing is provided.

DATES & DURATION: Summer; unlimited.

TO APPLY: Applications can be obtained by contacting the refuge office (see Contact) or by visiting the US Fish and Wildlife Service at www.fws.gov/volunteers.

FIELD NOTES: Both full- and part-time positions are available. All ages are welcome. Participants should be aware that volunteer duties may change to meet the reserve's current needs and goals. Positions are suitable for families, groups, and solo travelers.

CHARLES M. RUSSELL NATIONAL WILDLIFE REFUGE

MONTANA, USA

Within the more than 1 million acres that make up Montana's Charles M. Russell National Wildlife Refuge, visitors can hope to spot mule deer, pronghorn antelopes, sage grouses, prairie dogs, black-footed ferrets, and almost 240 species of birds. Volunteers help monitor the wildlife and maintain the grounds. The refuge conducts several species surveys and research projects to determine population dynamics, such as survival rates, sex ratios, and habitat preferences. Volunteers are welcome to take part in ongoing research studies on raptors, bats, mourning doves, spiny soft-shelled turtles, prairie dogs, black-footed ferrets, and burrowing owls.

CONTACT: Charles M. Russell National Wildlife Refuge, PO Box 110 Airport Rd, Lewistown, MT 59457; Tel: 4065388706; Fax: 4065387521; Web: www.fws.gov/cmr; Email: cmr@fws.gov.

LOCATION: Lewistown, MT.

CATEGORY: Conservation.

COST: Free in exchange for service. Trailer accommodations are provided.

DATES & DURATION: Summer; unlimited.

TO APPLY: Applications can be obtained by contacting the refuge office (see Contact) or by visiting the US Fish and Wildlife Service at www.fws.gov/volunteers.

FIELD NOTES: Both full- and part-time positions are available. Positions are suitable for families, groups, and solo travelers. All ages are welcome.

NATIONAL BISON RANGE

MONTANA, USA

Originally created as a reserve for the American bison, the National Bison Range refuge now hosts a variety of thriving species, including elk, white-tailed and mule deer, pronghorn antelope, bighorn sheep, and black bear. Working with the refuge staff, volunteers conduct wildlife surveys, maintain the beautiful landscape, help with visitor services, participate in educational programs, and work in the bookstore.

CONTACT: National Bison Range, 58355 Bison Range Rd, Moiese, MT 59824; Tel: 4066442211; Fax: 4066442661; Web: www .fws.gov/bisonrange; Email: bisonrange@ fws.gov.

LOCATION: Moiese, MT.

CATEGORY: Conservation.

COST: Free in exchange for service. Full RV hookups and other housing options are provided.

DATES & DURATION: Summer; unlimited.

TO APPLY: Applications can be obtained by contacting the refuge office (see Contact) or by visiting the US Fish and Wildlife Service at www.fws.gov/volunteers.

FIELD NOTES: All ages are welcome. Participants should be aware that volunteer duties may change to meet the reserve's current needs and goals. Positions are suitable for families, groups, and solo travelers.

ASH MEADOWS NATIONAL WILDLIFE REFUGE

NEVADA, USA

From spring-fed wetlands to desert uplands, Nevada's Ash Meadows National Wildlife Refuge offers a varied habitat for its 239 species of birds, 27 species of mammals, and 25 species of reptiles and amphibians. Refuge biologists work with volunteers on wildlife surveys focused on improving our understanding of these amazing animals. Participants also help restore habitats and work on environmental education programs.

CONTACT: Ash Meadows National Wildlife Refuge, HCR 70, Box 610Z, Amargosa Valley, NV 89020; Tel: 7753725435; Fax: 7753725436; Web: www.fws.gov/desertcomplex/ashmeadows; Email: sharon_mckelvey@fws.gov.

LOCATION: Amargosa Valley, NV.

CATEGORY: Conservation.

COST: Free in exchange for service. A small stipend and full RV hookups and mobile-home accommodations are provided.

DATES & DURATION: Year-round; unlimited.

TO APPLY: Applications can be obtained by contacting the refuge office (see Contact) or by visiting the US Fish and Wildlife Service at www.fws.gov/volunteers.

FIELD NOTES: Both full- and part-time positions are available. Positions are suitable for families, groups, and solo travelers.

DESERT NATIONAL WILDLIFE REFUGE

NEVADA, USA

The Desert National Wildlife Refuge was established to protect the desert bighorn sheep but is also a haven for 52 types of mammals, 31 kinds of amphibians and reptiles, and more than 240 species of birds. Volunteers help conservationists with wildlife surveys and with restoring wildlife habitats. Participants may also be involved with public education concerning the importance of conservation and may assist with interpretive services.

CONTACT: Desert National Wildlife Refuge, HCR 38, Box 700, Las Vegas, NV 89124; Tel: 7028796110; Fax: 7028796115; Web: www.fws.gov/desertcomplex; Email: talktous@fws.gov.

LOCATION: Las Vegas, NV.

CATEGORY: Conservation.

COST: Free in exchange for service. Full RV hookups are provided.

DATES & DURATION: Year-round; unlimited.

TO APPLY: Applications can be obtained by contacting the refuge office (see Contact) or by visiting the US Fish and Wildlife Service at www.fws.gov/volunteers.

FIELD NOTES: Both full- and part-time positions are available. Positions are suitable for families, groups, and solo travelers. All ages are welcome. Participants should be aware that volunteer duties may change to meet the reserve's current needs and goals.

MOAPA VALLEY NATIONAL WILDLIFE REFUGE

NEVADA, USA

Founded in 1979, the Moapa Valley National Wildlife Refuge offers visitors the unique chance to see the endangered Moapa dace, a small fish now found only on the refuge grounds. Lucky travelers will spot the rare desert tortoise. Volunteers at the site help survey the local wildlife, work on various habitat restoration projects, and assist with environmental education programs.

CONTACT: Moapa Valley National Wildlife Refuge, c/o Desert NWR, HCR 38, Box 700, Las Vegas, NV 89124; Tel: 7028796110; Fax: 7028796115; Web: www .fws.gov/desertcomplex/moapavalley; Email: talktous@fws.org.

LOCATION: Las Vegas, NV.

CATEGORY: Conservation.

COST: Free in exchange for service. Full RV hookups are provided.

DATES & DURATION: Year-round; unlimited.

TO APPLY: Applications can be obtained by contacting the refuge office (see Contact) or by visiting the US Fish and Wildlife Service at www.fws.gov/volunteers.

FIELD NOTES: All ages are welcome. Participants should be aware that volunteer duties may change to meet the reserve's current needs and goals. Positions are suitable for families, groups, and solo travelers.

PAHRANAGAT NATIONAL WILDLIFE REFUGE

NEVADA, USA

At Nevada's Pahranagat National Wildlife Refuge, visitors can spot over 230 species of birds, including the great blue heron, pintail duck, and greater sandhill crane. Mammals within the refuge include mule deer, foxes, coyotes, and mountain lions. Volunteers help with animal and plant surveys and with restoring the refuge's ecosystems. Participants may also work as campground hosts and as groundskeepers.

CONTACT: Pahranagat National Wildlife Refuge, Box 510, Alamo, NV 89001; Tel: 7757253443; Fax: 7757253417; Web: www .fws.gov/desertcomplex/pahranagat; Email: merry_maxwell@fws.gov.

LOCATION: Alamo, NV.

CATEGORY: Conservation.

COST: Free in exchange for service. Full RV hookups are provided.

DATES & DURATION: Year-round; unlimited.

TO APPLY: Applications can be obtained by contacting the refuge office (see Contact) or by visiting the US Fish and Wildlife Service at www.fws.gov/volunteers.

FIELD NOTES: Hunting, fishing, and picnicking are permitted in designated areas. Positions are suitable for families, groups, and solo travelers. All ages are welcome.

SHELDON NATIONAL WILDLIFE REFUGE

NEVADA, USA

More than 300 species of birds, mule deer, bighorn sheep, pronghorn antelopes, and fish are found within the boundaries of the Sheldon National Wildlife Refuge. The refuge is also home to an increasing population of feral horses. At the site, volunteers help refuge staff inventory the reserve's animal inhabitants and assist with general refuge maintenance. Participants may also get involved in efforts currently under way to restore damaged habitats.

CONTACT: Sheldon National Wildlife Refuge, Hwy 40, Denio, NV 89404; Tel: 7759410200; Web: www.fws.gov/sheldonhartmtn; Email: Contact form on website.

LOCATION: Denio, NV.

CATEGORY: Conservation.

COST: Free in exchange for service. Full RV hookups are provided.

DATES & DURATION: Year-round; unlimited.

TO APPLY: Applications can be obtained by contacting the refuge office (see Contact) or by visiting the US Fish and Wildlife Service at www.fws.gov/volunteers.

FIELD NOTES: Boating, fishing, and hunting are permitted in designated areas. Both full- and part-time positions are available. Families, groups, and solo travelers are all welcome. Participants should be aware that volunteer duties may change to meet the reserve's current needs and goals.

STILLWATER NATIONAL WILDLIFE REFUGE

NEVADA, USA

Named a Globally Important Bird Area by the American Bird Conservancy, Nevada's Stillwater National Wildlife Refuge plays host to more than 280 species of birds. The wetlands attract large concentrations of waterfowl as well as over 20,000 other water birds, including the pelican, ibis, egret, and gull. Working with the staff, volunteers help with wildlife surveys, bird-banding projects, and the elimination of invasive plant species. Participants can also take part in refuge maintenance, such as removing litter and debris.

CONTACT: Stillwater National Wildlife Refuge, 1000 Auction Rd, Fallon, NV 89406; Tel: 7754235128; Fax: 7754230416; Web: www.fws.gov/stillwater; Email: stillwater@fws.gov.

LOCATION: Fallon, NV.

CATEGORY: Conservation.

COST: Free in exchange for service. Housing is provided.

DATES & DURATION: Year-round; unlimited.

TO APPLY: Applications can be obtained by contacting the refuge office (see Contact) or by visiting the US Fish and Wildlife Service at www.fws.gov/volunteers.

FIELD NOTES: Due to high temperatures and few clouds, sunscreen and lightweight clothing are recommended. Both full- and part-time positions are available. Positions are suitable for families, groups, and solo travelers. All ages are welcome.

DIAMONDBACK TERRAPINS OF BARNEGAT BAY

NEW JERSEY, USA

Working with a dedicated team of scientists, volunteers study the magnificent diamondback terrapins of New Jersey's Barnegat Bay in an effort to determine the population status and viability of this unique species. Participants help track, capture, and tag terrapins in the wild. Volunteers collect samples and data to determine preferred habitats, monitor nesting habitats, and record hatchling success rates.

CONTACT: Earthwatch Institute, 3 Clock Tower Pl, Suite 100, Box 75, Maynard, MA 01754; Tel: 9784610081 or 8007760188; Fax: 9784612332; Web: www.earthwatch.org/exped/avery.html; Email: expeditions@earthwatch.org.

LOCATION: Barnegat Bay, NJ.

CATEGORY: Conservation.

COST: US$1,950 for 9 days. Fee includes accommodations, meals, ground transfers, training, and support.

DATES & DURATION: Varies; 9 days.

TO APPLY: Applications are accepted online and by fax and mail. Contact the office (see Contact).

FIELD NOTES: In the off-hours, volunteers may wish to canoe in the Pine Barrens or visit Old Barney, one of America's most famous lighthouses. Minimum age requirement of 18. A maximum of eight volunteers can participate at any one time. Training is provided on-site. Positions are suitable for adult groups and solo travelers.

WALLKILL RIVER NATIONAL WILDLIFE REFUGE

NEW JERSEY, USA

New Jersey's Wallkill River National Wildlife Refuge is home to forest-dwelling and grassland birds; waterfowl; and almost 40 species of mammals, including the bobcat, black bear, river otter, red and gray fox, and mink. Visitors have the chance to see some amazing creatures in their natural habitats. Working at the site, volunteers help with wildlife surveys, hiking-trail maintenance, and outdoor educational programs.

CONTACT: Wallkill River National Wildlife Refuge, 1547 Route 565, Sussex, NJ 07461; Tel: 9737027266; Fax: 9737027286; Web: www.fws.gov/northeast/wallkill river; Email: fran_stephenson@fws.gov.

LOCATION: Sussex, NJ.

CATEGORY: Conservation.

COST: Free in exchange for service. Complete RV hookups are provided.

DATES & DURATION: April through October; unlimited. To qualify, individuals must commit to a 24-hour workweek; couples and families, to 32 hours total per week.

TO APPLY: Applications can be obtained by contacting the refuge office (see Contact) or by visiting the US Fish and Wildlife Service at www.fws.gov/volunteers.

FIELD NOTES: All ages are welcome. Participants should be aware that volunteer duties may change to meet the reserve's current needs and goals. Positions are suitable for families, groups, and solo travelers.

BITTER LAKE NATIONAL WILDLIFE REFUGE

NEW MEXICO, USA

Established as a wintering habitat for migratory birds, including the lesser sandhill crane, New Mexico's Bitter Lake National Wildlife Refuge is now home to 357 bird species, 59 types of mammals, 50 kinds of reptiles and amphibians, and 24 species of fish. Volunteers help maintain the refuge's walking trails and conduct wildlife surveys. Participants may also help design the exhibits on display at the visitors center and assist with interpretive and educational programs.

CONTACT: Bitter Lake National Wildlife Refuge, 4067 Bitter Lake Rd, Roswell, NM 88201; Tel: 5756254009; Web: www.fws.gov/southwest/refuges/newmex/bitterlake; Email: steve_alvarez@fws.gov.

LOCATION: Roswell, NM.

CATEGORY: Conservation.

COST: Free in exchange for service. An RV hookup and other housing options are provided.

DATES & DURATION: Varies; long- and short-term commitments are available.

TO APPLY: Applications can be obtained by contacting the refuge office (see Contact) or by visiting the US Fish and Wildlife Service at www.fws.gov/volunteers.

FIELD NOTES:. Volunteers are most needed from spring through fall. All ages are welcome. Positions are suitable for families, groups, and solo travelers.

BOSQUE DEL APACHE NATIONAL WILDLIFE REFUGE

NEW MEXICO, USA

A leading center for wetland and riparian research, the Bosque del Apache National Wildlife Refuge offers more than 57,000 acres of protected lands for migratory birds, including the sandhill crane and Arctic goose. Volunteers help maintain the refuge's grounds and run environmental education and interpretive programs. Participants may be asked to take tour reservations, assist with special events and festivals, and provide tours to school groups.

CONTACT: Bosque del Apache National Wildlife Refuge, 500 Gold SW, 4th Floor, Albuquerque, NM 87102; Tel: 5052486635; Fax: 5052486874; Web: www.fws.gov/southwest/refuges/newmex/bosque; Email: Contact form on website.

LOCATION: Albuquerque, NM.

CATEGORY: Conservation.

COST: Free in exchange for service. Full RV hookups and apartments are provided.

DATES & DURATION: Year-round; unlimited. A 2-month stay is required for new volunteers. To qualify, volunteers must commit to a 40-hour workweek.

TO APPLY: Applications can be obtained by contacting the refuge office (see Contact) or by visiting the US Fish and Wildlife Service at www.fws.gov/volunteers.

FIELD NOTES: Positions fill fast during fall and winter, so apply early. All ages are welcome. Positions are suitable for families, groups, and solo travelers.

DEXTER NATIONAL FISH HATCHERY

NEW MEXICO, USA

Established in 1931, Dexter National Fish Hatchery and Technology Center houses more than 15 threatened or endangered fish species, including the desert pupfish, Colorado pike minnow, and Chihuahua chub. Volunteers help take care of the fish, the facility, and the grounds, and participate in public outreach activities. Volunteers participate in the fish-tagging program, which involves tagging more than 150,000 endangered or threatened fish each year.

CONTACT: Dexter National Fish Hatchery and Technology Center, 7116 Hatchery Rd, Dexter, NM 88230; Tel: 5757345910; Fax: 5757346130; Web: www .fws.gov/southwest/fisheries/dexter; Email: fw2_fr_dexter@fws.gov.

LOCATION: Dexter, NM.

CATEGORY: Conservation.

COST: Free in exchange for service. Full RV hookups and trailer housing are provided.

DATES & DURATION: Varies; unlimited.

TO APPLY: Applications can be obtained by contacting the hatchery office (see Contact) or by visiting the US Fish and Wildlife Service at www.fws.gov/volunteers.

FIELD NOTES: Positions are suitable for adult groups and solo travelers.

MORA NATIONAL FISH HATCHERY

NEW MEXICO, USA

Staff at Mora National Fish Hatchery work on restoration and recovery efforts of the endangered Gila trout. Volunteers participate in stocking programs, feeding and caring for resident fish, cleaning tanks and raceways, sample counting, and facility maintenance.

CONTACT: Mora National Fish Hatchery, PO Box 689, Mora, NM 87732; Tel: 5753876022; Fax: 5753879030; Web: www.fws.gov/southwest/fisheries/mora.html; Email: john_seal@fws.gov.

LOCATION: Mora, NM.

CATEGORY: Conservation.

COST: Free in exchange for service. Housing is provided.

DATES & DURATION: Varies; unlimited.

TO APPLY: Applications can be obtained by contacting the hatchery office (see Contact) or by visiting the US Fish and Wildlife Service at www.fws.gov/volunteers.

FIELD NOTES: Applicants must be at least 18 years of age. Positions are suitable for adult groups and solo travelers.

MONTEZUMA NATIONAL WILDLIFE REFUGE

NEW YORK, USA

A 7,000-acre reserve in New York's Finger Lakes region, the Montezuma National Wildlife Refuge provides a home for large populations of waterfowl, including snow geese, mallards, and American black ducks. Volunteers help scientists conduct species surveys and are called on to assist with general maintenance and gardening. Participants also work in the visitors center and lodge gift shop.

CONTACT: Montezuma National Wildlife Refuge, 3395 Route 5/20 E, Seneca Falls, NY 13148-9778; Tel: 3155685987; Web: www.fws.gov/r5mnwr; Email: andrea_vanbeusichem@fws.gov.

LOCATION: Seneca Falls, NY.

CATEGORY: Conservation.

COST: Free in exchange for service. Housing is provided.

DATES & DURATION: Year-round; unlimited. Commitment varies.

TO APPLY: Applications can be obtained by contacting the refuge office (see Contact) or by visiting the US Fish and Wildlife Service at www.fws.gov/volunteers.

FIELD NOTES: Training is provided. Both full- and part-time spots are available. Positions are suitable for families, groups, and solo travelers. All ages are welcome.

NEW YORK CITY WILDLIFE PROGRAM

NEW YORK, USA

New York may be the world's busiest city, but it's still got some incredible wildlife! Working with a team of scientists, volunteers study the impact of the urban environment on the city's animal life, including mammals, amphibians, and bird species. Participants help researchers collect data, create an animal inventory, and track native wildlife.

CONTACT: Earthwatch Institute, 3 Clock Tower Pl, Suite 100, Box 75, Maynard, MA 01754; Tel: 9784610081 or 8007760188; Fax: 9784612332; Web: www.earthwatch .org/exped/burns.html; Email: expedi tions@earthwatch.org.

LOCATION: Manhattan, NY

CATEGORY: Conservation.

COST: US$1,750 for 9 days. Fee includes accommodations, meals, ground transfers, training, and support.

DATES & DURATION: Varies; 9 days. Shorter-term assignments are available.

TO APPLY: Applications are accepted online or by fax or mail. Contact the office (see Contact).

FIELD NOTES: Minimum age requirement is 18. Maximum of eight volunteers at a time. Positions are suitable for adult groups and solo travelers. Information about the Teen Team is available on the website.

ALLIGATOR RIVER NATIONAL WILDLIFE REFUGE

NORTH CAROLINA, USA

North Carolina's Alligator River National Wildlife Refuge provides a home for many of the region's most endangered species, such as the red wolf, the red-cockaded woodpecker, and, of course, the American alligator. As part of the resident program, volunteers help maintain the reserve, study the local wildlife and surrounding forests, and work on environmental education programs. In the Red Wolf Recovery Program, participants help care for a captive breeding colony of these magnificent animals, feeding them and tracking them via radio telemetry equipment.

CONTACT: Alligator River National Wildlife Refuge, PO Box 1969, Manteo, NC 27954; Tel: 2524731131; Fax: 2524731668; Web: www.fws.gov/alligatorriver; Email: alligatorriver@fws.gov.

LOCATION: Manteo, NC.

CATEGORY: Conservation.

COST: Free in exchange for service. Full RV hookups are provided; laundry facilities are available on-site. Volunteers with the Red Wolf Recovery Program must commit to a 3-month stint and live in the caretaker cabin at the center of the refuge.

DATES & DURATION: Year-round; unlimited.

TO APPLY: Applications can be obtained by contacting the refuge office (see Contact) or by visiting the US Fish and Wildlife Service at www.fws.gov/volunteers.

FIELD NOTES: Training is provided upon arrival. Positions are suitable for families, groups, and solo travelers.

PEA ISLAND NATIONAL WILDLIFE REFUGE

NORTH CAROLINA, USA

From ocean beaches and dunes to salt flats and marshlands, Pea Island National Wildlife Refuge offers the ideal home for ducks, geese, swans, and wading birds. Working at this site, volunteers help monitor the local loggerhead turtle population and also assist with nest relocation projects. Participants may also conduct wildlife surveys, help conduct tours for park visitors, and restore damaged habitats.

CONTACT: Pea Island National Wildlife Refuge, PO Box 1969, Manteo, NC 27954; Tel: 2529871118; Web: www.fws.gov/peaisland. Email: alligatorriver@fws.gov.

LOCATION: Pea Island, NC.

CATEGORY: Conservation.

COST: Free in exchange for service. Housing is provided.

DATES & DURATION: May through September; unlimited.

TO APPLY: Applications can be obtained by contacting the refuge office (see Contact) or by visiting the US Fish and Wildlife Service at www.fws.gov/volunteers.

FIELD NOTES: Because the park contains marshlands, biting insects can be a problem; insect repellent is highly recommended during summer months. Positions are suitable for families, groups, and solo travelers. All ages are welcome and encouraged to participate.

PEE DEE NATIONAL WILDLIFE REFUGE

NORTH CAROLINA, USA

Pee Dee National Wildlife Refuge's more than 8,000 acres are home to a variety of migratory and resident birds, such as the common loon and horned grebe. Volunteers help with the park's bird-banding program, established to determine the population dynamics of wood ducks and migratory songbird species. Participants may also be asked to assist with educational and interpretive programs.

CONTACT: Pee Dee National Wildlife Refuge, 5770 US Hwy 52 N, Wadesboro, NC 28170; Tel: 7046944424; Fax: 7046946570; Web: www.fws.gov/peedee; Email: jeffrey_bricken@fws.gov.

LOCATION: Wadesboro, NC.

CATEGORY: Conservation.

COST: Free in exchange for service. Full RV hookups and rooming are provided.

DATES & DURATION: Year-round; unlimited.

TO APPLY: Applications can be obtained by contacting the refuge office (see Contact) or by visiting the US Fish and Wildlife Service at www.fws.gov/volunteers.

FIELD NOTES: Fishing and hunting are permitted in designated areas. The summers can be hot and humid; wearing sunscreen is highly advised. Both full- and part-time positions are available. Families, groups, and solo travelers are all welcome. Participants should be aware that volunteer duties may change to meet the reserve's current needs and goals.

ARROWWOOD NATIONAL WILDLIFE REFUGE

NORTH DAKOTA, USA

Established as a breeding ground for migratory birds and other wildlife, North Dakota's Arrowwood National Wildlife Refuge plays host to over 250 species of birds, including the sharp-tailed grouse and tundra swan, as well as some amazing mammals, such as the white-tailed deer and badger. Volunteers help conduct wildlife surveys and maintain the facilities. Participants may also assist with habitat restoration projects and environmental education and interpretive services.

CONTACT: Arrowwood National Wildlife Refuge, 7745 11th St SE, Pingree, ND 58476-8308; Tel: 7012853341; Fax: 7012853350; Web: www.fws.gov/arrowwood; Email: arrowwood@fws.gov.

LOCATION: Pingree, ND.

CATEGORY: Conservation.

COST: Free in exchange for service. Housing is provided.

DATES & DURATION: Varies; unlimited.

TO APPLY: Applications can be obtained by contacting the refuge office (see Contact) or by visiting the US Fish and Wildlife Service at www.fws.gov/volunteers.

FIELD NOTES: Hunting and fishing are permitted on the refuge grounds for certain species and in designated areas only. Before taking part in either activity, volunteers should check in with refuge staff on the current regulations. Since the refuge encompasses numerous bodies of water, insects can be a problem; repellent should be worn at all times. Both full- and part-time positions are available. All ages are welcome. Positions are suitable for families, groups, and solo travelers.

CHASE LAKE NATIONAL WILDLIFE REFUGE

NORTH DAKOTA, USA

Home to one of the largest white pelican nesting colonies in North America, Chase Lake National Wildlife Refuge needs volunteers to help with wildlife surveys. Each year, refuge staff bands over 2,500 pelicans to help learn more about the species' migrating and wintering habits. Participants of the program are welcome to take part in any pelican-banding projects under way at their time of service. Volunteers should also expect to help with reserve maintenance.

CONTACT: Chase Lake National Wildlife Refuge, 5924 19th St SE, Woodworth, ND 58496; Tel: 7017524218; Web: www.fws.gov/arrowwood/chaselake_nwr; Email: chaselake@fws.gov.

LOCATION: Woodworth, ND.

CATEGORY: Conservation.

COST: Free in exchange for service. Housing is provided.

DATES & DURATION: Varies; unlimited.

TO APPLY: Applications can be obtained by contacting the refuge office (see Contact) or by visiting the US Fish and Wildlife Service at www.fws.gov/volunteers.

FIELD NOTES: Hunting is permitted for white-tailed deer during specified seasons and in designated areas only. Both full- and part-time positions are available. All ages are welcome. Positions are suitable for families, groups, and solo travelers.

DES LACS NATIONAL WILDLIFE REFUGE

NORTH DAKOTA, USA

Des Lacs National Wildlife Refuge is one of America's top birding sites, hosting more than 250 species. The refuge provides a temporary home to large concentrations of migrating snow geese and tundra swans. Deer, moose, and other wildlife live on the refuge grounds. Volunteers help inventory wildlife and assist with general maintenance.

CONTACT: Des Lacs National Wildlife Refuge, Box 578, County Rd, Kenmare, ND 58746; Tel: 7013854046; Web: www.fws.gov/jclarksalyer/deslacs; Email: deslacs@fws.gov.

LOCATION: Kenmare, ND.

CATEGORY: Conservation.

COST: Free in exchange for service. Full RV hookups, trailers, and bunkhouse accommodations are provided.

DATES & DURATION: Varies; unlimited.

TO APPLY: Applications can be obtained by contacting the refuge office (see Contact) or by visiting the US Fish and Wildlife Service at www.fws.gov/volunteers.

FIELD NOTES: Hunting is permitted in designated areas only. Training is provided on-site. All ages are welcome. Positions are suitable for families, groups, and solo travelers.

GARRISON DAM NATIONAL FISH HATCHERY

NORTH DAKOTA, USA

Established in 1957, Garrison Dam National Fish Hatchery works to maintain migratory fish species and to restore endangered species, such as the pallid sturgeon. Hatchery species include brown trout, burbot, northern pike, and shovelnose sturgeon. Volunteers help with stocking, caring for the resident fish, cleaning tanks and raceways, and taking sample counts. Participants may also be asked to assist with facility maintenance, landscaping projects, and public outreach activities.

CONTACT: Garrison Dam National Fish Hatchery, PO Box 530, Riverdale, ND 58565; Tel: 7016547451; Web: www.fws .gov/garrisondam; Email: garrisondam@ fws.gov.

LOCATION: Riverdale, ND.

CATEGORY: Conservation.

COST: Free in exchange for service.

Full RV hookups and trailer housing are provided.

DATES & DURATION: Varies; unlimited.

TO APPLY: Applications can be obtained by contacting the hatchery office (see Contact) or by visiting the US Fish and Wildlife Service at www.fws.gov/ volunteers.

FIELD NOTES: Volunteers must be at least 18 years of age. Positions are suitable for adult groups and solo travelers.

J. CLARK SALYER NATIONAL WILDLIFE REFUGE

NORTH DAKOTA, USA

One of the most important duck-nesting sites in the United States, J. Clark Salyer National Wildlife Refuge provides a home for over 300 species of birds, including the ruddy duck, Wilson's phalarope, and pied-billed grebe. Participants survey the local bird populations and work on habitat restoration projects as needed. Volunteers should also expect to help with general refuge maintenance.

CONTACT: J. Clark Salyer National Wildlife Refuge, 681 Salyer Rd, Upham, ND 58789-0066; Tel: 7017682548; Web: www.fws.gov/jclarksalyer; Email: jclarksalyer @fws.gov.

LOCATION: Upham, ND.

CATEGORY: Conservation.

COST: Free in exchange for service. Full RV hookups and bunkhouse accommodations are provided.

DATES & DURATION: Varies; unlimited.

TO APPLY: Applications can be obtained by contacting the refuge office (see Contact) or by visiting the US Fish and Wildlife Service at www.fws.gov/volunteers.

FIELD NOTES: Canoeing is permitted in the refuge on the Souris River. Both full- and part-time positions are available. All ages are welcome. Positions are suitable for families, groups, and solo travelers.

LONG LAKE NATIONAL WILDLIFE REFUGE

NORTH DAKOTA, USA

Long Lake National Wildlife Refuge provides lake, marsh, and upland habitats to a variety of bird and other species. Franklin gulls can be observed in colossal concentrations, along with thousands of ducks and an assortment of geese. The endangered whooping crane has been spotted on refuge grounds. Volunteers are needed to participate in documenting breeding birds, duck production, and migratory birds. Volunteers may also help conduct tours and assist with educational programs.

CONTACT: Long Lake National Wildlife Refuge, US Fish and Wildlife Service, 12000 353rd St SE, Moffit, ND 58560-9704: Tel: 7013874397; Web: www.fws.gov/longlake; Email: longlake@fws.gov.

LOCATION: Moffit, ND.

CATEGORY: Conservation.

COST: Free in exchange for service. Accommodation is provided.

DATES & DURATION: Varies; unlimited.

TO APPLY: Applications can be obtained by contacting the refuge office (see Contact) or by visiting the US Fish and Wildlife Service at www.fws.gov/volunteers.

FIELD NOTES: Training is provided on-site. Both full- and part-time positions are available. All ages are welcome. Positions are suitable for families, groups, and solo travelers.

LOSTWOOD NATIONAL WILDLIFE REFUGE

NORTH DAKOTA, USA

Although home to 37 types of mammals—including the elk, pronghorn antelope, coyote and red fox—the Lostwood National Wildlife Refuge is perhaps best known for its 234 bird species. The common loon, black-billed cuckoo, and American white pelican can be found here. Volunteers help with bird surveys and nest monitoring. Working with park staff, participants also help maintain the refuge.

CONTACT: Lostwood National Wildlife Refuge, 8315 Hwy 8, Kenmare, ND 58746-9046; Tel: 7018482722; Web: www.fws.gov/lostwood; Email: lostwood@fws.gov.

LOCATION: Kenmare, ND.

CATEGORY: Conservation.

COST: Free in exchange for service. Full RV hookups and other housing options are provided.

DATES & DURATION: Varies; unlimited.

TO APPLY: Applications can be obtained by contacting the refuge office (see Contact) or by visiting the US Fish and Wildlife Service at www.fws.gov/volunteers.

FIELD NOTES: Hunting is permitted on refuge grounds in designated areas only. Hunting for waterfowl is prohibited. Both full- and part-time positions are available. Families are welcome. Participants should be aware that volunteer duties may change to meet the reserve's current needs and goals. Positions are suitable for families, groups, and solo travelers.

SULLYS HILL NATIONAL GAME PRESERVE

NORTH DAKOTA, USA

At over 1,600 acres, the Sullys Hill National Game Preserve plays host to mountain elk, white-tailed deer, prairie dogs, and over 200 different species of birds. Volunteers help park staff construct artificial nests and survey the local wildlife. Participants also help maintain the preserve's walking trails and other facilities. Volunteers also assist with any programs under way at their time of service.

CONTACT: Sullys Hill National Game Preserve, 221 2nd St W, Devils Lake, ND 58301; Tel: 7017664272; Web: www.fws.gov/sullyshill; Email: sullyshill@fws.gov.
LOCATION: Devils Lake, ND.
CATEGORY: Conservation.

COST: Free in exchange for service. Full RV hookups and other housing options are provided.
DATES & DURATION: Summer; unlimited.
TO APPLY: Applications can be obtained by contacting the refuge office (see Contact) or by visiting the US Fish and Wildlife Service at www.fws.gov/volunteers.
FIELD NOTES: The preserve conducts regular school programs, public workshops, guided nature hikes, bird-watching walks, and summer youth and conservation programs. All ages are welcome. Participants should be aware that volunteer duties may change to meet the preserve's current needs and goals. Positions are suitable for families, groups, and solo travelers.

TEWAUKON NATIONAL WILDLIFE REFUGE

NORTH DAKOTA, USA

Established in 1934, Tewaukon National Wildlife Refuge hosts over 243 bird species, including the snowy and great horned owl, blue-winged teal, and sharp-tailed grouse. Volunteers help with wildlife surveys, monitoring bird populations, and restoring natural habitats. Participants also assist with visitor services and general refuge maintenance.

CONTACT: Tewaukon National Wildlife Refuge, 9754 143½ Ave SE, Cayuga, ND 58013; Tel: 7017243598; Web: www.fws .gov/tewaukon; Email: tewaukon@ fws.gov.

LOCATION: Cayuga, ND.

CATEGORY: Conservation.

COST: Free in exchange for service. Trailer accommodations are provided.

DATES & DURATION: Varies; unlimited.

TO APPLY: Applications can be obtained by contacting the refuge office (see Contact) or by visiting the US Fish and Wildlife Service at www.fws.gov/volunteers.

FIELD NOTES: Both full- and part-time positions are available. All ages are welcome. Positions are suitable for families, groups, and solo travelers.

UPPER SOURIS NATIONAL WILDLIFE REFUGE

NORTH DAKOTA, USA

The Upper Souris National Wildlife Refuge, founded as a breeding ground for ducks and migratory birds, is home to more than 350,000 waterfowl during the spring and fall migration seasons. Visitors can expect to see large colonies of cormorants and great blue herons. Volunteers help with wildlife surveys and with restoring natural habitats. Participants may also remove invasive plant species and assist with general refuge maintenance and upkeep.

CONTACT: Upper Souris National Wildlife Refuge, 17705 212th Ave NW, Berthhold, ND 58718; Tel: 7014685467; Web: www.fws.gov/uppersouris; Email: upper souris@fws.gov.

LOCATION: Berthhold, ND.

CATEGORY: Conservation.

COST: Free in exchange for service. Full RV hookups and trailer accommodations are provided.

DATES & DURATION: Varies; unlimited.

TO APPLY: Applications can be obtained by contacting the refuge office (see Contact) or by visiting the US Fish and Wildlife Service at www.fws.gov/volunteers.

FIELD NOTES: The use of boats and canoes are prohibited on the refuge from October 1 to April 30. Collection of animal or plant species is prohibited year-round. Both full- and part-time positions are available. Positions are suitable for families, groups, and solo travelers. All ages are welcome.

VALLEY CITY NATIONAL FISH HATCHERY

NORTH DAKOTA, USA

The Valley City National Fish Hatchery rears various fish species, including northern pike, walleye, yellow perch, tiger muskies, small- and largemouth bass, blue gill, and pallid sturgeon. Volunteers participate in stocking programs and caring for the fish. Other tasks include cleaning tanks and raceways, and conducting species inventories. Volunteers also assist with facility maintenance and landscaping projects.

CONTACT: Valley City National Fish Hatchery, 11515 River Rd, Valley City, ND; Tel: 7018453464; Web: www.fws.gov/valleycity; Email: valleycity@fws.gov.

LOCATION: Valley City, ND.

CATEGORY: Conservation.

COST: Free in exchange for service. Full RV hookups and trailer housing are provided.

DATES & DURATION: Varies; unlimited.

TO APPLY: Applications can be obtained by contacting the hatchery office (see Contact) or by visiting the US Fish and Wildlife Service at www.fws.gov/volunteers.

FIELD NOTES: Participants must be at least 18 years of age. Positions are suitable for adult groups and solo travelers.

WOLF TIMBERS

OHIO, USA

Located in Bolivar, Ohio, Wolf Timbers offers safe haven for the endangered timber wolves and serves as an educational and research center. At Wolf Timbers, visitors can observe wolves in a protected but natural environment and learn more about these amazing creatures. Volunteers help prepare food for the wolves and clean their enclosures. Participants may also work on construction and maintenance projects.

CONTACT: Wolf Timbers, PO Box 107, Bolivar, OH 44612; Tel: 8668749653 or 3308747022; Web: www.wolftimbers.org; Email: wolftimbers@yahoo.com.

LOCATION: Bolivar, OH.

CATEGORY: Conservation.

COST: Free in exchange for service.

DATES & DURATION: Varies; long- and short-term placements are available.

TO APPLY: Applications are accepted by mail and can be downloaded from the website (see Contact).

FIELD NOTES: Not all participants have direct contact with wolves. Volunteers must participate in an orientation and training program before starting service. Positions are suitable for adult groups and solo travelers.

SEQUOYAH NATIONAL WILDLIFE REFUGE

OKLAHOMA, USA

Oklahoma's Sequoyah National Wildlife Refuge provides a home for many different types of waterfowl, including the snow goose (the largest population in the state), mallard, wood duck, teal, pintail, gadwall, and wigeon. Working with park staff, volunteers help conduct waterfowl surveys and may assist with other research projects and habitat improvement programs.

CONTACT: Sequoyah National Wildlife Refuge, Route 1, Box 18-A, Vian, OK 74962-9304: Tel: 9187735251 or 9187735252; Fax: 9187735598; Web: www.fws.gov/southwest/refuges/Oklahoma/Sequoyah; Email: fw2_rw_sequoyah@fws.gov.

LOCATION: Vian, OK.

CATEGORY: Conservation.

COST: Free in exchange for service. Full RV hookups and trailer accommodations are provided.

DATES & DURATION: March through October; unlimited.

TO APPLY: Applications can be obtained by contacting the refuge office (see Contact) or by visiting the US Fish and Wildlife Service at www.fws.gov/volunteers.

FIELD NOTES: Training is provided on-site. Positions are suitable for families, groups, and solo travelers. All ages are welcome.

ERIE NATIONAL WILDLIFE REFUGE

PENNSYLVANIA, USA

Within the boundaries of Pennsylvania's Erie National Wildlife Refuge, more than 230 species of birds, including nesting wood ducks, hooded mergansers, buffleheads, and American wigeons; 47 types of mammals; and 37 kinds of amphibians and reptiles can be found. Volunteers help with wildlife surveys and restore damaged habitats. Depending on interest and available time, participants can also assist with other biological, outreach, maintenance, public use, educational, and administrative programs.

CONTACT: Erie National Wildlife Refuge, 11296 Wood Duck Ln, Guys Mills, PA 16327; Tel: 8147893585; Fax: 8147892909; Web: www.fws.gov/northeast/erie; Email: fw5rw_ernwr@fws.gov.

LOCATION: Guys Mills, PA.

CATEGORY: Conservation.

COST: Free in exchange for service. Full RV hookups and other housing options are provided.

DATES & DURATION: Varies; unlimited.

TO APPLY: Applications can be obtained by contacting the refuge office (see Contact) or by visiting the US Fish and Wildlife Service at www.fws.gov/volunteers.

FIELD NOTES: Positions are suitable for families, groups, and solo travelers. All ages are welcome.

CABO ROJO NATIONAL WILDLIFE REFUGE

PUERTO RICO

Established in 1974, Puerto Rico's Cabo Rojo National Wildlife Refuge provides a temporary home for migratory shorebirds and a permanent residence for other animals, such as the endangered yellow-shouldered blackbird. Volunteers help with wildlife surveys and assist with laboratory research. Participants may also lead tours and maintain the refuge's facilities.

CONTACT: Cabo Rojo National Wildlife Refuge, PO Box 510, Boqueron, PR 00622; Tel: 7878517258; Web: www.fws.gov/refuges/profiles/index.cfm?id=41521; Email: caribbeanisland@fws.gov.

LOCATION: Boqueron, PR.

CATEGORY: Conservation.

COST: Free in exchange for service. Bunk rooms are provided.

DATES & DURATION: Year-round; unlimited.

TO APPLY: Applications can be obtained by contacting the refuge office (see Contact) or by visiting the US Fish and Wildlife Service at www.fws.gov/volunteers.

FIELD NOTES: Both full- and part-time positions are available. Positions are suitable for families, groups, and solo travelers. All ages are welcome.

PUERTO RICO'S RAIN FOREST PROGRAM

PUERTO RICO

Puerto Rico's rain forest has been severely depleted, destroying the habitats of many amphibians, including a variety of lizards and frogs. To help restore the environment, volunteers at Puerto Rico's Rain Forest Program work to replenish the rain forest and ensure the future of these amazing animals. Participants assist researchers by capturing lizards and frogs, which are then sexed, measured, and identified.

CONTACT: Earthwatch Institute, 3 Clock Tower Pl, Suite 100, Box 75, Maynard, MA 01754; Tel: 9784610081 or 8007760188; Fax: 9784612332; Web: www.earthwatch.org/exped/nelson.html; Email: expeditions@earthwatch.org.

LOCATION: San Juan, PR.

CATEGORY: Conservation.

COST: US$1750 for 10 days. Fee includes accommodations, meals, ground transfers, training, and support.

DATES & DURATION: Varies; 10 days.

TO APPLY: Applications are accepted online and by fax or mail. Contact the office (see Contact).

FIELD NOTES: Minimum age requirement of 18. A maximum of 12 volunteers at a time. Positions are suitable for adult groups and solo travelers. Teen programs are also available.

CAPE ROMAIN NATIONAL WILDLIFE REFUGE

SOUTH CAROLINA, USA

At more than 66,000 acres, South Carolina's Cape Romain National Wildlife Refuge provides a safe haven for many threatened and endangered animals, such as the loggerhead sea turtle, piping plover, and wood stork. Volunteers help with nest relocation, habitat modification, and invasive plant removal. Participants may also assist with visitor services and help run educational programs on the importance of conservation.

CONTACT: Cape Romain National Wildlife Refuge, 5801 Hwy 17 N, Awendaw, SC 29429; Tel: 8439283264; Fax: 8439283803; Web: www.fws.gov/caperomain; Email: caperomain@fws.gov.

LOCATION: Awendaw, SC.

CATEGORY: Conservation.

COST: Free in exchange for service. Trailer accommodations are provided.

DATES & DURATION: Year-round; unlimited.

TO APPLY: Applications can be obtained by contacting the refuge office (see Contact) or by visiting the US Fish and Wildlife Service at www.fws.gov/volunteers.

FIELD NOTES: Hunting and fishing are permitted on refuge grounds in designated areas during specified seasons. Positions are suitable for families, groups, and solo travelers. All ages are welcome.

CAROLINA SANDHILLS NATIONAL WILDLIFE REFUGE

SOUTH CAROLINA, USA

At more than 47,000 acres, Carolina Sandhills National Wildlife Refuge hosts the largest population of the endangered red-cockaded woodpecker in the United States. Volunteers help with wildlife surveys, build artificial nests, assist with general maintenance, and lead tours for visitors. Volunteers may participate in forest management activities, including inventorying refuge tree species, and help with clerical work and administrative duties.

CONTACT: Carolina Sandhills National Wildlife Refuge, 23734 US Hwy 1, McBee, SC 29101; Tel: 8433358401; Fax: 8433358406; Web: www.fws.gov/caroli nasandhills; Email: carolinasandhills@ fws.gov.

LOCATION: McBee, SC.

CATEGORY: Conservation.

COST: Free in exchange for service. Full RV hookups and other housing accommodations are provided.

DATES & DURATION: Year-round; unlimited.

TO APPLY: Applications can be obtained by contacting the refuge office (see Contact) or by visiting the US Fish and Wildlife Service at www.fws.gov/volunteers.

FIELD NOTES: Both full- and part-time positions are available. Positions are suitable for families, groups, and solo travelers. All ages are welcome.

D. C. BOOTH HISTORICAL NATIONAL FISH HATCHERY

SOUTH DAKOTA, USA

Although the D. C. Booth Historical National Fish Hatchery still produces some fish for stocking, it mostly operates as a museum and visitors center. More than 145,000 people visit the hatchery each year. Volunteers are involved with visitor services, interpretive programs, educational projects, facility maintenance, landscaping, and public outreach activities.

CONTACT: D. C. Booth Historical National Fish Hatchery, 423 Hatchery Circle, Spearfish, SD 57783; Tel: 6056427730; Fax: 6056422336; Web: www.fws.gov/dcbooth; Email: dcbooth@fws.gov.

LOCATION: Spearfish, SD.

CATEGORY: Conservation.

COST: Free in exchange for service. Housing and campsites are provided.

DATES & DURATION: Varies; unlimited.

TO APPLY: Applications can be obtained by contacting the hatchery office (see Contact) or by visiting the US Fish and Wildlife Service at www.fws.gov/volunteers.

FIELD NOTES: Participants must be 18 years of age. Positions are suitable for adult groups and solo travelers.

LAKE ANDES NATIONAL WILDLIFE REFUGE

SOUTH DAKOTA, USA

Home to 249 species of birds, such as the bald eagle, ring-necked pheasant, black tern, and Franklin gull, South Dakota's Lake Andes National Wildlife Refuge also plays hosts to large beaver and muskrat populations. Volunteers help survey this wildlife and help manage the animals' habitats. Working with the staff, participants also help maintain the refuge's grounds and facilities.

CONTACT: Lake Andes National Wildlife Refuge Complex, 38672 291st St, Lake Andes, SD 57356; Tel: 6054877603; Fax: 6054877604; Web: www.fws.gov/lakeandes.

LOCATION: Lake Andes, SD.

CATEGORY: Conservation.

COST: Free in exchange for service. Trailer accommodations are provided.

DATES & DURATION: Varies; unlimited.

TO APPLY: Applications can be obtained by contacting the refuge office (see Contact) or by visiting the US Fish and Wildlife Service at www.fws.gov/volunteers.

FIELD NOTES: Positions are suitable for families, groups, and solo travelers. All ages are welcome.

WAUBAY NATIONAL WILDLIFE REFUGE

SOUTH DAKOTA, USA

With marshlands, prairies, and forests, the Waubay National Wildlife Refuge is the ideal setting for a great variety of birds. Within the refuge's boundaries, visitors can spot Canada geese, blue-winged teals, and double-crested cormorants. Volunteers help with inventorying the bird populations. Participants may also assist with visitor services and general maintenance.

CONTACT: Waubay National Wildlife Refuge, 44401 134A St, Waubay, SD 57273; Tel: 6059474521; Fax: 6059474524; Web: www.fws.gov/waubay; Email: larry_d_martin@fws.gov.

LOCATION: Waubay, SD.

CATEGORY: Conservation.

COST: Free in exchange for service. Full RV hookups, trailers, and bunkhouse accommodations are provided.

DATES & DURATION: Varies; unlimited.

TO APPLY: Applications can be obtained by contacting the refuge office (see Contact) or by visiting the US Fish and Wildlife Service at www.fws.gov/volunteers.

FIELD NOTES: Positions are suitable for families, groups, and solo travelers. All ages are welcome.

ANAHUAC NATIONAL WILDLIFE REFUGE

TEXAS, USA

From its marshlands to its prairies, Texas's Anahuac National Wildlife Refuge offers visitors the chance to see an incredible range of animals in the wild, such as 27 types of ducks, snow geese, ibises, herons, bobcats, and even alligators. Volunteers help with park construction projects and general trail and refuge maintenance. Participants may also be asked to lead tours and run educational programs on the importance of conservation.

CONTACT: Anahuac National Wildlife Refuge, PO Box 278, Anahuac, TX 77514; Tel: 4092673337; Fax: 4092674314; Web: www.fws.gov/southwest/refuges/texas/anahuac; Email: fw2_rw_anahuac@fws.gov.

LOCATION: Anahuac, TX.

CATEGORY: Conservation.

COST: Free in exchange for service. Full RV hookups and other housing options are provided.

DATES & DURATION: Year-round; unlimited. To qualify, individuals must commit to a 32-hour workweek; couples, to 48 hours per week in total.

TO APPLY: Applications can be obtained by contacting the refuge office (see Contact) or by visiting the US Fish and Wildlife Service at www.fws.gov/volunteers.

FIELD NOTES: Both full- and part-time positions are available. Positions are suitable for families, groups, and solo travelers. All ages are welcome.

ARANSAS NATIONAL WILDLIFE REFUGE

TEXAS, USA

Pelicans, herons, egrets, and, in winter, the endangered whooping crane can all be seen in Texas's Aransas National Wildlife Refuge. Volunteers help conduct wildlife and waterfowl surveys. Participants may also be asked to take part in the interpretive van tours, which are offered from January through April.

CONTACT: US Fish and Wildlife Service, Aransas National Wildlife Refuge Complex, PO Box 100, Austwell, TX 77950; Tel: 3612863559; Fax: 3612863722; Web: www .fws.gov/southwest/refuges/texas/aransas; Email: fw2_rw_aransas@fws.gov.

LOCATION: Austwell, TX.

CATEGORY: Conservation.

COST: Free in exchange for service. Full RV hookups and other housing options are provided.

DATES & DURATION: Year-round; unlimited.

TO APPLY: Applications can be obtained by contacting the refuge office (see Contact) or by visiting the US Fish and Wildlife Service at www.fws.gov/volunteers.

FIELD NOTES: Fishing is permitted in designated areas during specified seasons. Bicycling is permitted on the auto tour loop only. Feeding of the wildlife is prohibited. Both full- and part-time positions are available. Positions are suitable for families, groups, and solo travelers. All ages are welcome.

BALCONES CANYONLANDS NATIONAL WILDLIFE REFUGE

TEXAS, USA

With over 270 resident and migratory birds, Balcones Canyonlands National Wildlife Refuge is the perfect site to spot some amazing species, including the black-capped vireo and the endangered golden-cheeked warbler. Volunteers help monitor these two species and also help construct artificial nests for bluebirds and boxes for bats. In October, participants help monitor the incredible monarch butterflies that migrate through the reserve each year. Volunteers may also help with general maintenance, and removing and recycling waste material found on the park grounds.

CONTACT: Balcones Canyonlands National Wildlife Refuge, 24518 FM 1431, Marble Falls, TX 78654; Tel: 5123399432; Fax: 5122676530; Web: www.fws.gov/southwest/refuges/texas/balcones; Email: fw2_rw_balcones@fws.gov.

LOCATION: Marble Falls, TX.

CATEGORY: Conservation.

COST: Free in exchange for service. Full RV hookups are provided.

DATES & DURATION: Year-round; unlimited. To qualify, volunteers must work 3 days a week.

TO APPLY: Applications can be obtained by contacting the refuge office (see Contact) or by visiting the US Fish and Wildlife Service at www.fws.gov/volunteers.

FIELD NOTES: Both full- and part-time positions are available. Positions are suitable for families, groups, and solo travelers. All ages are welcome.

BIG BOGGY NATIONAL WILDLIFE REFUGE

TEXAS, USA

Texas's Big Boggy National Wildlife Refuge provides an ideal coastal wetland habitat for a range of neotropical migratory birds, wintering waterfowl, and other resident wildlife. The refuge plays host to the white ibis, snowy egret, and endangered brown pelican. Although the refuge is closed to visitors, volunteers are welcome. Participants help with the development of freshwater impoundments, bird-banding projects, and general maintenance.

CONTACT: Big Boggy National Wildlife Refuge, 6801 County Rd 306, Brazoria, TX 77422; Tel: 9799643639; Fax: 9799643210; Web: www.fws.gov/south west/refuges/texas/texasmidcoast; Email: shane_kasson@fws.gov.

LOCATION: Brazoria, TX.

CATEGORY: Conservation.

COST: Free in exchange for service. Full RV hookups are provided.

DATES & DURATION: Varies; unlimited. To qualify, volunteers must commit to a 24-hour workweek.

TO APPLY: Applications can be obtained by contacting the refuge office (see Contact) or by visiting the US Fish and Wildlife Service at www.fws.gov/volunteers.

FIELD NOTES: Participants should be aware that volunteer duties may change to meet the reserve's current needs and goals. Positions are suitable for adult groups and solo travelers.

BRAZORIA NATIONAL WILDLIFE REFUGE

TEXAS, USA

As a wintering site for large concentrations of snow geese, mottled ducks, and American wigeons, Brazoria National Wildlife Refuge plays host to an array of over 200 bird species. Volunteers help conduct wildlife surveys and work on habitat modification programs. Participants may also be asked to take part in bird-banding programs, which help researchers determine species survival rates, sex ratios, and habitat preferences.

CONTACT: Brazoria National Wildlife Refuge, 24907 FM 2004, Angleton, TX 77515; Tel: 9799221037; Fax: 9799221539; Web: www.fws.gov/southwest/refuges/texas/texasmidcoast/brazoria.htm; Email: cody_dingee@fws.gov.

LOCATION: Angleton, TX.

CATEGORY: Conservation.

COST: Free in exchange for service. Full RV hookups are provided.

DATES & DURATION: Year-round; unlimited. To qualify, volunteers must commit to a 24-hour workweek.

TO APPLY: Applications can be obtained by contacting the refuge office (see Contact) or by visiting the US Fish and Wildlife Service at www.fws.gov/volunteers.

FIELD NOTES: Training is provided onsite. Participants should be aware that volunteer duties may change to meet the reserve's current needs and goals. Positions are suitable for families, groups, and solo travelers. All ages are welcome.

LAGUNA ATASCOSA NATIONAL WILDLIFE REFUGE

TEXAS, USA

Located in Texas's Lower Rio Grande Valley, the 45,000-acre Laguna Atascosa National Wildlife Refuge is home to many fascinating creatures, including over 400 species of birds and the endangered ocelot. Volunteers help with research projects focused on endangered animals, conduct surveys of local bird populations, and help with sea turtle recovery projects (including nest relocation efforts and species inventories). Volunteers may be asked to work at the visitors center and assist with general maintenance. Other duties relate to special events, tours, and education programs.

CONTACT: Laguna Atascosa National Wildlife Refuge, PO Box 450, Rio Hondo, TX 79834; Tel: 9567483607; Web: www .stateparks.com/laguna_atascosa .html; Email: fw2_rw_laguna_atascosa@ fws.gov.

LOCATION: Rio Hondo, TX.

CATEGORY: Conservation.

COST: Free in exchange for service. Full RV hookups are provided.

DATES & DURATION: Varies; unlimited.

TO APPLY: Applications can be obtained by contacting the refuge office (see Contact) or by visiting the US Fish and Wildlife Service at www.fws.gov/volunteers.

FIELD NOTES: Positions are suitable for families, groups, and solo travelers. All ages are welcome.

LOWER RIO GRANDE VALLEY NATIONAL WILDLIFE REFUGE

TEXAS, USA

More than 500 bird species and 300 different kinds of butterflies, including the zebra longwing and the Mexican bluewing, are found in the Lower Rio Grande Valley National Wildlife Refuge. Volunteers help survey the local wildlife, collect seeds and plantings, and maintain the grounds and facilities. Participants who work for the Kemp's ridley sea turtle program help conduct beach patrols to keep the animals safe, and run public education programs.

CONTACT: Lower Rio Grande Valley National Wildlife Refuge, Route 2, Box 202A, Alamo, TX 78516; Tel: 9567847521; Fax: 9567878338; Web: www.fws.gov/south west/refuges/texas/lrgv.html; Email: nancy_brown@fws.gov.

LOCATION: Alamo, TX.

CATEGORY: Conservation.

COST: Free in exchange for service. Full RV hookups are provided.

DATES & DURATION: Year-round; unlimited.

TO APPLY: Applications can be obtained by contacting the refuge office (see Contact) or by visiting the US Fish and Wildlife Service at www.fws.gov/volunteers.

FIELD NOTES: Training is provided onsite. Both full- and part-time positions are available. Positions are suitable for families, groups, and solo travelers. All ages are welcome.

MCFADDIN NATIONAL WILDLIFE REFUGE

TEXAS, USA

McFaddin National Wildlife Refuge, encompassing 55,000 acres, is home to the bobcat, gray fox, and American alligator. Thousands of geese and ducks can be observed along with a variety of neotropical migratory bird species, which arrive each year to nest on refuge lands. Volunteers help with migratory and resident bird surveys, refuge restoration and modification projects, construction and maintenance, and general upkeep.

CONTACT: McFaddin National Wildlife Refuge, PO Box 358, Sabine Pass, TX 77655; Tel: 4097362371; Fax: 4097362438; Web: www.fws.gov/southwest/refuges/texas/mcfaddin; Email: fw2_rw_mcfaddin@fws.gov.

LOCATION: Sabine Pass, TX.

CATEGORY: Conservation.

COST: Free in exchange for service. Full RV hookups are provided.

DATES & DURATION: Varies; unlimited.

TO APPLY: Applications can be obtained by contacting the refuge office (see Contact) or by visiting the US Fish and Wildlife Service at www.fws.gov/volunteers.

FIELD NOTES: Controlled hunting is allowed on refuge grounds during determined seasons. Volunteers are needed year-round for a variety of programs. Both full- and part-time positions are available. Training is provided on-site. Volunteers should have an interest in caring for the environment and its inhabitants. Participants under the age of 18 must have written parental consent. Positions are best suited for adult groups and solo travelers.

PRIDEROCK
WILDLIFE REFUGE

TEXAS, USA

Priderock Wildlife Refuge provides a safe haven for big cats (lions, tigers, and cougars) and wolf–dog mixes. The refuge's mission is to better the lives of animals that ended up as unwanted pets. Volunteers are needed to assist with feeding, cleaning enclosures, preparing meals, and general maintenance.

CONTACT: Priderock Wildlife Refuge, PO Box 1594, Terell, TX 75160; Tel: 2149260029; Web: www.priderock.org; Email: Contact form on website.

LOCATION: Terell, TX.

CATEGORY: Rehabilitation.

COST: Free in exchange for service. Volunteers must provide their own accommodations and transportation.

DATES & DURATION: Year-round; long- and short-term assignments are available.

TO APPLY: Applications can be obtained by contacting the refuge office (see Contact) or by visiting www.priderock.org.

FIELD NOTES: Participants must be at least 18 years of age. A moderate level of physical fitness is needed. Positions are suitable for adult groups and solo travelers.

SAN BERNARD NATIONAL WILDLIFE REFUGE

TEXAS, USA

The San Bernard National Wildlife Refuge provides habitat for more than 250 species of birds, such as the royal tern, laughing gull, and roseate spoonbill. The endangered brown pelican is occasionally spotted. Volunteers assist with habitat modification, upkeep and maintenance, and bird and wildlife surveys. Volunteers may also assist with office and educational duties and tours.

CONTACT: San Bernard National Wildlife Refuge, 6801 County Rd 306, Brazoria, TX 77422; Tel: 9799643639; Fax: 9799643210; Web: www.fws.gov/southwest/refuges/texas/texasmidcoast/sanbernard.htm; Email: lee_gaston@fws.gov.

LOCATION: Brazoria, TX.

CATEGORY: Conservation.

COST: Free in exchange for service. Full RV hookups are provided.

DATES & DURATION: Varies; unlimited. Volunteers must commit to a 24-hour workweek.

TO APPLY: Applications can be obtained by contacting the refuge office (see Contact) or by visiting the US Fish and Wildlife Service at www.fws.gov/volunteers.

FIELD NOTES: Controlled hunting is permitted on the refuge during determined seasons. Fishing is allowed year-round. Participation must be arranged in advance by contacting the refuge office (see Contact). Training is provided onsite. All volunteers should have an interest in wildlife and a willingness to learn. Participants under the age of 18 are required to have written parental consent. Positions are suitable for families, groups, and solo travelers.

SANTA ANA NATIONAL WILDLIFE REFUGE

TEXAS, USA

Established in 1943 to provide habitat for migratory birds, Santa Ana National Wildlife Refuge is home to more than 397 bird species, including waterfowl, marsh birds, and shorebirds. The bobcat, coyote, and armadillo can often be observed; the endangered ocelot and jaguarondi are known to the area but are rarely seen. Volunteers assist with interpretive services, construction and maintenance, animal and plant surveys and inventories, and visitor services.

CONTACT: Santa Ana National Wildlife Refuge, Rt. 2, Box 202A, Alamo, TX 78516; Tel: 9567847500; Fax: 9567878338; Web: www.fws.gov/southwest/refuges/texas/ santana.html; Email: patty_alexander@ fws.gov.

LOCATION: Alamo, TX.

CATEGORY: Conservation.

COST: Free in exchange for service. Full RV hookups are provided.

DATES & DURATION: Year-round; unlimited. Volunteers must commit to 3 months of service from November through April. To qualify, volunteers must commit to a 32-hour workweek.

TO APPLY: Applications can be obtained by contacting the refuge office (see Contact) or by visiting the US Fish and Wildlife Service at www.fws.gov/volunteers.

FIELD NOTES: Feeding of the wildlife is prohibited. Plants and animals are protected and should not be disturbed or collected. Bicycles and automobiles are limited to designated areas. Training is provided on-site. The staff works with volunteers to determine meaningful projects that suit both volunteer and refuge needs. Mosquitoes, chiggers, spiders, and scorpions are common in the refuge, so precautions should be taken. Positions are suitable for families, groups, and solo travelers.

UVALDE NATIONAL FISH HATCHERY

TEXAS, USA

Uvalde National Fish Hatchery works in an effort to rear imperiled fish species, such as the fountain darter, Comanche Springs fish, and Devils River minnow. Volunteers feed the fish, clean tanks and raceways, and conduct species inventories. Volunteers also help with general facility maintenance, landscaping, and public outreach activities.

CONTACT: Uvalde National Fish Hatchery, 754 County Rd 203, Uvalde, TX 78801-4563; Tel: 8302782419; Fax: 8302786042; Web: www.fws.gov/south west/fisheries/uvalde.html; Email: grant_weber@fws.gov.

LOCATION: Uvalde, TX.

CATEGORY: Conservation.

COST: Free in exchange for service. Full RV hookups are provided.

DATES & DURATION: Varies; unlimited.

TO APPLY: Applications can be obtained by contacting the hatchery office (see Contact) or by visiting the US Fish and Wildlife Service at www.fws.gov/volunteers.

FIELD NOTES: The hatchery is popular with volunteers, so apply in advance. Participants must be at least 18 years of age. Positions are suitable for adult groups and solo travelers.

BEAR RIVER MIGRATORY BIRD REFUGE

UTAH, USA

The more than 74,000 acres of the Bear River Migratory Bird Refuge serve as the wintering ground for a large variety of waterfowl, shorebirds, and songbirds. The great blue heron, snowy egret, and black-crowned heron are all known to nest in the refuge. Volunteers help with interpretive programs, visitor services, and educational outreach projects. Participants also staff the information desk and bookshop, help with landscaping and gardening, and participate in special events and tours.

CONTACT: Bear River Migratory Bird Refuge, 2155 West Forest St, Brigham City, UT 84302-4424; Tel: 4357346436; Web: www.fws.gov/bearriver; Email: bearriver@fws.gov.

LOCATION: Brigham City, UT.

CATEGORY: Conservation.

COST: Free in exchange for service. Full RV hookups and bunkhouse accommodations are provided.

DATES & DURATION: Varies; unlimited.

TO APPLY: Applications can be obtained by contacting the refuge office (see Contact) or by visiting the US Fish and Wildlife Service at www.fws.gov/volunteers.

FIELD NOTES: Controlled hunting is permitted on refuge grounds during determined seasons. Work schedules vary. Training is provided on-site. Participants must be at least 18 years of age or have written parental consent. Positions are suitable for families, groups, and solo travelers.

FISH SPRINGS NATIONAL WILDLIFE REFUGE

UTAH, USA

Home to the coyote, kit fox, and black-tailed jackrabbit, Fish Springs National Wildlife Refuge provides a safe haven to nesting waterfowl and wintering and migratory birds. Volunteers participate in wildlife surveys, maintenance and construction projects, and visitor services.

CONTACT: Fish Springs National Wildlife Refuge, PO Box 568, Dugway, UT 84022; Tel: 4358315353; Fax: 4358315354; Web: www.fws.gov/fishsprings; Email: robert_sims@fws.gov.

LOCATION: Dugway, UT.

CATEGORY: Conservation.

COST: Free in exchange for service. Bunkhouse accommodations, airport transfers, and a variety of subsistence support are provided.

DATES & DURATION: Year-round; unlimited.

TO APPLY: Applications can be obtained by contacting the refuge office (see Contact) or by visiting the US Fish and Wildlife Service at www.fws.gov/volunteers.

FIELD NOTES: No fishing, camping, or swimming is allowed on refuge grounds.

Plants and animals are protected and should not be disturbed or collected. Both full- and part-time positions are available. Training is provided on-site. Volunteer duties may vary according to current refuge needs. All ages are welcome. Positions are suitable for families, groups, and solo travelers.

JONES HOLE NATIONAL FISH HATCHERY

UTAH, USA

Established in 1956, Jones Hole National Fish Hatchery primarily rears cutthroat, rainbow, and brown trout, as well as Kokanee salmon. Volunteers work in stocking programs and caretaking positions. Participants feed fish, clean holding tanks, and conduct sample counts. Volunteers take part in the general day-to-day operations of the hatchery, including grounds and facility maintenance and public outreach programs. The hatchery hosts more than 7,000 visitors annually, and volunteers may be asked to lead tours and educational programs for school and community groups.

CONTACT: Jones Hole National Fish Hatchery, 24495 East Jones Hole Hatchery Rd, Vernal, UT. 84078-2042; Tel: 4357894481; Fax: 4357813024; Web: www .fws.gov/joneshole; Email: joneshole@ fws.gov.

LOCATION: Vernal, UT.

CATEGORY: Conservation.

COST: Free in exchange for service. Full RV hookups and trailer accommodations are provided.

DATES & DURATION: Varies; unlimited.

TO APPLY: Applications can be obtained by contacting the hatchery office (see Contact) or by visiting the US Fish and Wildlife Service at www.fws.gov/ volunteers.

FIELD NOTES: Participants must be at least 18 years of age. Positions are suitable for adult groups and solo travelers.

OURAY NATIONAL WILDLIFE REFUGE

UTAH, USA

Established in 1960, Ouray National Wildlife Refuge serves as a habitat for breeding and migratory waterfowl. Visitors to the refuge may observe 14 species of nesting ducks, 3 species of endangered fish (the Colorado pike minnow, bonytail, and humpback chub), as well as an assortment of mammals (the black bear, red fox, and lynx). Volunteers participate in wildlife surveys and inventories, habitat restoration and modification, refuge maintenance, and visitor services.

CONTACT: Ouray National Wildlife Refuge, HC 69, Box 232, Randlett, UT 84063; Tel: 4355452522; Fax: 4355452369; Web: www.fws.gov/ouray; Email: ouray@fws.gov.

LOCATION: Randlett, UT.

CATEGORY: Conservation.

COST: Free in exchange for service. Full RV hookups are provided.

DATES & DURATION: Varies; unlimited.

TO APPLY: Applications can be obtained by contacting the refuge office (see Contact) or by visiting the US Fish and Wildlife Service at www.fws.gov/volunteers.

FIELD NOTES: Controlled hunting is permitted on refuge grounds during determined seasons. Fishing is permitted in the river only. Refuge staff works with volunteers to place them in programs that best suit both the refuge's and volunteers' needs. Training is provided onsite. Volunteers can find opportunities for hiking, biking, horseback riding, and canoeing and rafting (river only). Mosquito activity is high during spring and summer months; repellent should be worn at all times. Positions are suitable for families, groups, and solo travelers.

WILDLIFE TRAILS OF THE AMERICAN WEST

UTAH, USA

Volunteers in the Wildlife Trails of the American West program document predators, survey wildlife, and monitor a variety of species, which means hiking in rugged mountain terrain among moose and elk. Volunteers identify and count tracks, and map game trails and kill sites; use of global positioning system (GPS) units is necessary.

CONTACT: Earthwatch Institute, 3 Clock Tower Pl, Suite 100, Box 75, Maynard, MA 01754; Tel: 9784610081 or 8007760188; Fax: 9784612332; Web: www.earthwatch .org; Email: expeditions@earthwatch.org.

LOCATION: Salt Lake City, UT; Idaho Falls, ID.

CATEGORY: Conservation.

COST: US$1,950 for 8 days. Fee includes accommodations, meals, ground transfers, training, and support.

DATES & DURATION: Varies; 8 days.

TO APPLY: Applications are accepted online and by fax or mail. Contact the office (see Contact).

FIELD NOTES: Volunteers must be physically fit to endure the long hikes that this program entails. Participants must be 18 years of age or older or traveling with a parent or guardian. Positions are suitable for families with older children, groups, and solo travelers.

BACK BAY NATIONAL WILDLIFE REFUGE

VIRGINIA, USA

Providing habitat to a variety of threatened or endangered species, including the loggerhead sea turtle, piping plover, peregrine falcon, and American bald eagle, Back Bay National Wildlife Refuge is also the temporary home of an assortment of geese and duck species during the fall migration season. Volunteers assist with wildlife surveys, visitor services, special projects and events, interpretive programs, trail maintenance, and general refuge upkeep.

CONTACT: US Fish and Wildlife Service, Back Bay National Wildlife Refuge, 4005 Sandpiper Rd, Virginia Beach, VA 23456-4325; Tel: 7577212412; Fax: 7577216141; Web: www.fws.gov/backbay; Email: walter_tegge@fws.gov.

LOCATION: Virginia Beach, VA.

CATEGORY: Conservation.

COST: Free in exchange for service. Housing is provided.

DATES & DURATION: Varies; unlimited.

TO APPLY: Applications can be obtained by contacting the refuge office (see Contact) or by visiting the US Fish and Wildlife Service at www.fws.gov/volunteers.

FIELD NOTES: Fishing, kayaking, and bicycling are permitted in designated areas. A sightseeing tram operates through the refuge from April through September. Volunteers under the age of 18 must have written parental consent; those under the age of 16 must be accompanied by a parent or guardian. No special skills are required; training is provided on-site. Organized group participation is welcomed and encouraged. Positions are suitable for families, groups, and solo travelers.

CHINCOTEAGUE NATIONAL WILDLIFE REFUGE

VIRGINIA, USA

Known for its famous annual pony swim, Chincoteague National Wildlife Refuge hosts an array of species, including the red fox, river otter, sika elk, white-tailed deer, bottlenose dolphin, and Delmarva fox squirrel. Volunteers conduct wildlife surveys, present interpretive walks and discussions, work on construction and maintenance projects, help with habitat modification and improvement projects, and participate in visitor services.

CONTACT: Chincoteague National Wildlife Refuge, PO Box 62, Chincoteague Island, VA 23336; Tel: 7573366122; Fax: 7573365273; Web: www.fws.gov/northeast/chinco; Email: fwrw_cnwr@fws.gov.

LOCATION: Chincoteague Island, VA.

CATEGORY: Conservation.

COST: Free in exchange for service.

DATES & DURATION: Year-round; unlimited.

TO APPLY: Applications can be obtained by contacting the refuge office (see Contact) or by visiting the US Fish and Wildlife Service at www.fws.gov/volunteers.

FIELD NOTES: Feeding of the wildlife is prohibited. Plants and animals are protected and should not be disturbed or collected. Fishing, crabbing, clamming, and kayaking are permitted in designated areas. The refuge maintains several miles of trails for hiking and biking. The use of alcohol while on refuge grounds is strictly prohibited. Training and uniforms are provided on-site. No special skills or requirements are needed to participate. Mosquitoes are abundant in the area, and repellent should be worn at all times. All ages are welcome. Positions are suitable for families, groups, and solo travelers.

EASTERN SHORE OF VIRGINIA NATIONAL WILDLIFE REFUGE

VIRGINIA, USA

Five marine mammals—the Atlantic right, finback, humpback, and sei whales, and the harbor seal—can be found in the waters of the Eastern Shore of Virginia National Wildlife Refuge. An assortment of bird, reptile and amphibian, and land mammal species also call these grounds home. Volunteers work in visitor services, greeting and educating visitors.

CONTACT: US Fish and Wildlife Service, Eastern Shore of Virginia National Wildlife Refuge, 5003 Hallett Circle, Cape Charles, VA 23310; Tel: 7573312760; Web: www.fws.gov/northeast/easternshore; Email: fw5rw_esvnwr@fws.gov.

LOCATION: Cape Charles, VA.

CATEGORY: Conservation.

COST: Free in exchange for service. Full RV hookups are provided.

DATES & DURATION: Year-round; unlimited. Volunteers must commit to a minimum 3-day workweek.

TO APPLY: Applications can be obtained by contacting the refuge office (see Contact) or by visiting the US Fish and Wildlife Service at www.fws.gov/volunteers.

FIELD NOTES: Boating, canoeing, and kayaking are permitted in designated areas. Controlled hunting is permitted during determined seasons. Training is provided on-site. Both full- and part-time positions are available. Positions are suitable for families, groups, and solo travelers.

LITTLE PEND OREILLE NATIONAL WILDLIFE REFUGE

WASHINGTON, USA

Little Pend Oreille National Wildlife Refuge is home to 206 bird, 8 reptile, 6 amphibian, and 58 mammal species—including the threatened Canada lynx. Volunteers participate in control of invasive plant species and general refuge maintenance and upkeep.

CONTACT: Little Pend Oreille National Wildlife Refuge, 1310 Bear Creek Rd, Colville, WA 99114; Tel: 5096848384; Fax: 5096848381; Web: www.fws.gov/littlependoreille; Email: lpo@fws.gov.

LOCATION: Colville, WA.

CATEGORY: Conservation.

COST: Free in exchange for service. Full RV hookups are provided.

DATES & DURATION: Varies; unlimited.

TO APPLY: Applications can be obtained by contacting the refuge office (see Contact) or by visiting the US Fish and Wildlife Service at www.fws.gov/volunteers.

FIELD NOTES: Permitted activities include camping, hiking, horseback riding, biking, cross-country skiing, and snowshoeing. Fishing and hunting are permitted in designated areas during determined seasons. Volunteer training is provided on-site. Participants under the age of 18 must have written parental consent; those 16 or under must be accompanied by a parent or guardian. Both full- and part-time positions are available. Positions are suitable for families, groups, and solo travelers.

CANAAN VALLEY NATIONAL WILDLIFE REFUGE

WEST VIRGINIA, USA

Established in 1994, Canaan Valley National Wildlife Refuge serves as a nesting ground for grassland nesting bird species. Volunteers assist with biological surveys, including anuran call counts, amphibian egg-mass surveys, and breeding-bird surveys.

CONTACT: Canaan Valley National Wildlife Refuge, HC 70, Box 200, Davis, WV 26260; Tel: 3048663858; Fax: 3048663852; Web: www.fws.gov/canaanvalley; Email: fw5rw_cvnwr@fws.gov.

LOCATION: Davis, WV.

CATEGORY: Conservation.

COST: Free in exchange for service. Full RV hookups and bunkhouse accommodations are provided.

DATES & DURATION: Year-round; unlimited.

TO APPLY: Applications can be obtained by contacting the refuge office (see Contact) or by visiting the US Fish and Wildlife Service at www.fws.gov/volunteers.

FIELD NOTES: Volunteer training is provided on-site. Volunteers are needed on a year-round basis. Both full- and part-time positions are available. All ages are welcome. Positions are suitable for families, groups, and solo travelers.

JACKSON NATIONAL FISH HATCHERY

WYOMING, USA

Established in 1950, Jackson National Fish Hatchery produces eggs and fish species for stocking. Volunteers participate in facility maintenance, gardening and landscaping, public outreach activities, and duties involved with raising fish.

CONTACT: Jackson National Fish Hatchery, 1455 Fish Hatchery Rd, Jackson, WY 83001; Tel: 3077332510; Web: www.fws.gov/Jackson; Email: jackson@fws.gov.

LOCATION: Jackson, WY.

CATEGORY: Conservation.

COST: Free in exchange for service. Full RV hookups are provided.

DATES & DURATION: May through September; unlimited.

TO APPLY: Applications can be obtained by contacting the hatchery office (see Contact) or by visiting the US Fish and Wildlife Service at www.fws.gov/volunteers.

FIELD NOTES: Work hours are generally 8 a.m. to 4 p.m. Volunteer shirts, hats, and jackets are provided. Participants must be 18 years of age or older if not accompanied by an adult. Positions are suitable for families, groups, and solo travelers.

NATIONAL ELK REFUGE

WYOMING, USA

Encompassing 25,000 acres, National Elk Refuge hosts more than 7,500 elk yearly. Volunteers assist with biological surveys, refuge maintenance and up-keep, and visitor services. Volunteers may be asked to participate in special events and festivals, depending on the time of service.

CONTACT: National Elk Refuge, PO Box 510, Jackson, WY 83002; Tel: 3077339212; Web: www.fws.gov/nationalelkrefuge; Email: nationalelkrefuge@fws.gov.

LOCATION: Jackson, WY.

CATEGORY: Conservation.

COST: Free in exchange for service. Full RV hookups and other housing options are provided.

DATES & DURATION: Varies. Volunteers must commit to a 32-hour workweek.

TO APPLY: Applications can be obtained by contacting the refuge office (see Con-tact) or by visiting the US Fish and Wild-life Service at www.fws.gov/volunteers.

FIELD NOTES: The refuge has a waiting list for volunteers seeking RV pads in ex-change for service. Applicants should apply well in advance. Training is pro-vided on-site. Both full- and part-time positions are available. All ages are wel-come. Positions are suitable for families, groups, and solo travelers.

SONGBIRDS OF THE TETONS PROGRAM

WYOMING, USA

The Jackson Hole area is home to a great variety of local and migratory songbirds. Volunteers in the Songbirds of the Tetons Program help locate and identify bird species. Participants may also assist with research involving bird species habitat use and the causes of population change.

CONTACT: Earthwatch Institute, 3 Clock Tower Pl, Suite 100, Box 75, Maynard, MA 01754; Tel: 9784610081 or 8007760188; Fax: 9784612332; Web: www.earthwatch .org; Email: expeditions@earthwatch.org.

LOCATION: Jackson Hole, WY.

CATEGORY: Conservation.

COST: US$2,150 for 9 days. Fee includes accommodations, meals, ground transfers, training, and support.

DATES & DURATION: Varies; 9 days.

TO APPLY: Applications are accepted online and by fax or mail. Contact the office (see Contact).

FIELD NOTES: A maximum of 12 volunteers at a time. Volunteers must be at least 18 years of age to participate. Positions are suitable for adult groups and solo travelers.

WHALES OF BRITISH COLUMBIA

BRITISH COLUMBIA, CANADA

Volunteers for the Whales of British Columbia project help conduct photo identification surveys as part of the ongoing research of gray whales in their summer feeding grounds. Participants also collect data on the abundance and distribution of prey available to these whales.

CONTACT: Earthwatch Institute, 3 Clock Tower Pl, Suite 100, Box 75, Maynard, MA 01754; Tel: 9784610081 or 8007760188; Fax: 9784612332; Web: www.earthwatch.org; Email: expeditions@earthwatch.org.
LOCATION: Tofino, BC, Canada.

CATEGORY: Conservation.

COST: US$2,850 for 7 days. Fee includes accommodations, meals, ground transfers, training, and support.

DATES & DURATION: Varies; 7 days.

TO APPLY: Applications are accepted online and by fax or mail. Contact the office (see Contact).

FIELD NOTES: Applicants must be at least 18 years of age. Volunteers should be in good physical condition because they are required to spend time in kayaks and other boats. Positions are suitable for adult groups and solo travelers.

CLIMATE CHANGE AT THE ARCTIC'S EDGE PROGRAM

MANITOBA, CANADA

Volunteers in the Climate Change at the Arctic's Edge Program participate in an expedition to study how climate change is affecting the arctic region. This unique experience features both field and laboratory components. Groups of volunteers help with specific field tasks and then work on data entry and analysis of the information they gathered. Participants help set up and monitor equipment and collect data on snowpack, permafrost, vascular plant species, lichens, mosses, and mammals.

CONTACT: Earthwatch Institute, 3 Clock Tower Pl, Suite 100, Box 75, Maynard, MA 01754; Tel: 9784610081 or 8007760188; Fax: 9784612332; Web: www.earthwatch.org; Email: expeditions@earthwatch.org.

LOCATION: Churchill, MB, Canada.

CATEGORY: Conservation.

COST: US$2,950 for 11 days. Fee includes accommodations, meals, ground transfers, orientation, training, and support.

DATES & DURATION: Varies; 11 days.

TO APPLY: Applications are accepted online and by fax or mail. Contact the office (see Contact).

FIELD NOTES: Because fieldwork occurs in polar bear country, participants must sign a polar bear acknowledgment form. Volunteers must be at least 18 years of age. A maximum of 15 volunteers at a time. Training is provided on-site. Positions are suitable for adult groups and solo travelers.

MAMMALS OF NOVA SCOTIA

NOVA SCOTIA, CANADA

On the peninsula of Nova Scotia, volunteers can participate in a study of the affect of climate change and habitat loss on a variety of animals, from beavers to bats. Volunteers in the Mammals of Nova Scotia project use a variety of monitoring techniques, including live trapping and surveillance equipment, to learn more about population densities and animal behavior.

CONTACT: Earthwatch Institute, 3 Clock Tower Pl, Suite 100, Box 75, Maynard, MA 01754; Tel: 9784610081 or 8007760188; Fax: 9784612332; Web: www.earthwatch.org; Email: expeditions@earthwatch.org.

LOCATION: Halifax, NS, Canada.

CATEGORY: Conservation.

COST: US$2,750 for 14 days. Fee includes accommodations, meals, ground transfers, orientation, training, and support.

DATES & DURATION: Summer; 14 days.

TO APPLY: Applications are accepted online and by fax or mail. Contact the office (see Contact).

FIELD NOTES: Participants must be at least 18 years of age. A maximum of 12 volunteers at a time. A moderate level of physical fitness is required. Positions are suitable for adult groups and solo travelers.

MINKE WHALE PROJECT

QUEBEC, CANADA

The Minke Whale Project offers the opportunity to work alongside marine biologists who are observing and studying one of the most accessible marine mammals in the world. Participants are involved in all aspects of the study, helping with behavioral and foraging research, observing population ecology, and participating in photo identification programs.

CONTACT: Eco Volunteer Organization, c/o The Great Canadian Travel Company Ltd, 158 Fort St, Winnipeg, MB, Canada R3C 1C9; Tel: 2049490199 or 8006613830; Web: www.ecovolunteer.org or www.greatcanadiantravel.com; Email: ecovolunteer@gctc-mst.com.

LOCATION: Gulf of St. Lawrence, QC, Canada.

CATEGORY: Conservation.

COST: US$1,586 for 13 days. Fee includes accommodations, ground transfers, lectures and presentations, training, and support.

DATES & DURATION: Summer; 13 days.

TO APPLY: Applications are accepted online by contacting the office (see Contact).

FIELD NOTES: Volunteers must be at least 18 years of age and speak English. Daily outings require the use of modern inflatable boats; thus, participants should be in good physical shape. Positions are suitable for adult groups and solo travelers.

CLIMATE CHANGE IN THE MACKENZIE MOUNTAINS

YUKON, CANADA

The Mackenzie Mountains play host to Canada's largest herd of mountain caribou. Moose, subarctic wolves, wolverines, and grizzlies are among many other species that can be observed in the region. Volunteers in the Climate Change in the Mackenzie Mountains program participate in all aspects of a study focused on the affects of climate change in the mountains. Volunteers are needed for both field and laboratory assignments.

CONTACT: Earthwatch Institute, 3 Clock Tower Pl, Suite 100, Box 75, Maynard, MA 01754; Tel: 9784610081 or 8007760188; Fax: 9784612332; Web: www.earthwatch.org; Email: expeditions@earthwatch.org.

LOCATION: Whitehorse, YT, Canada.

CATEGORY: Conservation.

COST: US$5,050 for 11 days. Fee includes accommodations, meals, ground transfers, training, and support.

DATES & DURATION: Varies; 11 days.

TO APPLY: Applications are accepted online and by fax or mail. Contact the office (see Contact).

FIELD NOTES: On-site travel is by 4-wheel-drive vehicle, though some hiking is required. Participants should be physically fit. Volunteers must be at least 18 years of age. Training is provided on-site. Because this program is stationed in polar bear country, volunteers need to sign a polar bear acknowledgment form. Positions are suitable for adults traveling solo or by group.

TRACKING BAJA'S BLACK SEA TURTLES

BAJA CALIFORNIA SUR, MEXICO

Kayak around the pristine waters of San Ignacio Lagoon while participating in the Tracking Baja's Black Sea Turtles project. Volunteers assist scientists who are working to better understand black sea turtle behavior. Volunteers take part in capturing turtles, collecting data, tracking turtles, and collecting samples.

CONTACT: Earthwatch Institute, 3 Clock Tower Pl, Suite 100, Box 75, Maynard, MA 01754; Tel: 9784610081 or 8007760188; Fax: 9784612332; Web: www.earthwatch.org; Email: expeditions@earthwatch.org.

LOCATION: Loreta, Baja California Sur, Mexico.

CATEGORY: Conservation.

COST: US$2,550 for 7 days. Fee includes accommodations, meals, ground transfers, training, and support.

DATES & DURATION: Varies; 7 days.

TO APPLY: Applications are accepted online and by fax or mail. Contact the office (see Contact).

FIELD NOTES: Participants must be 18 years of age and be able to swim. A moderate level of physical fitness is required for participation. Positions are suitable for adult groups and solo travelers.

MARINE EXPEDITION IN MEXICO

YUCATÁN PENINSULA, MEXICO

Learn how to scuba dive and earn your Professional Association of Diving Instructors (PADI) certificate while taking part in a marine conservation study of the world's second largest barrier reef. Volunteers on the Marine Expedition in Mexico assist with reef and fish species monitoring, turtle nesting and crocodile surveys, and community awareness programs.

CONTACT: Global Vision International, 252 Newbury St, #4, Boston, MA 02116; Tel: 8886536028; Fax: 6176742109; Web: www.gviusa.com; Email: info@gviworld.com.

LOCATION: Yucatán Peninsula, Mexico.

CATEGORY: Conservation.

COST: US$3,150–$5,190 for 5–10 weeks. Fee includes cabana-style accommodations or tents, meals, ground transfers, training, and support.

DATES & DURATION: Year-round; 5 or 10 weeks. To qualify, volunteers must commit to a 5- or 10-week stay.

TO APPLY: Applications are accepted online and by fax or mail. Contact the office (see Contact).

FIELD NOTES: No previous diving experience is needed. Volunteers must be able to pass a medical examination and be physically fit to dive. All volunteers must pass a swim test upon arrival. Positions are suitable for adult groups and solo travelers.

COASTAL ECOLOGY OF THE BAHAMAS

LONG ISLAND, GEORGETOWN; MATTHEW TOWN, BAHAMAS

The Coastal Ecology of the Bahamas program is focused on protecting the island habitats. The archipelago includes more than 30 settlements and towns. Volunteers help measure the shoreline using GPS equipment and participate in wildlife surveys. Participants also assist in plant identification and transplant measures.

CONTACT: Earthwatch Institute, 3 Clock Tower Pl, Suite 100, Box 75, Maynard, MA 01754; Tel: 9784610081 or 8007760188; Fax: 9784612332; Web: www .earthwatch.org; Email: expeditions@ earthwatch.org.

LOCATION: Long Island, Georgetown; Matthew Town, Bahamas.

CATEGORY: Conservation.

COST: US$2,350 for 12 days. Fee includes accommodations, meals, ground transfers, training, and support.

DATES & DURATION: Varies; 12 days.

TO APPLY: Applications are accepted online and by fax or mail. Contact the office (see Contact).

FIELD NOTES: Volunteers must be at least 18 years of age and must be comfortable snorkeling in shallow waters for up to 3 hours at a time. During free time, participants are encouraged to learn to fish for bonefish or take a tour of the islands. Positions are suitable for adult groups and solo travelers.

DOLPHINS AND WHALES OF ABACO ISLAND

MARSH HARBOR, GREAT ABACO ISLAND, BAHAMAS

The Dolphins and Whales of Abaco Island program focuses on the study of the bottlenose dolphin and beaked and sperm whale. Volunteers work with resident staff, who are studying the abundance, distribution, and seasonality of these majestic marine mammals.

CONTACT: Earthwatch Institute, 3 Clock Tower Pl, Suite 100, Box 75, Maynard, MA 01754; Tel: 9784610081 or 8007760188; Fax: 9784612332; Web: www .earthwatch.org; Email: expeditions@ earthwatch.org.

LOCATION: Marsh Harbor, Great Abaco Island, Bahamas.

CATEGORY: Conservation.

COST: US$2,650 for 11 days. Fee includes accommodations, meals, ground transfers, training, and support.

DATES & DURATION: Varies; 11 days.

TO APPLY: Applications are accepted online and by fax or mail. Contact the office (see Contact).

FIELD NOTES: Applicants must be at least 18 years of age. A reasonable level of physical fitness is needed because volunteers are required to spend much of their time on watercraft and in the water. Positions are suitable for adult groups and solo travelers.

BAHAMIAN REEF SURVEY

SAN SALVADOR ISLAND, BAHAMAS

San Salvador Island, where Christopher Columbus made landfall in 1492, is known for its crystal clear blue waters and history. Unfortunately, tourism has adversely affected the coral reefs. Volunteers in the Bahamian Reef Survey program join a study that is determining what can be done to save these pristine waters and the inhabitants that live there. Participants must snorkel in order to conduct water-life surveys, collect data, and engage in restoration efforts.

CONTACT: Earthwatch Institute, 3 Clock Tower Pl, Suite 100, Box 75, Maynard, MA 01754; Tel: 9784610081 or 8007760188; Fax: 9784612332; Web: www .earthwatch.org; Email: expeditions@ earthwatch.org.

LOCATION: San Salvador Island, Bahamas.

CATEGORY: Conservation.

COST: US$2,450 for 8 days. Fee includes accommodations, meals, ground transfers, training, and support.

DATES & DURATION: Varies; 8 days.

TO APPLY: Applications are accepted online and by fax or mail. Contact the. office (see Contact).

FIELD NOTES: Participants must be at least 18 years of age. A moderate level of physical fitness and the ability to swim are required. Positions are suitable for adult groups and solo travelers.

REEF FISH OF THE VIRGIN ISLANDS

ST. THOMAS, US VIRGIN ISLANDS

Volunteers participating in the Reef Fish of the Virgin Islands program help collect fish, remove and count parasites, assist with observational data collection, and participate in laboratory studies.

CONTACT: Earthwatch Institute, 3 Clock Tower Pl, Suite 100, Box 75, Maynard, MA 01754; Tel: 9784610081 or 8007760188; Fax: 9784612332; Web: www .earthwatch.org; Email: expeditions@ earthwatch.org.

LOCATION: St. Thomas, US VI.

CATEGORY: Conservation.

COST: US $2,750 for 9 days. Fee includes accommodations, meals, ground transfers, training, and support.

DATES & DURATION: Varies; 9 days.

TO APPLY: Applications are accepted online and by fax or mail. Contact the office (see Contact).

FIELD NOTES: Volunteers must be at least 18 years of age. A maximum of 12 volunteers at a time. This program requires an open-water scuba certification before service. Night snorkeling may be required for species collection. Positions are suitable for adult groups and solo travelers.

SOUTH AMERICA

Bolivia, Brazil, Colombia, Costa Rica, Ecuador,
Guatemala, Nicaragua, Panama, Peru, Tobago

COCHABAMBA CONSERVATION PROJECT

BOLIVIA

Participants in the Cochabamba Conservation Project help rehabilitate rescued, injured, sick, and orphaned animals in Bolivia. Volunteers participate in the feeding and care of a variety of species, including monkeys, snakes, tigers, birds, and turtles. The project houses over 300 monkeys, so volunteers are needed year-round.

CONTACT: Twin Work & Volunteer Abroad, 2nd Floor, 67-71 Lewisham, London, SE13 5JX, UK; Tel: 08008048380; Fax: 08707775206; Web: www.workand volunteer.com; Email: Contact form on website.

LOCATION: Cochabamba, Bolivia.

CATEGORY: Rescue and rehabilitation.

COST: US$650 for 2 weeks; US$300 per extra week. Fee includes accommodations, breakfast, ground transfers, and training.

DATES & DURATION: Year-round; 2 weeks. To qualify, volunteers must commit to a 2-week stay.

TO APPLY: Applications are accepted online and by fax or mail. Contact the office (see Contact).

FIELD NOTES: Volunteers must be at least 18 years of age. Basic Spanish-language skills preferred. Positions are suitable for adult groups and solo travelers.

BRAZIL RAIN FOREST ADVENTURE

BRAZIL

Volunteers in the Brazil Rain Forest Adventure program have the opportunity not only to experience wildlife at its best but also to stop the destruction of the rain forests. The Brazilian rain forest is in desperate need of help. Deforestation has caused irreversible damage, leaving animals with little or no place to live and the bare minimum of food sources. Volunteers help with reforestation projects.

CONTACT: The Society for Environmental Exploration (operating as Frontier), 50-52 Rivington St, London, EC2A 3QP, UK; Tel: 4402076132422; Fax: 4402076132992; Web: www.frontier.ac .uk/gap_year_projects/Brazil/Brazil_ Rainforest_Adventure; Email: info@ frontier.ac.uk.

LOCATION: Brazil.

CATEGORY: Conservation.

COST: US$1,686 for 4 weeks; US$352 per extra week. Fee includes accommodations, meals, orientation, project training, equipment, and in-country emergency support.

DATES & DURATION: Year-round; 4–20 weeks. Programs begin monthly.

TO APPLY: Applications are accepted online and by fax or mail. Contact the office (see Contact).

FIELD NOTES: Minimum age requirement of 18 years; 16- and 17-year-olds may participate if accompanied by a parent or guardian. Positions are suitable for adult groups and solo travelers.

HUMPBACK WHALE PROJECT

BRAZIL

Each year, from July to November, a population of humpback whales arrives in Brazil's Abrolhos National Park for their mating and calving season. Volunteers on the Humpback Whale Project have the opportunity to watch these majestic, endangered creatures in action, while helping protect them. Volunteers are asked to record behavioral data, maintain the site's picture identification library, collect biopsies, and conduct bio-acoustic monitoring to record the sounds and songs of the whales.

CONTACT: Eco Volunteer Organization, c/o The Great Canadian Travel Company Ltd, 158 Fort St, Winnipeg, MB, Canada R3C 1C9; Tel: 2049490199 or 8006613830; Web: www.ecovolunteer.org; Email: ecovolunteer@gctc-mst.com.

LOCATION: Caravelas, Brazil.

CATEGORY: Conservation.

COST: US$1,400 for 2 weeks. Fee includes accommodations, breakfast, and project training.

DATES & DURATION: July through November; 2-week minimum.

TO APPLY: Applications are accepted online by contacting the office (see Contact).

FIELD NOTES: Participants must be at least 18 years of age, speak English, and be able to tolerate rough seas. Positions are suitable for adult groups and solo travelers.

JAGUAR PROJECT

BRAZIL

Get involved in the Jaguar Project, a long-term program committed to the protection of Brazil's jaguars and pumas. Volunteers work in the field, monitoring the cats' movements and activities.

CONTACT: Eco Volunteer Organization c/o The Great Canadian Travel Company Ltd, 158 Fort St, Winnipeg, MB, Canada R3C 1C9; Tel: 2049490199 or 8006613830; Web: www.ecovolunteer.org; Email: ecovolunteer@gctc-mst.com.

LOCATION: Miranda Town, Brazil.

CATEGORY: Conservation.

COST: US$1,080 for 2 weeks. Fee includes accommodations, breakfast and dinners, and project training.

DATES & DURATION: Varies; 2 weeks.

TO APPLY: Applications are accepted online by contacting the office (see Contact).

FIELD NOTES: Volunteers must be at least 21 years old, have a working knowledge of English, be in good health, and be able to walk long distances. Positions are suitable for adults traveling both solo or in small groups. A maximum of four volunteers at a time.

LOST WORLD EXPEDITION

BRAZIL

Set in Brazil's Atlantic rain forest, the Lost World Expedition offers amateur explorers a unique opportunity: the chance to research two fascinating carnivores—the jaguar and the puma—in a remote, little-studied area. Participants assist scientists with fieldwork, conducting observational surveys to determine these animals' distribution patterns in one of earth's most threatened ecosystems. Participants also conduct interviews in local communities to assess individual concerns regarding these species and to aid in the future development of community-based conservation plans.

CONTACT: Biosphere Expeditions, PO Box 917750, Longwood, FL 32791; Tel: 8004075761; Fax: 8004075766; Web: www .biosphere-expeditions.org; Email: north america@biosphere-expeditions.org.

LOCATION: Curitiba, Brazil.

CATEGORY: Conservation.

COST: US$1,690 for 12 nights. Fee includes accommodations, meals, training, and in-country emergency support.

DATES & DURATION: Varies; 12 nights.

TO APPLY: Applications are accepted online and by fax or mail. Contact the office (see Contact).

FIELD NOTES: No specific skills are required. The program is open to all ages. Participants must feel comfortable hiking through mountainous terrain. Positions are suitable for families, groups, and solo travelers.

PINK RIVER DOLPHIN PROJECT

BRAZIL

Though severely endangered, the majestic pink river dolphin still has a fighting chance for recovery. Volunteers in the Pink River Dolphin Project live on a houseboat on the Amazon. Participants help research this amazing creature and are involved with public awareness campaigns to disseminate information about sustainable development and the importance of conservation. Participants also conduct daily small-boat surveys lasting 5–7 hours, recording sightings and behavioral data of the pink river dolphin.

CONTACT: Global Vision International, 252 Newbury St, #4, Boston, MA 02116; Tel: 8886536028; Fax: 6176742109; Web: www.gviusa.com/projects/south-america/brazil/volunteer-pink-river-dolphins-project-brazil/the-program; Email: info@gviworld.com.

LOCATION: Amazon region, Brazil.

CATEGORY: Conservation.

COST: US$2,690–$3,790 for 2–4 weeks; extended stays available for additional fee. Fee includes accommodations, meals, ground transfers, orientation, project training, equipment, and in-country emergency support.

DATES & DURATION: Year-round; 2–4 weeks.

TO APPLY: Applications are accepted online and by fax or mail. Contact the office (see Contact).

FIELD NOTES: No previous experience or skills are required, but participants must be team oriented, physically fit, and willing to spend long hours on small research boats. Positions are suitable for adult groups and solo travelers.

RED-BREASTED TOUCAN PROJECT

BRAZIL

Now endangered, the red-breasted toucan needs our support. Scientists in the Red-Breasted Toucan Project are gathering much-needed information about this gorgeous creature and its natural habitat. Volunteers work in the rain forest of southeastern Brazil, using GPS to locate the toucans, collecting behavioral data for further analysis, and monitoring nests to ensure the safety of hatchlings.

CONTACT: Eco Volunteer Organization, c/o The Great Canadian Travel Company Ltd, 158 Fort St, Winnipeg, MB, Canada R3C 1C9; Tel: 2049490199 or 8006613830;

Web: www.ecovolunteer.org; Email: ecovolunteer@gctc-mst.com.

LOCATION: Santa Catarina Island, Brazil.

CATEGORY: Conservation.

COST: US$1,080 for 2 weeks; extended stays available for an additional fee. Fee includes accommodations, two meals per day, and project training.

DATES & DURATION: Year-round; 2 weeks.

TO APPLY: Applications are accepted online by contacting the office (see Contact).

FIELD NOTES: Participants must be 18 years old and fluent in Portuguese, English, or Spanish. Positions are suitable for adult groups and solo travelers.

RIVER OTTER PROJECT

BRAZIL

With much of its habitat destroyed by river pollution, the once-thriving river otter has now joined the endangered species list. To help improve the chances of these struggling creatures, volunteers in the River Otter Project track the wild mammals in the water and on the land, and monitor and record the behavior of captive otters. Volunteers also assist with daily feedings, cleaning of enclosures, and general maintenance procedures.

CONTACT: Eco Volunteer Organization, c/o The Great Canadian Travel Company Ltd, 158 Fort St, Winnipeg, MB, Canada R3C 1C9; Tel: 2049490199 or 8006613830; Web: www.ecovolunteer.org; Email: ecovolunteer@gctc-mst.com.

LOCATION: Piri, Brazil.

CATEGORY: Conservation.

COST: US$1,053 for 2 weeks; extended stays available for additional fee. Fee includes accommodations, meals, and project training.

DATES & DURATION: Year-round; 2 weeks.

TO APPLY: Applications are accepted online by contacting the office (see Contact).

FIELD NOTES: Participants must be at least 18 years of age, speak English, and be in good health. Younger children (over 6) are welcome when accompanied by a parent or guardian. Positions are suitable for families, groups, and solo travelers.

TRACKING BRAZIL'S ELUSIVE JAGUAR

BRAZIL

The Tracking Brazil's Elusive Jaguar expedition is situated in Emas National Park, home to an amazing diversity of species. Volunteers work alongside leading biologists and conservationists to track the jaguars and collect data on survival rates, habitat preferences, and basic nutritional needs. With the help of trained dogs, volunteers conduct mammal surveys, identify prey populations, and collect and analyze jaguar scat and kills to determine the jaguar's diet.

CONTACT: Earthwatch Institute, 3 Clock Tower Pl, Suite 100, Box 75, Maynard, MA 01754; Tel: 9784610081 or 8007760188; Fax: 9784612332; Web: www.earthwatch.org/europe/exped/silveira.html; Email: expeditions@earthwatch.org.

LOCATION: Campo Grande, Mato Grosso do Sul, Brazil.

CATEGORY: Conservation.

COST: US$2,950 for 13 days. Fee includes accommodations, meals, ground transfers, orientation, project training, and in-country emergency support.

DATES & DURATION: Varies; 13 days.

TO APPLY: Applications are accepted online and by fax or mail. Contact the office (see Contact).

FIELD NOTES: Volunteers must be at least 18 years old; 16- to 17-year-olds may participate if accompanied by a parent or guardian. Volunteers should expect moderate activity throughout their stay. Participants must work with or among dogs; volunteers with allergies should take the proper precautions. Positions are suitable for adult groups and solo travelers.

WHALES OF BRAZIL

BRAZIL

Based off of one of Brazil's most beautiful beaches, the Whales of Brazil project aims to improve our understanding of the majestic humpback whale. Volunteers help researchers collect behavioral data, conduct acoustic monitoring, and maintain the site's already-extensive picture library. Participants may also spend time in the historic fishing village of Praia do Forte.

CONTACT: Global Vision International, 252 Newbury St, #4, Boston, MA 02116; Tel: 8886536028; Fax: 6176742109; Web: www.gviusa.com/projects/south-america/brazil/volunteer-humpback-whale-project-brazil/home; Email: info@gviworld.com.

LOCATION: Praia do Forte, Brazil.

CATEGORY: Conservation.

COST: US$1,800–$2,780 for 2–4 weeks; extended stays available for additional fee. Fee includes accommodations, breakfast, ground transfers, orientation, project training, equipment, and in-country emergency support.

DATES & DURATION: July through October; 2–4 weeks.

TO APPLY: Applications are accepted online and by fax or mail. Contact the office (see Contact).

FIELD NOTES: A maximum of four volunteers at a time. Positions suited for families with older children, groups, and solo travelers.

WILDLIFE OF THE PANTANAL

BRAZIL

With four research projects to choose from, the Wildlife of the Pantanal program offers a variety of eco-rich experiences. Participants can focus on amphibians and reptiles, bats, birds, or otters—all four exceptional opportunities to explore the world's largest freshwater wetlands. Volunteers help researchers in their efforts to better understand the area's species by conducting biodiversity surveys, monitoring wildlife behavior, and collecting other data.

CONTACT: Earthwatch Institute, 3 Clock Tower Pl, Suite 100, Box 75, Maynard, MA 01754; Tel: 9784610081 or 8007760188; Fax: 9784612332; Web: www.earthwatch .org/europe/exped/pantanal.html; Email: expeditions@earthwatch.org.

LOCATION: Campo Grande, Mato Grosso do Sul, Brazil.

CATEGORY: Conservation.

COST: US$2,950 for 13 days. Fee includes accommodations, meals, ground transfers, orientation, project training, and in-country emergency support.

DATES & DURATION: Varies; 13 days.

TO APPLY: Applications are accepted online and by fax or mail. Contact the office (see Contact).

FIELD NOTES: Volunteers must be at least 18 years old; 16- to 17-year-olds may also participate if accompanied by a parent or guardian. Volunteers who wish to handle bats must have a rabies vaccination before the trip. Positions are suitable for adult groups and solo travelers.

WILDLIFE SANCTUARY PROJECT

BRAZIL

Brazil's Wildlife Sanctuary plays hosts to a variety of animals who have suffered as a result of deforestation, encroachment, and mistreatment; the illegal pet, circus, and skin trades; and a wide variety of other abuses. Participants in the Wildlife Sanctuary Project can lend a hand in bettering the lives of these once-tortured animals. Volunteers help create a safe environment, help with daily feedings, clean enclosures, and help build shelters for the new arrivals.

CONTACT: Eco Volunteer Organization, c/o The Great Canadian Travel Company Ltd, 158 Fort St, Winnipeg, MB, Canada R3C 1C9; Tel: 2049490199 or 8006613830; Web: www.ecovolunteer.org; Email: ecovolunteer@gctc-mst.com.

LOCATION: Cotia, Brazil.

CATEGORY: Rehabilitation.

COST: US$1,697 for 2 weeks. Fee includes accommodations, meals (vegetarian only), and project training.

DATES & DURATION: Year-round; 2 weeks.

Arrivals and departures on Saturdays only.

TO APPLY: Applications are accepted online by contacting the office (see Contact).

FIELD NOTES: Volunteers must be 18 years old and have a basic knowledge of English, Portuguese, or Spanish. In order to work with the nonhuman primates, participants must show a negative tuberculosis test dated within 12 months of service or have documentation of a TB vaccination. Positions are suitable for adult groups and solo travelers.

CERULEAN WARBLER BIRD RESERVE

COLOMBIA

Bordering the Yariguíes National Park, the Cerulean Warbler Bird Reserve is home to a variety of critically endangered species, such as the gorgeted wood quail, chestnut-bellied hummingbird, and Colombian mountain grackle. Here volunteers can work in the Bird Monitoring Program or the Conservation Support Program or participate in both. Bird monitors' are particularly interested in the violet-bellied and indigo-capped hummingbird; yellow-throated, mustached, and Yariguíes brush-finch; bar-crested antshrike; and Parker's antbird. Volunteers with the Conservation Support Program help keep the bird habitats free and clear of debris and invasive species.

CONTACT: ProAves Foundation, Carrera 20, No 36-61, Bogotá, DC, Colombia; Tel: 5713403229, 5713403261, or 5712455134; Fax: 5713403285; Web: www.eco-volunteer.com/index.php?lang=en&page=ceruleanwarblerbirdreserve; Email: direct through website.

LOCATION: Eastern Andes, Colombia.

CATEGORY: Conservation.

COST: US$550 for 4 weeks. Fee includes accommodations, meals, training, and in-country emergency support.

DATES & DURATION: Year-round; 4 weeks. To qualify, volunteers must commit to a 40-hour workweek.

TO APPLY: Applications are accepted online and by fax or mail. Contact the office (see Contact).

FIELD NOTES: Volunteers must be at

least 18 years of age, physically fit, and able to work without supervision. Positions are suitable for adult groups and solo travelers.

EL DORADO BIRD RESERVE
COLOMBIA

Situated in the subtropical to montane forest of the Sierra Nevada de Santa Marta, the 1,600-acre El Dorado Bird Reserve boasts over 415 bird species. In an effort to rebuild habitats for these native birds, volunteers help with reforestation. Duties include clearing non-native species and debris, collecting seeds, and maintaining footpaths.

CONTACT: ProAves Foundation, Carrera 20, No 36-61, Bogotá, DC, Colombia; Tel: 5713403229, 5713403261, or 5712455134; Fax: 5713403285; Web: www.proaves.org/index.php?lang=en&page=eldoradobirdreserve; Email: Contact form on website.

LOCATION: Sierra Nevada de Santa Marta, Colombia.

CATEGORY: Conservation.

COST: US$590 for 4 weeks. Fee includes accommodations, meals, training, and in-country emergency support.

DATES & DURATION: Year-round; 4 weeks. To qualify, volunteers must commit to a 40-hour workweek.

TO APPLY: Applications are accepted online and by fax or mail. Contact the office (see Contact).

FIELD NOTES: Volunteers must be at least 18 years of age, physically fit, and able to work without supervision. Positions are suitable for adult groups and solo travelers.

EL PAUJIL BIRD RESERVE

COLOMBIA

The curassow, an ancient symbol of Colombian culture, was a species that had all but disappeared. With support from the American Bird Conservancy, volunteers at the El Paujil Bird Reserve, in the Magdalena Valley, help protect the critically endangered blue-billed curassow, a species that was rediscovered in 2003. A dedicated band of local conservationists deserve the credit for reviving the curassow population, and they welcome volunteers. Participants collect field data, take surveys, and document local bird species via photography and audiorecordings. The reserve is also one of the few places where the spider monkey and lowland tapir can be spotted.

CONTACT: ProAves Foundation, Carrera 20, No 36-61, Bogotá, DC, Colombia; Tel: 5713403229, 5713403261, or 5712455134; Fax: 5713403285; Web: www.proaves.org/index.php?lang=en&page=elpaujilbirdreserve; Email: Contact form on website.

LOCATION: Magdalena Valley, Colombia.

CATEGORY: Conservation.

COST: US$520 for 4 weeks. Fee includes accommodations, meals, training, and in-country emergency support.

DATES & DURATION: Year-round; 4 weeks. To qualify, volunteers must commit to a 40-hour workweek.

TO APPLY: Applications are accepted online and by fax or mail. Contact the office (see Contact).

FIELD NOTES: Volunteers must be at least 18 years of age, physically fit, and able to work without supervision. Experience associated with bird surveying, monitoring, and banding is preferred. Positions are suitable for adult groups and solo travelers.

TROPICAL RAIN FOREST PROJECT

COLOMBIA

Participants in the Tropical Rain Forest Project help preserve the area's rich natural resources by measuring and marking trees, sampling plants, recording birdsongs, and constructing footpaths for local use. To ensure the area's future, volunteers also help design new methods for sustainable development, determining which crops are best suited for this lush environment.

CONTACT: Eco Volunteer Organization, c/o The Great Canadian Travel Company Ltd, 158 Fort St, Winnipeg, MB, Canada R3C 1C9; Tel: 2049490199 or 8006613830; Web: www.ecovolunteer.org; Email: ecovolunteer@gctc-mst.com.

LOCATION: Gulf of Tribugá, Colombia.

CATEGORY: Conservation.

COST: US$1,272 for 3 weeks; extended stays available for additional fee. Fee includes accommodation, three meals per day, and training.

DATES & DURATION: Varies; 3 weeks.

TO APPLY: Applications are accepted online by contacting the office (see Contact).

FIELD NOTES: There are no specific skills required other than the ability to swim and walk without assistance. Participants must be at least 18 years of age and speak English, Spanish, or French. Positions are suitable for adult groups and solo travelers.

BARBILLA NATIONAL PARK

COSTA RICA

Nestled in the virgin rain forest, Barbilla National Park hosts a great collection of endangered plant and animal species. Participants take part in a variety of projects, including gardening, working with butterflies, and collecting data. Volunteers conduct wildlife surveys to inventory native populations and define the area's current conservation needs and efforts.

CONTACT: A Broader View, 1001 Dell Ln, Suite B, Wyncote, PA 19095; Tel: 2157801845; Fax: 2158870915; Web: www .abroaderview.org/caribbean.php; Email: volunteers@abroaderview.org.

LOCATION: Cartago and Limón Provinces, Costa Rica.

CATEGORY: Conservation.

COST: US$925–$1,015 for 1–2 weeks. Fee includes accommodations, meals, ground transfers, training, and in-country emergency support.

DATES & DURATION: Varies; 1–24 weeks.

TO APPLY: Applications are accepted online and by fax or mail. Contact the office (see Contact).

FIELD NOTES: Applicants must be at least 18 years of age, be physically fit, and have a general knowledge of Spanish. Work hours are Monday through Friday, 8 hours per day. Positions are suitable for adult groups and solo travelers.

CAHUITA NATIONAL PARK

COSTA RICA

B est known for its close-to-shore coral reefs, Cahuita National Park is home to over 500 fish species, including the angel and blue parrot fish. Volunteers assist with general park maintenance, including the cleaning of debris from marsh and other areas, trail construction and maintenance, and assisting visitors to the park.

CONTACT: A Broader View, 1001 Dell Ln, Suite B, Wyncote, PA 19095; Tel: 2157801845; Fax: 2158870915; Web: www .abroaderview.org/caribbean.php; Email: volunteers@abroaderview.org.

LOCATION: Limón Province, Costa Rica.

CATEGORY: Conservation.

COST: US$925–$1,015 for 1–2 weeks. Fee includes accommodations, meals, ground transfers, training, and in-country emergency support.

DATES & DURATION: Varies; 1–24 weeks.

TO APPLY: Applications are accepted online and by fax or mail. Contact the office (see Contact).

FIELD NOTES: Applicants must be at least 18 years of age, be physically fit, and have a general knowledge of Spanish to participate. Work hours are Monday through Friday, 8 hours per day. Positions are suitable for adult groups and solo travelers.

CAMARONAL SEA TURTLE PROJECT

COSTA RICA

Working to protect sea turtles—such as the Olive Ridley, hawksbill, leatherback, and black—in Costa Rica's National Wildlife Reserve of Camaronal, volunteers help locate nesting sites, measure and tag different turtle species, and collect eggs. Participants may even have the opportunity to participate in the release of hundreds of hatchlings into the sea. Other duties include digging holes and the general cleanup of the beach nesting area. Participants may be asked to patrol the area for poachers or to stand guard at the hatchery.

CONTACT: Tropical Adventures, 1775 East Palm Canyon Dr, Suite 110-341, Palm Springs, CA 92264-1613; Tel: 8008329419 (USA & CAN) or 50625744412 (INT); Web: www.tropicaladventures .com/projects.php; Email: info@tropical adventures.com.

LOCATION: Guanacaste Province, Costa Rica.

CATEGORY: Conservation.

COST: US$995–$1,895 for 1–2 weeks; US$399 per extra week. Fee includes airport pickup, accommodations, meals, orientation and training, and 24-hour in-country emergency service.

DATES & DURATION: Year-round; 1–2 weeks. To qualify, volunteers must commit to a 48-hour workweek.

TO APPLY: Applications are accepted through the website (see Contact).

FIELD NOTES: This trip is a great project for families, groups, and solo travelers. All ages welcome. The work, however, can be physically challenging.

CLIMATE CHANGE AND CATERPILLARS PROJECT

COSTA RICA

Participants in the Climate Change and Caterpillars Project work in a tropical heaven while studying more than 300 species of caterpillar and the plants that keep them alive. Volunteers work with a small group of researchers in an effort to collect species and their host plants, to identify and collect data, and to observe and analyze toxins known to these species.

CONTACT: Earthwatch Institute, 3 Clock Tower Pl, Suite 100, Box 75, Maynard, MA 01754; Tel: 9784610081 or 8007760188; Fax: 9784612332; Web: www.earthwatch .org/europe/exped/dyer_costarica.html; Email: expeditions@earthwatch.org.

LOCATION: San Jose, Costa Rica.
CATEGORY: Conservation.
COST: US$2,350 for 11 days. Fee includes accommodations, meals, ground transfers, orientation, project training, and in-country emergency support.
DATES & DURATION: Varies; 11 days.
TO APPLY: Applications are accepted online and by fax or mail. Contact the office (see Contact).
FIELD NOTES: Participants must be 18 years old; 16- to 17-year-olds may participate if accompanied by a parent or guardian. Positions are suitable for adult groups and solo travelers.

COSTA RICA BIG CATS, TURTLES, AND CLIMATE CHANGE PROJECT

COSTA RICA

The jaguar, sloth, howler monkey, and harpy eagle are all feeling the repercussions of the world's warming trend. Participants in the Costa Rica Big Cats, Turtles, and Climate Change Project learn how climate change is taking its toll on endangered species and threatened habitats. The project's mission is to save these and other species from extinction. Volunteers take part in a variety of extensive biodiversity surveys, which are conducted in a range of major habitats.

CONTACT: The Society for Environmental Exploration (operating as Frontier), 50-52 Rivington St, London, EC2A 3QP, UK; Tel: 4402076132422; Fax: 4402076132992; Web: www.frontier.ac.uk/gap_year_projects/Costa%20Rica/Costa_Rica_Big_Cats,_Turtles_and_Climate_Change; Email: info@frontier.ac.uk.

LOCATION: Costa Rica.

CATEGORY: Conservation.

COST: US$1,265–$4,660 for 4–20 weeks. Fee includes accommodations, meals, ground transfers, orientation, project training, equipment, and in-country emergency support.

DATES & DURATION: Year-round; 4–20 weeks. Programs begin monthly.

TO APPLY: Applications are accepted online and by fax or mail. Contact the office (see Contact).

FIELD NOTES: Participants must be at least 18 years old; 16- to 17-year-olds may participate if accompanied by a parent or guardian. Positions are suitable for adult groups and solo travelers.

COSTA RICA CLOUD FOREST PROJECT

COSTA RICA

Home to more than 500,000 different animal species, including howler monkeys, jaguars, and sloths, Costa Rica is famous for its biodiversity. This natural paradise, however, is in dire danger from deforestation. At the Costa Rica Cloud Forest Project, volunteers team with local conservationists in an effort to save this wildlife haven and preserve the land for future generations. Volunteers take part in a variety of projects, including maintaining and conserving the area, building trails, making signs, and marking and patrolling the boundaries.

CONTACT: The Society for Environmental Exploration (operating as Frontier), 50-52 Rivington St, London, EC2A 3QP, UK; Tel: 4402076132422; Fax: 4402076132992; Web: www.frontier.ac .uk/gap_year_projects/Costa%20Rica/ Costa_Rica_Cloud_Forest_Project; Email: info@frontier.ac.uk.

LOCATION: Heredia, Costa Rica.

CATEGORY: Conservation.

COST: US$1,124 for 4 weeks; extended stays available for an extra fee.

DATES & DURATION: Year-round; 4 weeks. Programs begin weekly, starting on Saturdays.

TO APPLY: Applications are accepted online and by fax or mail. Contact the office (see Contact).

FIELD NOTES: Participants must be at least 18 years old; 16- to 17-year-olds may participate if accompanied by a parent or guardian. Positions are suitable for adult groups and solo travelers.

COSTA RICAN SEA TURTLES

COSTA RICA

While Costa Rica may be paradise for humans, the country's leatherback turtles are now endangered. Volunteers in the Costa Rican Sea Turtles program work to save this species from extinction by monitoring nesting turtles, measuring and tagging animals, recording nest location data, and performing egg counts. Volunteers may also be called on to relocate nests threatened by flooding, protect hatchlings, and place transmitters on adults to monitor behavior and migration.

CONTACT: Earthwatch Institute, 3 Clock Tower Pl, Suite 100, Box 75, Maynard, MA 01754; Tel: 9784610081 or 8007760188; Fax: 9784612332; Web: www.earthwatch.org/europe/exped/paladino.html; Email: expeditions@earthwatch.org.

LOCATION: Guanacaste Province, Costa Rica.

CATEGORY: Conservation.

COST: US$2,650 for 9 days. Fee includes accommodations, meals, ground transfers, orientation, project training, and in-country emergency support.

DATES & DURATION: October through February; 9 days.

TO APPLY: Applications are accepted online and by fax or mail. Contact the office (see Contact).

FIELD NOTES: Participants must be at least 18 years old; 16- to 17-year-olds may participate if accompanied by a parent or guardian. Positions are suitable for adult groups and solo travelers.

LAS BAULAS NATIONAL PARK

COSTA RICA

As a primary nesting ground for the leatherback turtle, Langosta Beach, located in Costa Rica's Las Baulas National Park, offers volunteers the unique opportunity to work with these majestic creatures firsthand. Volunteers can assist with a variety of tasks, including monitoring and registering nesting patterns, patrolling the beach, and even releasing hatchlings into the sea.

CONTACT: A Broader View, 1001 Dell Ln, Suite B, Wyncote, PA 19095; Tel: 2157801845; Fax: 2158870915; Web: www.abroaderview.org/pacific.php; Email: volunteers@abroaderview.org.

LOCATION: Guanacaste Province, Costa Rica.

CATEGORY: Conservation.

COST: US$925–$1,015 for 1–2 weeks. Fee includes accommodations, meals, ground transfers, training, and in-country emergency support.

DATES & DURATION: Varies; 1–24 weeks.

TO APPLY: Applications are accepted online and by fax or mail. Contact the office (see Contact).

FIELD NOTES: Applicants must be at least 18 years of age, be physically fit, and have a general knowledge of Spanish. Work hours are Monday through Friday, 8 hours per day. Positions are suitable for adult groups and solo travelers.

NATIONAL PARK DIRIA

COSTA RICA

At more than 13,000 acres, Costa Rica's National Park Diria is home to a stunning collection of wildlife, including the howler monkey, coatis, peccary, and white-faced monkey. Volunteers help with general park maintenance, trail construction, and debris removal in an effort to preserve this land for its wildlife and visitors alike. Participants may also be called on to assist with interpretive programs.

CONTACT: A Broader View, 1001 Dell Ln, Suite B, Wyncote, PA 19095; Tel: 2157801845; Fax: 2158870915; Web: www .abroaderview.org/pacific.php; Email: volunteers@abroaderview.org.

LOCATION: Guanacaste Province, Costa Rica.

CATEGORY: Conservation.

COST: US$925–$1,015 for 1–2 weeks. Fee includes accommodations, meals, ground transfers, training, and in-country emergency support.

DATES & DURATION: Varies; 1–24 weeks.

TO APPLY: Applications are accepted online and by fax or mail. Contact the office (see Contact).

FIELD NOTES: Applicants must be at least 18 years of age, be physically fit, and have a general knowledge of Spanish. Work hours are Monday through Friday, 8 hours per day. Positions are suitable for adult groups and solo travelers.

TORTUGUERO NATIONAL PARK

COSTA RICA

Tortuguero National Park is a preferred nesting site of the endangered green sea turtle. Volunteers assist with a variety of duties, such as monitoring and registering nesting patterns, conducting beach patrols, and releasing newborns back into the sea. Experience is not required, though long and variable hours are a must for participation.

CONTACT: A Broader View, 1001 Dell Ln, Suite B, Wyncote, PA 19095; Tel: 2157801845; Fax: 2158870915; Web: www .abroaderview.org/caribbean.php; Email: volunteers@abroaderview.org.

LOCATION: Limón Province, Costa Rica.

CATEGORY: Conservation.

COST: US$925–$1,015 for 1–2 weeks. Fee includes accommodations, meals, ground transfers, training, and in-country emergency support.

DATES & DURATION: Varies; 1–24 weeks.

TO APPLY: Applications are accepted online and by fax or mail. Contact the office (see Contact).

FIELD NOTES: Applicants must be at least 18 years of age, be physically fit, and have a general knowledge of Spanish. Work hours are Monday through Friday, 8 hours per day. Experience is not required, but the ability to work variable hours, including late nights, is desired. Positions are suitable for adult groups and solo travelers.

AMAZON CONSERVATION ECUADOR PROGRAM

ECUADOR

Volunteers in the Amazon Conservation Ecuador Program have the unique opportunity to help develop new methods for conserving the Amazon rain forest. Participants collect seedlings, work in the Amazon Plant Conservation Center and the organic farm, and take long treks through the rain forest in search of seeds for reforestation.

CONTACT: Twin Work & Volunteer Abroad, 2nd Floor, 67-71 Lewisham, London, SE13 5JX, UK; Tel: 08008048380; Fax: 08707775206; Web: www.workand volunteer.com/programme/?pgid=67; Email: Contact form on website.

LOCATION: Amazon basin, Ecuador.

CATEGORY: Conservation.

COST: US$1,150 for 8 weeks. Fee includes accommodations, meals, ground transfers, and training.

DATES & DURATION: Year-round; 8 weeks.

TO APPLY: Applications are accepted online and by fax or mail. Contact the office (see Contact).

FIELD NOTES: Volunteers need to be at least 18 years of age and in good physical shape. A basic understanding of Spanish is beneficial. Positions are suitable for adult groups and solo travelers.

CLIMATE CHANGE, CANOPIES, AND WILDLIFE PROGRAM

ECUADOR

Declared a protected forest in 1988, Santa Lucia Reserve is a flora and fauna haven hosting over 320 species of tropical birds, thousands of plant species, and at least 45 different types of mammals. Volunteers for the Climate Change, Canopies, and Wildlife Program help conduct rain forest surveys and search for spectacled bears, jaguars, and ocelots. Canopies are monitored by camera to survey the abundant bird life in an effort to determine the effects of global warming on this rather pristine habitat.

CONTACT: Earthwatch Institute, 3 Clock Tower Pl, Suite 100, Box 75, Maynard, MA 01754; Tel: 9784610081 or 8007760188; Fax: 9784612332; Web: www.earthwatch .org/europe/exped/peck.html; Email: expeditions@earthwatch.org.

LOCATION: Quito, Ecuador.

CATEGORY: Conservation.

COST: US$2,550 for 11 days. Fee in-cludes accommodations, meals, ground transfers, orientation, project training, and in-country emergency support.

DATES & DURATION: Varies; 11 days.

TO APPLY: Applications are accepted online and by fax or mail. Contact the office (see Contact).

FIELD NOTES: Participants must be at least 18 years old; 16- to 17-year-olds may participate if accompanied by a parent or guardian. Positions are suitable for adult groups and solo travelers.

GALÁPAGOS CONSERVATION ECUADOR

ECUADOR

Population growth has taken its toll on the highland forests of the Galápagos. Now the once-thriving habitats of Galápagos's easternmost island, San Cristóbal, are riddled with invasive species. To help save the island's unique wildlife, participants in Galápagos Conservation Ecuador contribute to the habitat reconstruction plan already under way by restoring the highlands of this and other Galápagos islands.

CONTACT: Twin Work & Volunteer Abroad, 2nd Floor, 67-71 Lewisham, London, SE13 5JX, UK; Tel: 08008048380; Fax: 08707775206; Web: www.workandvolunteer.com/programme/?pgid=89; Email: Contact form on website.

LOCATION: San Cristóbal Island, Galápagos.

CATEGORY: Conservation.

COST: US$2,010 for 8 weeks; US$800 for 4-week extension. Fee includes accommodations, meals, ground transfers, and training.

DATES & DURATION: Year-round; 8 weeks. Programs begin on Monday. Extended stays are available in 4-week intervals.

TO APPLY: Applications are accepted online and by fax or mail. Contact the office (see Contact).

FIELD NOTES: Volunteers must be at least 18 years old and willing to work as a team. Positions are suitable for adult groups and solo travelers.

SHIRIPUNO
RESEARCH CENTER

ECUADOR

Working in the lowland jungles of Ecuador, volunteers at the Shiripuno Research Center help study the diverse butterflies that gather on the Rio Shiripuno, collecting and identifying them for scientific research. An avifauna haven, the center also boats an impressive variety of rare birds; visitors can expect to see antbirds, woodcreepers, manakins, and white-throated toucans.

CONTACT: Ecuador Volunteer Foundation, Yánez Pinzón N25-106 y Av. Colón, Quito, Ecuador; Tel: 59322557749; Fax: 59322226544; Web: www.ecuadorvolunteer.org; Email: info@ecuadorvolunteer.org.

LOCATION: Amazonian jungle, Ecuador.

CATEGORY: Conservation.

COST: US$470 for 4 weeks; extended stays available for additional fee. Fee includes accommodations, meals, training, and in-country emergency support.

DATES & DURATION: Year-round; 4 weeks.

TO APPLY: Applications are accepted online and by fax or mail. Contact the office (see Contact).

FIELD NOTES: An intermediate level of Spanish is required. Participants must be at least 18 years of age and in good physical condition. Positions are suitable for adult groups and solo travelers.

GUATEMALA ANIMAL RESCUE CENTER

GUATEMALA

At the Guatemala Animal Rescue Center, volunteers have a chance to protect some of Guatemala's most rare and fascinating species: jaguars, spider monkeys, and scarlet macaws. Participants work with animals that suffered from human activities, including poaching, the illegal pet trade, and deforestation. Volunteers may help with feeding the animals, cleaning enclosures, maintaining trails, and making and recording behavioral observations. Participants also assist with general maintenance and work with quarantined animals that are awaiting release into the wild.

CONTACT: The Society for Environmental Exploration (operating as Frontier), 50-52 Rivington St, London, EC2A 3QP, UK; Tel: 4402076132422; Fax: 4402076132992; Web: www.frontier.ac.uk/gap_year_projects/Guatemala/Guatemala_Animal_Rescue_Centre; Email: info@frontier.ac.uk.

LOCATION: Guatemala.

CATEGORY: Rehabilitation.

COST: US$1,122 for 4 weeks; extended stays available for additional fee. Fee includes accommodations, meals, ground transfers, orientation, project training, equipment, and in-country emergency support.

DATES & DURATION: Year-round; 4 weeks.

TO APPLY: Applications are accepted online and by fax or mail. Contact the office (see Contact).

FIELD NOTES: Participants must be at least 18 years old; 16- to 17-year-olds may participate if accompanied by a parent or guardian. Positions are suitable for adult groups and solo travelers.

GUATEMALA CROCODILE BREEDING PROGRAM

GUATEMALA

Situated in one of Guatemala's most pristine habitats, the Guatemala Crocodile Breeding Program is perfect for volunteers who want to be directly involved in the care and breeding of the world's most elusive reptiles: the caiman and the iguana. Volunteers prepare food, conduct feeding, treat sick and injured animals, clean enclosures, and may even help release these fascinating reptiles back into their native habitat.

CONTACT: The Society for Environmental Exploration (operating as Frontier), 50-52 Rivington St, London, EC2A 3QP, UK; Tel: 4402076132422; Fax: 4402076132992; Web: www.frontier.ac .uk/gap_year_projects/Guatemala/ Guatemala_Crocodile_Breeding_ Programme; Email: info@frontier.ac.uk.
LOCATION: Pacific south coast, Guatemala.

CATEGORY: Conservation.
COST: US$1,123 for 4 weeks. Fee includes accommodations, meals, orientation, project training, equipment, and in-country emergency support.
DATES & DURATION: Year-round; 4 weeks.
TO APPLY: Applications are accepted online and by fax or mail. Contact the office (see Contact).
FIELD NOTES: In their spare time, volunteers may wish to take part in a variety of local activities, including river fishing, horseback riding, hang gliding, and volcano climbing. Cycling, rafting, and diving opportunities are also nearby. Participants must be at least 18 years old; 16- to 17-year-olds may participate if accompanied by a parent or guardian. Positions are suitable for adult groups and solo travelers.

NICARAGUA SEA TURTLE AND FOREST CONSERVATION PROGRAM

NICARAGUA

Working with a dedicated team of local conservationists on the pristine beaches of Nicaragua, participants in the Nicaragua Sea Turtle and Forest Conservation Program help with surveys of the park's diverse array of turtles, which include the green nesting, loggerhead, hawksbill, leatherback, and Olive Ridley. Volunteers conduct biodiversity surveys and monitor beaches during the breeding seasons. Participants also assist researchers with compiling inventory data on a range of other large and small species that inhabit the area, including butterflies, birds, and bats.

CONTACT: The Society for Environmental Exploration (operating as Frontier), 50-52 Rivington St, London, EC2A 3QP, UK; Tel: 4402076132422; Fax: 4402076132992; Web: www.frontier.ac.uk/gap_year_proj ects/Nicaragua/Nicaragua_Sea_Turtle _Forest_Conservation; Email: info@ frontier.ac.uk.

LOCATION: Nicaragua.

CATEGORY: Conservation.

COST: US$1,500–$4,300 for 3–20 weeks. Fee includes airport pickup, accommodations, meals (2 per day), ground transfers, orientation, project training, equipment, and in-country emergency support.

DATES & DURATION: Varies; 4–20 weeks. Programs begin monthly.

TO APPLY: Applications are accepted online and by fax or mail. Contact the office (see Contact).

FIELD NOTES: During their free time, volunteers may wish to take part in one of the many guided volcano tours offered from a variety of nearby sources. Participants must be at least 18 years old; 16- to 17-year-olds may participate if accompanied by a parent or guardian. Positions are suitable for adult groups and solo travelers.

LEATHERBACKS OF PANAMA PROJECT

PANAMA

As recently as 2002, the beaches of Panama's Bocas del Toro were a death sentence for the endangered leatherback turtle. But thanks to the Leatherbacks of Panama Project, these islands once again offer a secure habitat for the world's heaviest reptile. Participants help monitor, tag, and measure the turtles as part of an effort to ensure their continued safety. Volunteers also help patrol the beaches, looking for potential threats and relocating nests when necessary.

CONTACT: Global Vision International, 252 Newbury St, #4, Boston, MA 02116; Tel: 8886536028; Fax: 6176742109; Web: www.gviusa.com/projects/central-america/panama/volunteer-turtles-project-panama/home; Email: info@gviworld.com.

LOCATION: Bocas del Toro, Panama.

CATEGORY: Conservation.

COST: US$1,690–$3,410 for 2–10 weeks. Fee includes accommodations, meals, ground transfers, orientation, project training, equipment, and in-country emergency support.

DATES & DURATION: March through June; 2–10 weeks.

TO APPLY: Applications are accepted

online and by fax or mail. Contact the office (see Contact).

FIELD NOTES: A maximum of 12 volunteers at a time. Volunteers rotate among field sites, spending about a week at each location. Positions are suitable for families with older children, groups, and solo travelers.

AMAZON RIVERBOAT EXPLORATION

PERU

Situated in the western Amazon basin, the rain forests of Loreto, Peru, harbor a rich diversity of flora and fauna. The Amazon Riverboat Exploration is a good match for volunteers who want to observe a diversity of species, interact with indigenous people, and get involved with conservation. Volunteers collect data on ungulates, macaws, large-bodied primates, caimans, dolphins, giant river otters, manatees, river turtles, game birds, large cats and other large mammals, and fish in one of two areas: the Samiria River in the Pacaya-Samiria National Reserve, or the Yavarí River.

CONTACT: Earthwatch (Europe), Mayfield House, 256 Banbury Rd, Oxford, OX2 7DE, UK; Tel: 4401865318838 or 8007760188 (USA); Fax: 4401865311383; Web: www .earthwatch.org/europe/exped/bodmer .html; Email: info@earthwatch.org.uk.

LOCATION: Western Amazon basin, Peru.

CATEGORY: Conservation and research.

COST: US$2,790 for 15 days. Fee includes accommodation, three meals per day, bottled water, coffee, tea, and field training.

DATES & DURATION: Varies on an annual basis; 15 days.

TO APPLY: Applications are accepted online and by fax or mail. Contact Earthwatch (www.earthwatch.org/Europe). A US$300 deposit is required to secure placement.

FIELD NOTES: Participants must be at least 18 years old; 16- to 17-year-olds may participate if accompanied by a parent or guardian. Positions are suitable for adult groups and solo travelers.

ANDEAN CONSERVATION PROJECT

PERU

The Andean Conservation Project's aim is to reduce the impact of deforestation, which has put much of Peru's diverse wildlife at risk. Volunteers help with reforestation of the rain forest and conservation of native Peruvian species. Participants may conduct timber audits to help locate new reforestation sites.

CONTACT: Volunteer Adventures, 915 South Colorado Blvd, Denver, CO 80246; Tel: 3032428705 or 8665748606; Fax: 3037858893; Web: www.volunteer adventures.com/proj_peru_an_cp.htm; Email: Contact form on website.

LOCATION: Peru.

CATEGORY: Conservation.

COST: US$1,090 for 2 weeks; US$205 per extra week. Fee includes airport pickup and drop-off, accommodations, meals, training, and in-country emergency support.

DATES & DURATION: March through December; 2 weeks.

TO APPLY: Applications are accepted online and by fax or mail. Contact the office (see Contact).

FIELD NOTES: Volunteers need to be physically fit. The work schedule is generally Monday through Friday, 6 hours per day. Positions are suitable for adults traveling in small groups or alone.

ICONS OF THE AMAZON

PERU

Set deep in the heart of the Peruvian jungle, the Icons of the Amazon offers lucky participants the opportunity to see the four major species of the Amazon rain forest in action: jaguars, pumas, parrots, and peccaries. Adventurous volunteers help local conservationists identify animals, record behavioral data, and design new plans for future use of the site. In addition, participants identify prey species of the puma and peccary, and determine the patterns of species occurrence in relation to known feeding sites.

CONTACT: Biosphere Expeditions, PO Box 917750, Longwood, FL 32791; Tel: 8004075761; Fax: 8004075766; Web: www.biosphere-expeditions.org; Email: northamerica@biosphere-expeditions.org.

LOCATION: Madre de Dios, Peru.

CATEGORY: Conservation.

COST: US$1,620 for 12 nights. Fee includes accommodations, meals, training, and in-country emergency support.

DATES & DURATION: Varies; 12 nights.

TO APPLY: Applications are accepted online and by fax or mail. Contact the office (see Contact).

FIELD NOTES: No specific skills are required. The program is open to all ages, but volunteers must be able to walk over mountainous terrain. Positions are suitable for families, groups, and solo travelers.

MACAWS OF THE PERUVIAN AMAZON

PERU

Victims of deforestation and poaching, the brilliantly colored macaws of the Peruvian Amazon are now endangered and desperately need our support. The Macaws of the Peruvian Amazon program offers volunteers the chance to help. Working alongside professional researchers, participants collect behavioral data, record feeding frequencies of chicks, and make note of other parent–chick interactions. These data help scientists better understand these macaws so that they are better able to secure the birds' habitats for the future.

CONTACT: Earthwatch Institute, 3 Clock Tower Pl, Suite 100, Box 75, Maynard, MA 01754; Tel: 9784610081 or 8007760188;

Fax: 9784612332; Web: www.earthwatch.org/europe/exped/brightsmith.html; Email: expeditions@earthwatch.org.

LOCATION: Puerto Maldonado, Peru.

CATEGORY: Conservation.

COST: US$2,750 for 13 days. Fee includes accommodations, meals, ground transfers, orientation, project training, and in-country emergency support.

DATES & DURATION: Varies; 13 days.

TO APPLY: Applications are accepted online and by fax or mail. Contact the office (see Contact).

FIELD NOTES: Participants must be at least 18 years old; 16- to 17-year-olds may participate if accompanied by a parent or guardian. Positions are suitable for adult groups and solo travelers.

TOBAGO COASTAL ECOSYSTEM MAPPING PROJECT

TOBAGO

As a result of global warming, the world's coral-reef systems are suffering. Coral bleaching and disease are spreading and must be stopped before these precious resources diminish and die off. The Tobago Coastal Ecosystem Mapping Project is working to help solve this pressing problem. Volunteers map the benthic zones and local fish communities so that researchers can assess the current state of the reef and create sustainable management plans for the future.

CONTACT: Coral Cay Conservation, 1st Floor, Block 1, Elizabeth House, 39 York Rd, London, SE1 7NQ, UK; Tel: 02076201411; Fax: 02079210469; Web: www.coralcay.org/content/view/192/618; Email: info@coralcay.org.

LOCATION: Charlotteville, Tobago.

CATEGORY: Conservation.

COST: US$2,045 for 4 weeks; extended stays available for an additional fee. Fee includes accommodations, meals, and training.

DATES & DURATION: Varies; 4 weeks.

TO APPLY: Applications are accepted online and by fax or mail. Contact the office (see Contact).

FIELD NOTES: Participants must be 16 years of age. Positions are suitable for families with older children, groups, and solo travelers.

AFRICA

Botswana, Cameroon, Ghana, Kenya, Madagascar,
Malawi, Mauritius, Mozambique, Namibia,
Seychelles, South Africa, Tanzania,
Uganda, Zimbabwe

BOTSWANA WILDLIFE CONSERVATION PROJECT

BOTSWANA

Amid the gorgeous, untouched landscape of Bostwana, volunteers on the Botswana Wildlife Conservation Project work with a variety of Africa's biggest animals: elephants, giraffes, and rhinos. Participants help monitor and rescue animals in need and patrol the lands to ensure the safety of the reserve and its inhabitants.

CONTACT: The Society for Environmental Exploration (operating as Frontier), 50-52 Rivington St, London, EC2A 3QP, UK; Tel: 4402076132422; Fax: 4402076132992; Web: www.frontier.ac.uk; Email: info@frontier.ac.uk.

LOCATION: Botswana.

CATEGORY: Conservation.

COST: US$2,500 for 4 weeks; extended stays available on request. Fee includes accommodations, meals, ground transfers, equipment, and in-country emergency support.

DATES & DURATION: Varies. Programs begin monthly. To qualify, volunteers must commit to 4 weeks.

TO APPLY: Applications are accepted through the website (see Contact).

FIELD NOTES: Training is provided onsite. Participants should be in moderately good shape. Positions are suitable for adult groups and solo travelers.

TULI CONSERVATION PROJECT

BOTSWANA

At the Tuli Conservation Project in breathtaking Botswana, volunteers get up close and personal with two of Africa's famed "Big Five": the leopard and the African elephant. To help protect the elephants, participants assess the damage that's been done to local vegetation—the animals' main source of food—and track the reserve's resident herds. Volunteers also monitor the local leopard population, mapping territories and documenting interactions with other species.

CONTACT: African Conservation Experience, Unit 1, Manor Farm, Churchend Ln, Charfield, Gloucester, GL12 8LJ, UK; Tel: 08455200888; Web: www.conservationafrica.net; Email: Contact form on website.

LOCATION: Southern Botswana.

CATEGORY: Conservation.

COST: US$3,198–$7,361 for 2–12 weeks.

Fee includes round-trip flight from London, ground transfers, accommodations, meals, and emergency support.

DATES & DURATION: Year-round; 2–12 weeks.

TO APPLY: Applications are accepted through the website (see Contact).

FIELD NOTES: This project requires a great deal of walking and climbing, so participants must be physically fit. Positions are suitable for adult groups and solo travelers.

CROSS RIVER GORILLA PROJECT

CAMEROON

While some tourists may choose to spend their vacation lounging on Cameroon's gorgeous beaches, volunteers for the Cross River Gorilla Project help protect the local Cross River gorillas and Nigeria Cameroon chimpanzees. The project hopes to establish community wildlife reserves, creating safe havens for these and other animals. Participants help with wildlife surveys.

CONTACT: Global Vision International, 252 Newbury St, #4, Boston, MA 02116; Tel: 8886536028; Fax: 6176742109; Web: www.gviusa.com/projects/africa/cameroon/gorillas-survey-project-cameroon/home; Email: info@gviworld.com.

LOCATION: Southwest Cameroon.

CATEGORY: Conservation.

COST: US$1,990–$2,830 for 2–4 weeks. Fee includes accommodations, meals, ground transfers, training, and in-country emergency support.

DATES & DURATION: Varies; 2–4 weeks.

TO APPLY: Applications are accepted online and by fax or mail. To apply, contact the office (see Contact).

FIELD NOTES: This program hosts a maximum of four volunteers at a time; book well in advance. No special skills are required; training is provided on-site. This trip is very demanding, so volunteers must be physically fit. Positions are suitable for adult groups and solo travelers.

FLORA, FAUNA, AND WILDLIFE OF GHANA PROJECT

GHANA

Participants in the Flora, Fauna, and Wildlife of Ghana Project help local communities understand the importance of conserving rivers and lakes, preserving habitats and wildlife, and maintaining a disease-free environment for all—humans and wildlife. Volunteers work side by side with park rangers throughout Ghana's National Park system planting trees, preserving the wetlands, and developing methods to keep rivers pollution free.

CONTACT: U Volunteer Ltd, 202B Muswell Hill Rd, London, N10 3NH, UK; Tel: 442081449031 (Europe) or 9712521334 (USA); Fax: 448000073062 (Europe) or 8882678236 (USA); Web: www.uvolunteer .org/ghana/animals-wildlife-accra -ghana.php; Email: info@uvolunteer.org.

LOCATION: Ghana.

CATEGORY: Conservation.

COST: US$1,300 for 4 weeks. Fee includes accommodations, meals, ground transfers, training, and support.

DATES & DURATION: Varies; 4 weeks.

TO APPLY: Applications are accepted online and by fax or mail. Contact the office (see Contact).

FIELD NOTES: Minimum age requirement of 18. Volunteers work Monday through Friday, 6 hours per day. Positions are suitable for adult groups and solo travelers.

COLOBUS MONKEY PROJECT

KENYA

Set on the breathtaking Indian Ocean, Kenya's Colobus Monkey Project offers volunteers the chance to experience the natural beauty of East Africa while helping protect local wildlife. Living in a traditional Swahili village, participants help study the Angolan black and white colobus monkeys, conduct wildlife surveys, and collect behavioral data.

CONTACT: Global Vision International, 252 Newbury St, #4, Boston, MA 02116; Tel: 8886536028; Fax: 6176742109; Web: www.gviusa.com/projects/africa/kenya/ Volunteer-Colobus-monkeys-Kenya/ home; Email: info@gviworld.com.

LOCATION: Shimoni Peninsula, Kenya.

CATEGORY: Conservation.

COST: US$1,300–$3,000+ for 2–10 weeks; extended stays available for additional fee. Fee includes accommodations, meals, ground transfers, orientation, project training, equipment, and in-country emergency support.

DATES & DURATION: Year-round; 2–10 weeks.

TO APPLY: Applications are accepted online and by fax or mail. Contact the office (see Contact).

FIELD NOTES: Participants must be at least 18 years old; 16- to 17-year-olds may participate if accompanied by a parent or guardian. Positions are suitable for adult groups and solo travelers.

DOLPHIN RESEARCH PROJECT

KENYA

Volunteers in the Dolphin Research Project work on the beautiful Shimoni Archipelago, home to whales, whale sharks, manta rays, dolphins, and other marine creatures. Participants collect data that help researchers determine how the animals interact with their environment. Volunteers also help assess the current human impact on the area's marine mammals. The project is principally interested in identifying problem issues that are affecting the area's inhabitants. Volunteers may be asked to participate in species identification and critical habitat identification as well as to identify sites that should be considered priority conservation areas.

CONTACT: Global Vision International, 252 Newbury St, #4, Boston, MA 02116; Tel: 8886536028; Fax: 6176742109; Web: www.gviusa.com/projects/Africa/Kenya/volunteering-dolphin-kenya/home; Email: info@gviworld.com.

LOCATION: Wasini Island, Kenya.

CATEGORY: Conservation.

COST: US$1,390 for 2 weeks. Fee includes accommodations, meals, ground transfers, orientation and training, and in-country emergency support.

DATES & DURATION: Year-round, varies; 2 weeks.

TO APPLY: Applications are accepted online and by fax or mail. To apply, contact the office (see Contact).

FIELD NOTES: Participants should be in moderately good shape and must complete a swim test on arrival. Positions are suitable for adult groups and solo travelers.

KENYA FOREST WILDLIFE PROJECT

KENYA

Trekking through the lush Kenyan forest, volunteers on the Kenya Forest Wildlife Project will come across an incredible world of wildlife—numerous species of birds, zebras, elephants, and many more amazing creatures. Participants help staff determine what diseases and other ailments might threaten the local flora and fauna. Participants also plant trees and work on maintenance projects.

CONTACT: The Society for Environmental Exploration (operating as Frontier), 50-52 Rivington St, London, EC2A 3QP, UK; Tel: 4402076132422; Fax: 4402076132992; Web: www.frontier.ac.uk/gap_year_projects/Kenya/Kenya_Forest_Wildlife_Project; Email: info@frontier.ac.uk.

LOCATION: Malindi, Kenya.

CATEGORY: Conservation.

COST: US$1,685 for 4 weeks; US$317 per extra week. Fee includes airport pickup and drop-off, accommodations, meals, ground transfers, project training, and in-country emergency support.

DATES & DURATION: Year-round; 2–52 weeks.

TO APPLY: Applications are accepted online and by fax or mail. Contact the office (see Contact).

FIELD NOTES: This project includes a great deal of daily travel, and a moderate level of physical fitness is needed. Positions are suitable for adult groups and solo travelers.

KENYA GREAT RIFT VALLEY CONSERVATION PROJECT

KENYA

Home to giraffes, lions, and elephants, Kenya's Great Rift Valley Conservation Project provides volunteers with an opportunity to experience a diverse range of ecosystems and landscapes, including savannas, forests, woodlands, and lakes, while helping save the area's wildlife. Participants help identify and group lion prides, monitor and track other species, and collect behavioral data. Volunteers participate in daily treks to research sites to conduct field surveys, and may take part in nighttime game drives. Participants must also help with camp maintenance.

CONTACT: The Society for Environmental Exploration (operating as Frontier), 50-52 Rivington St, London, EC2A 3QP, UK; Tel: 4402076132422; Fax: 4402076132992; Web: www.frontier.ac .uk/gap_year_projects/Kenya/Kenya_ Great_Rift_Valley_Conservation_Project; Email: info@frontier.ac.uk.

LOCATION: Lake Magadi, Kenya.

CATEGORY: Conservation.

COST: US$2,091 for 4 weeks. Fee includes airport pickup, accommodations, meals, ground transfers, project training and orientation, and in-country emergency support.

DATES & DURATION: Varies; 4 weeks. Projects begin monthly.

TO APPLY: Applications are accepted through the website (see Contact).

FIELD NOTES: Volunteers must be 18 years old and moderately physically fit because hikes to locate animals can be demanding. Positions are suitable for adult groups and solo travelers.

SAVING KENYA'S BLACK RHINOS

KENYA

Kenya's black rhinos are in danger. While their population totaled an impressive 20,000 only 20 years ago, poaching has reduced their number to a mere 400. Luckily, volunteers in the Saving Kenya's Black Rhinos project are helping. At the Ol Pejeta Conservancy, volunteers manage the local vegetation—the main food source of the black rhino—and observe the animals to improve further conservation efforts.

CONTACT: Earthwatch Institute, 3 Clock Tower Pl, Suite 100, Box 75, Maynard, MA 01754; Tel: 9784610081 or 8007760188; Fax: 9784612332; Web: www.earthwatch.org/exped/wahungu.html; Email: expeditions@earthwatch.org.

LOCATION: Nairobi, Kenya.

CATEGORY: Conservation.

COST: US$2,850 for 15 days. Fee includes accommodations, meals, and training.

DATES & DURATION: Varies; 15 days.

TO APPLY: Applications are accepted through the Earthwatch Institute. Contact the office (see Contact).

FIELD NOTES: Participants must be at least 18 years old; 16- to 17-year-olds may participate if accompanied by a parent or guardian. Positions are suitable for adult groups and solo travelers.

WILDLIFE EXPEDITION TO KENYA

KENYA

Wildlife Expedition to Kenya, based in the Shimoni Archipelago, lets volunteers experience the best of both land and sea: They not only study terrestrial wildlife, such as the black and white colobus monkey, but also explore the sea, monitoring the whales and dolphins that populate the islands' surrounding waters. Volunteers also participate in public education programs about current and future conservation efforts.

CONTACT: Global Vision International, 252 Newbury St, #4, Boston, MA 02116; Tel: 8886536028; Fax: 6176742109; Web: www.gviusa.com/expeditions/africa/kenya/conservation-community-development-expedition/home; Email: info@gviworld.com.

LOCATION: Shimoni Archipelago, Kenya.

CATEGORY: Conservation.

COST: US$3,150–$5,170 for 5–10 weeks. Fee includes accommodations, meals, ground transfers, training, and in-country emergency support.

DATES & DURATION: Varies; 5–10 weeks.

TO APPLY: Applications are accepted online and by fax or mail. Contact the office (see Contact).

FIELD NOTES: Upon arrival, volunteers must complete a swim test at the expedition base (including a 10-minute open sea float). All other training is provided on-site. Positions are suitable for adult groups and solo travelers.

CARNIVORES OF MADAGASCAR

MADAGASCAR

With less than 7% of its original habitat remaining, Madagascar's largest mammalian carnivore—the fossa, a relative of the mongoose—needs our support. However, scientists need more information about these unusual creatures. Volunteers with Carnivores of Madagascar help researchers learn more about the fossa's behavior and its habitat to inform future conservation efforts. Participants help set up traps and check for captured animals, conduct surveys of the local forest, and collect radiotelemetry data. Volunteers may also handle the animals directly, measuring and tagging them before they're released back into the wild.

CONTACT: Earthwatch Institute, 3 Clock Tower Pl, Suite 100, Box 75, Maynard, MA 01754; Tel: 9784610081 or 8007760188; Fax: 9784612332; Web: www.earthwatch .org/exped/dollar.html; Email: expedi tions@earthwatch.org.

LOCATION: Mahajanga, Madagascar.

CATEGORY: Research.

COST: US$2,550 for 13 days. Fee includes accommodations, meals, and training.

DATES & DURATION: Varies; 13 days.

TO APPLY: Applications are accepted through the website (see Contact).

FIELD NOTES: Participants must be able to hike and stay on their feet for long periods of time. Volunteers must be at least 18 years old; teen trips are available for 16- and 17-year-olds. Positions are suitable for adult groups and solo travelers.

LEMURS OF MADAGASCAR

MADAGASCAR

Deforestation has left many of Madagascar's 71 lemur species severely endangered. Working in some of the island's most remote and gorgeous areas, volunteers with the Lemurs of Madagascar study observe lemur behavior to improve our understanding of these amazing creatures. Participants collect data on animal abundance and diversity, and the effects of human disturbance on the forest.

CONTACT: Global Vision International, 252 Newbury St, #4, Boston, MA 02116; Tel: 8886536028; Fax: 6176742109; Web: www.gviusa.com/projects/africa/mada gascar/volunteer-lemurs-project-Mada gascar/home; Email: info@gviworld.com.
LOCATION: Southeastern Madagascar.
CATEGORY: Conservation.
COST: US$3,200–$4,400 for 4–8 weeks. Fee includes accommodations, meals, ground transfers, training, and in-country emergency support.

DATES & DURATION: Varies; 4–8 weeks.
TO APPLY: Applications are accepted online and by fax or mail. Contact the office (see Contact).
FIELD NOTES: Participants must be moderately physically fit because they will be on their feet for long periods of time. A maximum of 14 volunteers at a time; early booking is suggested, as programs fill up fast. Positions are suitable for adult groups and solo travelers.

MADAGASCAR MARINE CONSERVATION AND DIVING PROGRAM

MADAGASCAR

At the Madagascar Marine Conservation and Diving Program, volunteers enjoy crystal-clear waters and remote beaches while working to protect the environment. Teaming up with the local government, participants map coral reefs and record underwater wildlife to better our understanding of this incredible ecosystem. Volunteers identify marine mammals and intertidal life, survey mangroves, and document coastal bird and reptile populations.

CONTACT: The Society for Environmental Exploration (operating as Frontier), 50-52 Rivington St, London, EC2A 3QP, UK; Tel: 4402076132422; Fax: 4402076132992; Web: www.frontier.ac .uk/gap_year_projects/Madagascar/ Madagascar_Marine_Conservation_ Diving; Email: info@frontier.ac.uk.

LOCATION: Baie de Diego-Suarez, Madagascar.

CATEGORY: Conservation.

COST: US$2,000–$6,000 for 3–20 weeks.

Fee includes accommodations, meals, ground transfers, orientation and training, project equipment and materials, and in-country emergency support.

DATES & DURATION: January through November; 3–20 weeks. Programs begin monthly on the first Monday.

TO APPLY: Applications are accepted through the website (see Contact).

FIELD NOTES: Scuba certification is required to participate; dive training and certification is provided on-site at no additional cost. Positions are suitable for adult groups and solo travelers.

MADAGASCAR WILDLIFE CONSERVATION ADVENTURE

MADAGASCAR

With over 80% of its native species found nowhere else on earth, Madagascar offers unparalleled opportunity for eco-adventures. The Madagascar Wildlife Conservation Adventure asks volunteers to help survey the island's diverse wildlife—mammals, birds, reptiles, and amphibians. Volunteers may observe 63 species of lemur, dozens of chameleons, and the rare and beautiful fossa. Participants help with trapping, species collection and identification, and forest mapping in an effort to assess the biodiversity of this amazing area.

CONTACT: The Society for Environmental Exploration (operating as Frontier), 50-52 Rivington St, London, EC2A 3QP, UK; Tel: 4402076132422; Fax: 4402076132992; Web: www.frontier .ac.uk/gap_year_projects/Madagascar/ Madagascar_Wildlife_Conservation_ Adventure; Email: info@frontier.ac.uk.

LOCATION: Montagne des Français, Madagascar.

CATEGORY: Conservation.

COST: US$1,665–$5,149 for 3–20 weeks. Fee includes accommodations, meals, ground transfers, training and orientation, equipment and materials, and in-country emergency support.

DATES & DURATION: Varies; 3–20 weeks. Projects begin monthly on first Monday.

TO APPLY: Applications are accepted through the website (see Contact).

FIELD NOTES: Volunteers must be at least 18 years old. Positions are suitable for adult groups and solo travelers.

MALAWI HIPPO CONSERVATION PROGRAM

MALAWI

Malawi's hippopotamus populations are in decline, and the Malawi Hippo Conservation Program is working to reverse the trend. Working in this amazing creature's natural habitat, volunteers study, observe, and record its behavior on a 4-week boat expedition. Lucky participants also participate in a 4-day safari at Liwonde National Park, where they can see the hippo, baboon, and even leopard in the wild.

CONTACT: The Society for Environmental Exploration (operating as Frontier), 50-52 Rivington St, London, EC2A 3QP, UK; Tel: 4402076132422; Fax: 4402076132992; Web: www.frontier.ac .uk/gap_year_projects/Malawi/Malawi_ Hippo_Conservation; Email: info@ frontier.ac.uk.

LOCATION: Senga Bay or Palmbeach, Malawi.

CATEGORY: Environmental impact.

COST: US$2,085 for 4 weeks. Fee includes airport pickup, ground transfers, local orientation, and training.

DATES & DURATION: Year-round; 4 weeks. Programs begin monthly.

TO APPLY: Applications are accepted through the website (see Contact).

FIELD NOTES: Participants are required to bring their own tents and sleeping bags. This program is suitable for families with older children, groups, and solo travelers.

MAURITIUS DOLPHIN CONSERVATION PROJECT

MAURITIUS

Working with a small research team in Tamarin Bay, volunteers on the Mauritius Dolphin Conservation Project study the impact of tourism on the local spinner and bottlenose dolphin populations. To help scientists improve their understanding of these magnificent creatures, participants record population movements, population data, and behavioral data. Participants also take part in photo identification procedures and the cataloging of individual species.

CONTACT: African Conservation Experience, Unit 1, Manor Farm, Churchend Ln, Charfield, Gloucester, GL12 8LJ, UK; Tel: 08455200888; Web: www.conservationafrica.net; Email: Contact form on website.
LOCATION: Tamarin Bay, Mauritius.
CATEGORY: Conservation.
COST: US$3,980–$8,410 for 2–12 weeks.

Fee includes accommodations, meals, training, round-trip flight from London, and in-country emergency support.
DATES & DURATION: Varies; 2–12 weeks.
TO APPLY: Applications are accepted through the website (see Contact).
FIELD NOTES: Volunteers work approximately 3 days per week. Volunteers must be at least 17 years old. Positions are suitable for adult groups and solo travelers.

MOZAMBIQUE WHALE SHARK PROJECT

MOZAMBIQUE

Based in Mozambique, the Whale Shark Project tracks these majestic creatures as they travel along the country's eastern coast. Working alongside a team of professional scientists, volunteers study whale shark behavior in the wild to improve our understanding of these amazing animals. Participants also study the nesting activities of the loggerhead turtle and collect data on the current condition of the coral reefs.

CONTACT: The Society for Environmental Exploration (operating as Frontier), 50-52 Rivington St, London, EC2A 3QP, UK; Tel: 4402076132422; Fax: 4402076132992; Web: www.frontier.ac .uk/gap_year_projects/Mozambique/ Mozambique_Whale_Sharks; Email: info@frontier.ac.uk.

LOCATION: Eastern coast, Mozambique.

CATEGORY: Conservation.

COST: US$2,299 for 4 weeks; longer stays available on request. Fee includes airport pickup and drop-off, accommodations, meals, ground transfers, equipment, and in-country emergency support.

DATES & DURATION: January through November; 4 weeks. Projects begin monthly on the first Monday.

TO APPLY: Applications are accepted through the website (see Contact).

FIELD NOTES: All training is provided on-site. Volunteers are required to cook for themselves on Sundays. Because this project is constantly moving with the whale shark migration, volunteers must keep in contact with the provider up until the time of their arrival. Positions are suitable for adult groups and solo travelers.

CHEETAH PROJECT

NAMIBIA

Namibia, home to the world's largest cheetah population, is working to save the world's fastest mammal from extinction. Volunteers for the Cheetah Project help feed and care for captive cats, conduct wildlife surveys, and may be lucky enough to help collect biomedical samples. Participants may be asked to conduct 24-hour water-hole surveys and assist staff with public education programs focused on cheetah conservation efforts.

CONTACT: Earthwatch Institute, 3 Clock Tower Pl, Suite 100, Box 75, Maynard, MA 01754; Tel: 9784610081 or 8007760188; Fax: 9784612332; Web: www.earthwatch.org/exped/marker.html; Email: expeditions@earthwatch.org.

LOCATION: Windhoek, Namibia.

CATEGORY: Conservation.

COST: US$4,050 for 15 days. Fee includes accommodations, meals, and training.

DATES & DURATION: Varies; 15 days.

TO APPLY: Applications are accepted through the website (see Contact).

FIELD NOTES: Participants must be at least 18 years old; 16- to 17-year-olds may participate if accompanied by a parent or guardian. Positions are suitable for adult groups and solo travelers.

DESERT ELEPHANTS

NAMIBIA

In an effort to resolve the constant conflict between farmers and elephants in the Namibian desert, volunteers on the Desert Elephants project help develop and facilitate cohabitation programs, so that both species can share the local resources and land. Participants help farmers build protective walls around water sources and teach eco-friendly farming methods. Volunteers also help study elephant herds to improve future conservation efforts.

CONTACT: *Africa Office:* Enkosini Eco Experience, PO Box 1197, Lydenburg 1120, South Africa; Tel: 27824426773; *US Office:* Enkosini Eco Experience, PO Box 15355, Seattle, WA 98115; Tel: 2066042664; Fax: 3103590269; Web: www.enkosini ecoexperience.com; Email: info@enko sini.com and enkosini@yahoo.com (send email to both addresses).

LOCATION: Damaraland, Namibia.

CATEGORY: Research, education, and development.

COST: US$1,295–$1,995 for 2–4 weeks. Fee includes accommodations, meals, activities, and project donation.

DATES & DURATION: Year-round; 2–4 weeks.

TO APPLY: Applications are accepted directly by Enkosini; contact one of the offices (see Contact).

FIELD NOTES: Participants must be physically fit because much of the work involves manual labor. Volunteers are required to obtain travel insurance that covers medical evacuation by air and road from a remote area, and doing manual labor during the building phase of service. Positions are suitable for adult groups and solo travelers.

NAMIBIA LEOPARD AND CHEETAH CONSERVATION PROGRAM

NAMIBIA

Working alongside biologists in Namibia's breathtaking bushveld, volunteers in the Leopard and Cheetah Conservation Program team up to save Africa's big cat populations. Participants study leopards and cheetahs both in their natural habitat and in captivity. Volunteers can expect to assist in capturing large carnivores, collecting behavioral data, and tracking radio-collared individuals. Volunteers also participate in the setting up and monitoring of box traps and in species identification procedures.

CONTACT: The Society for Environmental Exploration (operating as Frontier), 50-52 Rivington St, London, EC2A 3QP, UK; Tel: 4402076132422; Fax: 4402076132992; Web: www.frontier.ac.uk/gap_year_projects/Namibia/Namibia_Leopard_Cheetah_Conservation_Programme; Email: info@frontier.ac.uk.

LOCATION: Windhoek, Namibia.

CATEGORY: Conservation.

COST: US$2,063 for 4 weeks. Fee includes accommodations, meals, airport pickup and drop-offs, ground transfers, orientation and training, and in-country emergency support.

DATES & DURATION: Varies; 4 weeks. Programs begin monthly.

TO APPLY: Applications are accepted online and by fax or mail. Contact the office (see Contact).

FIELD NOTES: Participants must be at least 18 years old. Positions are suitable for adult groups and solo travelers.

NAMIBIA WILDLIFE RESEARCH AND SANCTUARY PROGRAM

NAMIBIA

The Namibia Wildlife Research and Sanctuary Program offers volunteers the unique chance to help rehabilitate injured and orphaned animals—such as the cheetah, wild dog, baboon, leopard, and even lion—while studying these same animals in the wild. Volunteers also help monitor cheetahs and leopards that have been reintroduced back into the wild. Owing to habit destruction, many of these species are severely endangered, but this program's staff and volunteers can make a difference, not only rescuing animals today but also contributing to future conservation efforts through research.

CONTACT: The Society for Environmental Exploration (operating as Frontier), 50-52 Rivington St, London, EC2A 3QP, UK; Tel: 4402076132422; Fax: 4402076132992; Web: www.frontier.ac .uk/gap_year_projects/Namibia/ Namibia_Wildlife_Research_and_ Sanctuary; Email: info@frontier.ac.uk.
LOCATION: Windhoek, Namibia.

CATEGORY: Rehabilitation and conservation.

COST: US$2,083 for 4 weeks; US$411 per extra week. Fee includes accommodations, meals, airport pickup, orientation and training, and in-country emergency support.

DATES & DURATION: Year-round; 4 weeks. Programs begin monthly.

TO APPLY: Applications are accepted through the website (see Contact).

FIELD NOTES: No special skills are required. Positions are suitable for adult groups and solo travelers.

NAMIBIA WILDLIFE SANCTUARY

NAMIBIA

At the Namibia Wildlife Sanctuary, visitors can enjoy any of three available programs. Working with the Wildlife Project, volunteers help care for the sanctuary's diverse wildlife, including the lion, leopard, wild dog, cheetah, baboon, meerkat, and jackal. At the Research Project, participants help researchers monitor the reserve's five study animals, currently two leopards and three cheetahs (study animals are subject to change without notice). And with the Medical Project, volunteers can help doctors and other healthcare professionals provide care for the bushmen who live in the area.

CONTACT: *Africa Office:* Enkosini Eco Experience, PO Box 1197, Lydenburg 1120, South Africa; Tel: 27824426773; *US Office:* Enkosini Eco Experience, PO Box 15355, Seattle, WA 98115; Tel: 2066042664;

Fax: 3103590269; Web: www .enkosiniecoexperience.com; Email: info@enkosini.com and enkosini@yahoo .com (send email to both addresses).

LOCATION: Windhoek, Namibia.

CATEGORY: Research and conservation.

COST: US$1,000–$5,000 for 1–8 weeks. Fee includes accommodations, meals, activities, airport transfers, training, and volunteer contribution.

DATES & DURATION: Varies, depending on volunteer's needs.

TO APPLY: Applications are accepted directly by Enkosini; contact one of the offices (see Contact).

FIELD NOTES: These are popular programs, and volunteers are encouraged to make arrangements well in advance. Volunteers must be at least 17 years old. All training is provided on-site. Positions are suitable for adult groups and solo travelers.

NOAH'S ARK PROJECT

NAMIBIA

At the appropriately named Noah's Ark Project, volunteers work with orphaned, injured, neglected, abused, and abandoned cheetahs and baboons at a Namibian wildlife refuge. Participants help prepare meals, feed the animals, bottle-feed the infants, and maintain the center's facilities.

Participants may also have the chance to work with the Rehabilitation and Reintroduction Program, which focuses on the release of recently rehabilitated animals into reserve settings, where continuous monitoring is conducted, or with the African Wild Dog Program, which releases captive dogs back into the wild in an effort to increase the population.

CONTACT: *Africa Office:* Enkosini Eco Experience, PO Box 1197, Lydenburg 1120, South Africa; Tel: 27824426773; *US Office:* Enkosini Eco Experience, PO Box 15355, Seattle, WA 98115; Tel: 2066042664; Fax: 3103590269; Web: www .enkosiniecoexperience.com; Email: info@enkosini.com and enkosini@yahoo .com (send email to both addresses).

LOCATION: Gobabis, Namibia.

CATEGORY: Rehabilitation.

COST: US$1,400–$5,000 for 2–8 weeks. Fee includes accommodations, meals, activities, transfers, training, and volunteer contribution.

DATES & DURATION: Year-round; 2–8 weeks. Programs begin on Friday mornings.

TO APPLY: Applications are accepted directly by Enkosini; contact one of the offices (see Contact).

FIELD NOTES: Volunteers must be between ages 18 and 40. Training is provided on-site. Each volunteer is assigned a supervisor, who monitors his or her work throughout the stay. Positions are suitable for adult groups and solo travelers.

MARINE CONSERVATION PROJECT

SEYCHELLES

Based in the Seychelles islands in the Indian Ocean, the Marine Conservation Project offers volunteers a chance to participate in local efforts to preserve the area's coral reefs and diverse marine wildlife. To improve our understanding of this remarkable ecosystem, volunteers dive deep underwater, helping researchers monitor the reefs. Lucky participants will observe whale sharks, survey sea turtle nesting sites, and collect plankton samples for further research projects.

CONTACT: Global Vision International, 252 Newbury St, #4, Boston, MA 02116; Tel: 8886536028; Fax: 6176742109; Web: www.gviusa.com/expeditions/africa/seychelles/marine-conservation-expedition-seychelles/home; Email: info@gviworld.com.

LOCATION: Seychelles islands.

CATEGORY: Conservation.

COST: US$2,787–$4,185 for 5–10 weeks. Fee includes accommodations, meals, ground transfers, orientation and training, and in-country emergency support.

DATES & DURATION: Varies; 5–10 weeks.

TO APPLY: Applications are accepted online and by fax and mail. Contact the office (see Contact).

FIELD NOTES: Volunteers with no diving experience need to be qualified for Professional Association of Diving Instructors (PADI) open-water certification by completing a required swim test upon arrival. Global Vision International can book volunteers for certification through one of their local dive centers before the expedition. Positions are suitable for adult groups and solo travelers.

AMAKHALA GAME RESERVE

SOUTH AFRICA

Home to Africa's "Big 5"—the lion, rhinoceros, leopard, buffalo, and elephant—the Amakhala Game Reserve offers visitors the chance to see some of the region's most incredible wildlife. Volunteers help track and manage the park's animals; assist with game capture, breeding, and health initiatives; and work on vehicle maintenance and other related tasks. Participants primarily work with the newly introduced lions of the reserve.

CONTACT: *Africa Office:* Enkosini Eco Experience, PO Box 1197, Lydenburg 1120, South Africa; Tel: 27824426773; *US Office:* Enkosini Eco Experience, PO Box 15355, Seattle, WA 98115; Tel: 2066042664; Fax: 3103590269; Web: www .enkosiniecoexperience.com; Email: info@enkosini.com and enkosini@yahoo .com (send email to both addresses).

LOCATION: Port Elizabeth, South Africa.

CATEGORY: Conservation.

COST: US$1,295–$1,995 for 2–4 weeks. Fee includes accommodation, meals, activities, and project donation.

DATES & DURATION: Varies, depending on volunteer's needs; 2–4 weeks.

TO APPLY: Applications are accepted directly by Enkosini; contact one of the offices (see Contact).

FIELD NOTES: This popular program takes a maximum of eight volunteers at a time; volunteers are encouraged to make arrangements well in advance. Participants are required to sign an indemnity form acknowledging and accepting the consequences of working with wild animals. Volunteers must be at least 18 years of age. Positions are suitable for adult groups and solo travelers.

BABOON ORPHANAGE PROGRAM

SOUTH AFRICA

Working deep in the South African jungle, volunteers with the Baboon Orphanage Program help rehabilitate orphaned, sick, and injured baboons. Participants work closely with baby baboons, bottle-feeding them, cleaning their enclosures, and even changing their diapers. Volunteers also interact with older baboons, many of whom have behavioral problems from years of human abuse. Volunteers are also expected to maintain the animal quarters, help in the general care of housed animals, and assist in reserve maintenance.

CONTACT: The Society for Environmental Exploration (operating as Frontier), 50-52 Rivington St, London, EC2A 3QP, UK; Tel: 4402076132422; Fax: 4402076132992; Web: www.frontier.ac .uk/gap_year_projects/South%20Africa/ South_African_Baboon_Orphanage_ Adventure; Email: info@frontier.ac.uk.

LOCATION: Limpopo region, South Africa.

CATEGORY: Rehabilitation.

COST: US$1,530 for 1 month. Fee includes accommodations, ground transfers, project training and orientation, and in-country emergency support. Volunteers must provide their own meals.

DATES & DURATION: Year-round. To qualify, volunteers must commit to 1 month.

TO APPLY: Applications are accepted through the website (see Contact).

FIELD NOTES: Training is provided onsite. Positions are suitable for adult groups and solo travelers.

BABOON SANCTUARY

SOUTH AFRICA

As seen on Animal Planet and the Discovery Channel, the Baboon Sanctuary of South Africa is a one-of-a-kind facility. Founded in 1989, the sanctuary houses over 400 abandoned or orphaned baboons. At the center, volunteers help rehabilitate baby baboons and care for older baboons that have previously lived as laboratory specimens. Participants work with the animals and help maintain the sanctuary's facilities.

CONTACT: *Africa Office:* Enkosini Eco Experience, PO Box 1197, Lydenburg 1120, South Africa; Tel: 27824426773; *US Office:* Enkosini Eco Experience, PO Box 15355, Seattle, WA 98115; Tel: 2066042664; Fax: 3103590269; Web: www.enkosini ecoexperience.com; Email: info@enko

sini.com and enkosini@yahoo.com (send email to both addresses).

LOCATION: Phalaborwa, South Africa.

CATEGORY: Conservation and rehabilitation.

COST: US$1,695–$3,995 for 4–12 weeks. Fee includes accommodations, meals, activities, transfers, and project donation.

DATES & DURATION: Year-round; 4–12 weeks.

TO APPLY: Applications are accepted directly by Enkosini; contact one of the offices (see Contact).

FIELD NOTES: Visitors can expect to learn a great deal about the life and behavioral patterns of baboons. Training is provided on-site. Volunteers should be reasonably fit. Positions are suitable for adult groups and solo travelers.

BLACK AND WHITE RHINO PROJECT

SOUTH AFRICA

Home to a remarkable array of animals, including elephants, tsessebes, and sable antelope, South Africa's Mkhaya Game Reserve is one of the only places in the world where black and white rhinos live together. Volunteers on the Black and White Rhino Project help park staff with game counts, species identification, foot patrols, and animal monitoring. The project is an ideal program for anyone wanting to learn more about Africa's conservation efforts or for those interested wildlife management. On occasion, volunteers are asked to participate in the capture and translocation of game. Road and fence maintenance and a variety of other duties may be required.

CONTACT: Eco Volunteer Organization, c/o The Great Canadian Travel Company Ltd, 158 Fort St, Winnipeg, MB, Canada R3C 1C9; Tel: 2049490199 or 8006613830; Web: www.ecovolunteer.org; Email: ecovolunteer@gctc-mst.com.
LOCATION: Swaziland, South Africa.
CATEGORY: Preservation.

COST: US$1,400–$1,875 for 2–4 weeks; week 5 is free. Fee includes accommodations, meals, supervision, and ground transfers.

DATES & DURATION: Year-round; 2–5 weeks.

TO APPLY: Applications accepted through the website (see Contact).

FIELD NOTES: Participants must be at least 18 years old. The program can accommodate up to six volunteers at a time. Participants must be in good physical condition and be able to walk long distances. Positions are suitable for adult groups and solo travelers.

BROWN HYENA PROJECT

SOUTH AFRICA

Volunteers with the Brown Hyena Project help scientists determine how South Africa's brown hyenas are faring outside of the country's protected areas and reserves. Volunteer involvement consists of spoor and sign surveys, camera trap setting, and night drives. Participants also take part in prey assessment studies, data collection, and den searching activities.

CONTACT: Earthwatch Institute, 3 Clock Tower Pl, Suite 100, Box 75, Maynard, MA 01754; Tel: 9784610081 or 8007760188; Fax: 9784612332; Web: www.earthwatch.org/exped/scott.html; Email: expeditions@earthwatch.org.
LOCATION: Johannesburg, South Africa.

CATEGORY: Environmental impact.
COST: US$2,950 for 12 days. Fee includes accommodations, meals, and training.
DATES & DURATION: Varies; 12 days.
TO APPLY: Applications are accepted online and by fax or mail. Contact the office (see Contact).
FIELD NOTES: Volunteers must be at least 18 years of age. Training is provided on-site. The project works out of three main study sites: Pilanesberg National Park, Kgaswane Mountain Reserve, and Mankwe Wildlife Reserve. Participants should expect a moderate level of physical activity. Positions are suitable for adult groups and solo travelers; couples can be accommodated.

DOLPHIN AND WHALE RESEARCH CENTER

SOUTH AFRICA

Set on South Africa's Plettenberg Bay, the Dolphin and Whale Research Center was founded to help protect marine wildlife, such as dolphins and whales, that call the western Indian Ocean home. Participants study bottlenose and humpback dolphins, humpback and southern right whales, and seals. Participants observe marine species while collecting data on species movements, population numbers, and habitat use.

CONTACT: African Conservation Experience, Unit 1, Manor Farm, Churchend Ln, Charfield, Gloucester, GL12 8LJ, UK; Tel: 08455200888; Web: www.conservationafrica.net; Email: Contact form on website.

LOCATION: Plettenberg Bay, South Africa.

CATEGORY: Conservation.

COST: US$5,150–$8,430 for 4–12 weeks. Fee includes accommodations, meals, ground transfers, training, and in-country emergency support.

DATES & DURATION: Varies; 4–12 weeks.

TO APPLY: Applications are accepted through the website (see Contact).

FIELD NOTES: Participants must be at least 18 years old. Positions are suitable for adult groups and solo travelers.

ENKOSINI RANGER PROGRAM

SOUTH AFRICA

On its 15,000 acres, the Enkosini Wild-life Reserve provides volunteers in the Ranger Program with an exceptional hands-on experience of a startup game reserve. Working as rangers, volunteers help reintroduce zebra, wildebeest, impala, rhino, giraffe, cheetah, lion, and other species from captivity into a reserve setting. Participants assist with fencing, construction, bush encroachment, alien plant control, security, and anti-poaching efforts.

CONTACT: *Africa Office:* Enkosini Eco Experience, PO Box 1197, Lydenburg 1120, South Africa; Tel: 27824426773; *US Office:* Enkosini Eco Experience, PO Box 15355, Seattle, WA 98115; Tel: 2066042664; Fax: 3103590269; Web: www.enkosiniecoexperience.com; Email: info@enkosini.com and enkosini@yahoo.com (send email to both addresses).

LOCATION: Lydenburg, South Africa.

CATEGORY: Conservation.

COST: US$7,545–$8,895 for 24–48 weeks.

Fee includes accommodations, meals, training, and purchase of a quad bike (required).

DATES & DURATION: Year-round; 24–48 weeks. Programs begin on Mondays.

TO APPLY: Applications are accepted online and by fax or mail. Contact the office (see Contact).

FIELD NOTES: Participants should be in good physical condition in order to handle a wide range of demanding tasks. Positions are suitable for adult groups and solo travelers.

ENKOSINI WILDLIFE RESERVE

SOUTH AFRICA

Established in 2001, South Africa's Enkosini Wildlife Reserve offers protection for orphaned, injured, and displaced wildlife. Volunteers work to reintroduce wildlife to their natural habitat, assist with vegetation management in an effort to remove invasive species, and build fences and conduct maintenance procedures to provide a safe habitat. Participants also assist staff with ongoing habitat restoration projects, construction needs, and educational outreach programs.

CONTACT: *Africa Office:* Enkosini Eco Experience, PO Box 1197, Lydenburg 1120, South Africa; Tel: 27824426773; *US Office:* Enkosini Eco Experience, PO Box 15355, Seattle, WA 98115; Tel: 2066042664; Fax: 3103590269; Web: www.enkosiniecoexperience.com; Email: info@enkosini.com and enkosini@yahoo.com (send email to both addresses).

LOCATION: Lydenburg, South Africa.

CATEGORY: Conservation and rehabilitation.

COST: US$700–$6,000 for 1–24 weeks.

Fee includes accommodations, meals, training, and supervision.

DATES & DURATION: Year-round; 1–24 weeks.

TO APPLY: Applications are accepted online and by fax or mail. Contact the appropriate office (see Contact).

FIELD NOTES: Discounts are available for volunteers joining multiple service projects. There is no minimum age requirement to participate. Positions are suitable for families, groups, and solo travelers.

GAME CAPTURE PROJECT

SOUTH AFRICA

To help conserve South Africa's native wildlife, the African Conservation Experience's Game Capture Project breeds and restocks reserves with locally endangered species. Volunteers for this project literally take to the air—riding in helicopters to help capture animals for breeding and tracking. Participants may also help tranquilize wildlife, set up *bomas* (enclosures used to capture the animals), and rerelease animals back into the wild.

CONTACT: African Conservation Experience, Unit 1, Manor Farm, Churchend Ln, Charfield, Gloucester, GL12 8LJ, UK; Tel: 08455200888; Web: www.conservationafrica.net; Email: Contact form on website.

LOCATION: South Africa.

CATEGORY: Conservation.

COST: US$3,228–$7,430 for 2–12 weeks. Fee includes accommodations, meals, round-trip flight from London, ground transfers, project training, and in-country emergency support.

DATES & DURATION: April through September; 2–12 weeks. Volunteers are encouraged to commit to 6 weeks so as to experience all that this program has to offer.

TO APPLY: Applications are accepted through the website (see Contact).

FIELD NOTES: Participants must be physically fit because the program is somewhat strenuous. Participants must be at least 18 years old. Positions are suitable for adults wishing to have a real hands-on experience.

HANDS-ON BIG FIVE PROGRAM

SOUTH AFRICA

At one of South Africa's most scenic reserves, volunteers in the Hands-On Big Five Program can catch sight of all the "Big 5" animals—lions, elephants, rhinos, buffalo, and leopards. Participants also monitor elephants, track lions and hyenas, catalog bird species, and survey the entire wildlife population. Volunteers may also be asked to help with game counts and capture efforts, soil erosion control, habitat rehabilitation, and reserve cleanup and maintenance.

CONTACT: Twin Work & Volunteer Abroad, 2nd Floor, 67-71 Lewisham, London, SE13 5JX, UK; Tel: 08008048380; Fax: 08707775206; Web: www.workand volunteer.com/programme/?pgid=91; Email: Contact form on website.

LOCATION: Kenton-on-Sea, South Africa.

CATEGORY: Conservation.

COST: US$1,605 for 2 weeks; US$400 per extra week. Fee includes accommodations, food (meals are self-prepared), laundry, ground transfers, training, and in-country emergency support.

DATES & DURATION: Varies; 2–12 weeks.

TO APPLY: Applications are accepted online through the website (see Contact).

FIELD NOTES: Participants must be at least 18 years old. All training is provided on-site. This program requires hard physical work, so participants should be physically fit. Pregnant women are advised not to participate. Positions are suitable for adult groups and solo travelers.

KARIEGA GAME RESERVE

SOUTH AFRICA

On the 21,000-acre Kariega Game Reserve, volunteers work on various research, conservation, educational, and community development projects. Participants track elephants and hyenas, study wild lions and their prey, and help manage vegetation alien to the local ecosystem.

CONTACT: *Africa Office:* Enkosini Eco Experience, PO Box 1197, Lydenburg 1120, South Africa; Tel: 27824426773; *US Office:* Enkosini Eco Experience, PO Box 15355, Seattle, WA 98115; Tel: 2066042664; Fax: 3103590269; Web: www.enkosiniecoexperience.com; Email: info@enkosini.com and enkosini@yahoo .com (send email to both addresses).

LOCATION: Port Elizabeth, South Africa.

CATEGORY: Conservation.

COST: US$1,395–$1,995 for 2–4 weeks. Fee includes accommodations, meals, excursions, and volunteer contribution.

DATES & DURATION: Year-round; 2–4 weeks. Arrivals and departures are on Mondays.

TO APPLY: Applications are accepted directly by Enkosini; contact one of the offices (see Contact).

FIELD NOTES: Volunteers work from Monday to Friday, 7 to 9 hours per day. On Saturdays, participants take trips into town to shop, eat out, and visit local sites, such as Port Alfred. On Sundays, volunteers and staff are free to do as they please. Positions are suitable for adult groups and solo travelers.

LION ADVENTURE PROGRAM

SOUTH AFRICA

Set deep in the African savanna, the Lion Adventure Program offers volunteers the unique chance to work firsthand with lions and their cubs. Participants help feed, study, and care for these amazing creatures in captivity. Volunteers may also patrol the reserve grounds to protect the local wildlife from poachers.

CONTACT: The Society for Environmental Exploration (operating as Frontier), 50-52 Rivington St, London, EC2A 3QP, UK; Tel: 4402076132422; Fax: 4402076132992; Web: www.frontier.ac.uk/gap_year_projects/South%20Africa/South_Africa_Lion_Adventure; Email: info@frontier.ac.uk.

LOCATION: Port Elizabeth, South Africa.

CATEGORY: Conservation.

COST: US$1,530 for 2 weeks; extended stays available. Fee includes airport pickup and drop-off, accommodations, meals, ground transfers, project equipment, and emergency support.

DATES & DURATION: Monthly; 2 weeks.

TO APPLY: Applications are accepted through the website (see Contact).

FIELD NOTES: Positions are suitable for adult groups and solo travelers.

MAKALALI GAME RESERVE

SOUTH AFRICA

On the amazing 61,000-acre Makalali Game Reserve, volunteers enjoy the very best of South African wildlife while working to protect the sanctuary's incredible creatures. Volunteers work in the areas of elephant and lion contraception, monitoring the range and behavior of animals taking part in a newly introduced contraception program. Participants assist with leopard and African wildcat monitoring to acquire data on foraging and reproductive behavior of newly released offspring and general species demography.

CONTACT: *Africa Office:* Enkosini Eco Experience, PO Box 1197, Lydenburg 1120, South Africa; Tel: 27824426773; *US Office:* Enkosini Eco Experience, PO Box 15355, Seattle, WA 98115; Tel: 2066042664; Fax: 3103590269; Web: www.enkosini ecoexperience.com; Email: info@enko sini.com and enkosini@yahoo.com (send email to both addresses).

LOCATION: Hoedspruit, South Africa.

CATEGORY: Conservation.

COST: US$900–$2,000 for 1–4 weeks. Fee includes accommodations, meals, activities, transfers from Hoedspruit (on Mondays only), and volunteer contribution.

DATES & DURATION: Varies; 1–4 weeks.

TO APPLY: Applications are accepted directly by Enkosini; contact one of the offices (see Contact).

FIELD NOTES: Training is provided in all aspects of wildlife conservation, tracking, and research. Positions are suitable for adult groups and solo travelers.

MOHOLOHOLO WILDLIFE REHABILITATION CENTER

SOUTH AFRICA

South Africa's Moholoholo Wildlife Rehabilitation Center was recently featured in a *National Geographic* documentary. Staff rehabilitate injured, sick, and orphaned wildlife—including cheetah, servals, and warthogs—and, if possible, reintroduce them into the wild. Volunteers feed and care for the animals at the center. Volunteers also help with animal capture, relocation, and release when deemed necessary.

CONTACT: *Africa Office:* Enkosini Eco Experience, PO Box 1197, Lydenburg 1120, South Africa; Tel: 27824426773; *US Office:* Enkosini Eco Experience, PO Box 15355, Seattle, WA 98115; Tel: 2066042664; Fax: 3103590269; Web: www.enkosini ecoexperience.com; Email: info@enko sini.com and enkosini@yahoo.com (send email to both addresses).

LOCATION: Hoedspruit, South Africa.

CATEGORY: Rehabilitation.

COST: US$1,595–$2,795 for 2–4 weeks; extended stays (up to 12 weeks) avail-

able on request. Fee includes accommodations, three meals per day, laundry, activities, transfers, and volunteer contribution.

DATES & DURATION: Year-round; 2–4 weeks.

TO APPLY: Applications are accepted directly by Enkosini; contact one of the offices (see Contact).

FIELD NOTES: Training is provided on-site. The center provides volunteers with T-shirts that are to be worn as uniforms while volunteering. Positions are suitable for adult groups and solo travelers.

PENGUIN CONSERVATION CENTER

SOUTH AFRICA

Internationally recognized for its care of the endangered African penguin, the Penguin Conservation Center provides volunteers with a one-of-a-kind opportunity to rehabilitate injured, sick, and orphaned penguins. Volunteers catch and tube-feed seabirds, help prepare fish, and bathe and hand-raise birds. Participants also clean enclosures, pools, and mats.

CONTACT: *Africa Office:* Enkosini Eco Experience, PO Box 1197, Lydenburg 1120, South Africa; Tel: 27824426773; *US Office:* Enkosini Eco Experience, PO Box 15355, Seattle, WA 98115; Tel: 2066042664; Fax: 3103590269; Web: www.enkosiniecoexperience.com; Email: info@enkosini.com and enkosini@yahoo .com (send email to both addresses).

LOCATION: Cape Town, South Africa.

CATEGORY: Rehabilitation.

COST: *Guest House:* US$1,200 for 6 weeks; extended stays available on request. Fee includes dorm-style accommodations, project donation, cleaning and linen change, and laundry. No meals are provided. *Family Home Stay:* US$1,400 for 6 weeks. Fee includes accommodations, meals, project donation, laundry, and daily transport to the center.

DATES & DURATION: Year-round. To qualify, volunteers must commit to a minimum of 6 weeks.

TO APPLY: Applications are accepted directly by Enkosini; contact one of the offices (see Contact).

FIELD NOTES: All training is provided on-site. Applicants must be at least 16 years of age. This trip is suitable for families with older children, groups, and solo travelers. Couples can be accommodated.

PENGUIN PROJECT

SOUTH AFRICA

With the second-largest colony of African penguins on earth, Robben Island offers visitors the incredible opportunity to see these amazing seabirds in breeding season. To help scientists improve their understanding of these marvelous creatures, volunteers in the Penguin Project survey the penguin population, gathering data on their breeding practices and survival rates. Participants may also assist staff members in working to monitor the health of this unique island environment.

CONTACT: Earthwatch Institute, 3 Clock Tower Pl, Suite 100, Box 75, Maynard, MA 01754; Tel: 9784610081 or 8007760188; Fax: 9784612332; Web: www.earthwatch .org/exped/barham.html; Email: expeditions@earthwatch.org.

LOCATION: Cape Town, South Africa.

CATEGORY: Conservation.

COST: US$2,850 for 12 days. Fee includes accommodations, meals, and training.

DATES & DURATION: Varies; 12 days.

TO APPLY: Applications are accepted through the Earthwatch Institute. Contact the office (see Contact).

FIELD NOTES: Participants must be at least 18 years old; 16- to 17-year-olds may participate if accompanied by a parent or guardian. Positions are suitable for adult groups and solo travelers.

PHINDA WILDLIFE RESEARCH PROJECT

SOUTH AFRICA

Renowned for its incredible biodiversity, South Africa's Phinda Game Reserve is an ideal environment for many of Africa's rarest species, such as the white rhino and the remarkable Suni, a rare type of antelope. In the Phinda Wildlife Research Project, volunteers help reintroduce these and other animals, such as the majestic African elephant, to an area that is once again thriving. Volunteers also have the option to take part in a research program focused on reestablishing cheetah, leopard, and serval populations.

CONTACT: African Conservation Experience, Unit 1, Manor Farm, Churchend Ln, Charfield, Gloucester, GL12 8LJ, UK; Tel: 08455200888; Web: www.conservationafrica.net; Email: Contact form on website.

LOCATION: Phinda Game Reserve, South Africa.

CATEGORY: Conservation.

COST: US$4,579 for 4 weeks. Fee includes round-trip flight from London, ground transfers, meals, accommodations, project training, and in-country emergency support.

DATES & DURATION: Year-round; 4 weeks.

TO APPLY: Applications are accepted through the website (see Contact).

FIELD NOTES: Participants must be at least 18 years old. Positions are suitable for adult groups and solo travelers.

PRIMATE SANCTUARY PROGRAM

SOUTH AFRICA

Hunted for their meat, sold illegally as exotic pets, and otherwise victimized by humans, South Africa's primates need our support now more than ever. Volunteers at the Primate Sanctuary Program feed and care for injured orphaned primates and help maintain the center's facilities. Participants may also be asked to lead tours and educate visitors of the sanctuary on the problems facing these magnificent creatures.

CONTACT: The Society for Environmental Exploration (operating as Frontier), 50-52 Rivington St, London, EC2A 3QP, UK; Tel: 4402076132422; Fax: 4402076132992; Web: www.frontier.ac .uk/gap_year_projects/South%20Africa/ South_African_Primate_Sanctuary; Email: info@frontier.ac.uk.

LOCATION: Plettenberg Bay, South Africa.

CATEGORY: Conservation.

COST: US$1,400 for 1 month. Fee includes accommodations, project equipment, training and orientation, and in-country emergency support. Volunteers must prepare their own meals; food can be purchased inexpensively from a local grocer.

DATES & DURATION: Year-round; 1-month minimum.

TO APPLY: Applications are accepted through the website (see Contact).

FIELD NOTES: Plettenberg Bay offers a variety of activities that volunteers may want to take advantage of in their spare time: horseback riding, windsurfing, and hang gliding. Training is provided onsite. A moderate level of physical fitness is needed. Positions are suitable for adult groups and solo travelers.

SHIMONGWE WILDLIFE VETERINARY EXPERIENCE

SOUTH AFRICA

Working with a dedicated team of big-game veterinarians at a South African reserve, volunteers with the Shimongwe Wildlife Veterinary Experience work with a number of incredible animals, including antelope, elephants, rhinos, giraffes, and lions. Participants assist with game capture and relocation efforts, and help the vets treat sick animals. This project will particularly appeal to volunteers with an interest in veterinary work or animal care.

CONTACT: African Conservation Experience, Unit 1, Manor Farm, Churchend Ln, Charfield, Gloucester, GL12 8LJ, UK; Tel: 08455200888; Web: www.conservationafrica.net; Email: Contact form on website.

LOCATION: South Africa.

CATEGORY: Rehabilitation.

COST: US$3,660–$9,260 for 2–12 weeks. Fee includes round-trip flight from London, accommodations, meals, ground transfers, project training and orientation, and in-country emergency support.

DATES & DURATION: April through September; 2–12 weeks.

TO APPLY: Applications are accepted through the office (see Contact).

FIELD NOTES: Participants should be reasonably fit because the work can be very demanding. Positions are suitable for adult groups and solo travelers.

SIYAFUNDA BUSH EXPERIENCE

SOUTH AFRICA

Ever since Discovery Channel's *Man vs. Wild* debuted in 2006, viewers have wanted to know what it really takes to live in the wild. At South Africa's Makalali Game Reserve, lucky participants in the Siyafunda Bush Experience find out. Living in the bush, volunteers learn basic survival skills, including navigation and animal tracking, and learn the proper way to approach and interact with otherwise dangerous creatures. To help conserve this amazing wilderness, volunteers also help conduct a census of the local wildlife.

CONTACT: *Africa Office:* Enkosini Eco Experience, PO Box 1197, Lydenburg 1120, South Africa; Tel: 27824426773; *US Office:* Enkosini Eco Experience, PO Box 15355, Seattle, WA 98115; Tel: 2066042664; Fax: 3103590269; Web: www.enkosini ecoexperience.com; Email: info@enko sini.com and enkosini@yahoo.com (send email to both addresses).

LOCATION: Makalali Game Reserve, Hoedspruit, South Africa.

CATEGORY: Conservation.

COST: US$895–$1,995 for 1–4 weeks. Fee includes accommodations, meals, activities, transfers from Hoedspruit (Mondays only), and project donation.

DATES & DURATION: Varies; 1–4 weeks.

TO APPLY: Applications are accepted directly by Enkosini; contact one of the offices (see Contact).

FIELD NOTES: All training is provided on-site. Positions are suitable for adult groups and solo travelers.

SWAZILAND GAME CONSERVANCY PROGRAM

SOUTH AFRICA

Working at various sites throughout the kingdom of Swaziland, volunteers in the Swaziland Game Conservancy Program help protect southern Africa's amazing animals. Volunteers might help scientists observe the nocturnal activity of big-game predators; others might help capture live birds and bats for further study. Volunteers should be prepared to work with captive animals, preparing them for reintroduction into the wild, and to take part in a variety of other conservation tasks.

CONTACT: The Society for Environmental Exploration (operating as Frontier), 50-52 Rivington St, London, EC2A 3QP, UK; Tel: 4402076132422; Fax: 4402076132992; Web: www.frontier.ac .uk/gap_year_projects/Swaziland/ Swaziland_Game_Conservancy; Email: info@frontier.ac.uk.

LOCATION: Swaziland, South Africa.

CATEGORY: Conservation.

COST: US$2,362 for 4 weeks; from US$348 per extra week. Fee includes airport pickup and drop-off, accommodations, meals, ground transfers, orientation and project training, and in-country emergency support.

DATES & DURATION: Year-round; 4+ weeks.

TO APPLY: Applications are accepted through the website (see Contact).

FIELD NOTES: In their spare time, volunteers may wish to take part in white-water rafting, mountain biking, or horseback riding. The area hosts a wealth of tribal festivals, such as the Reed Dance (August or September) and the Inewala Ceremony (December or January). Positions are suitable for adult groups and solo travelers.

TAMBOTIE WILDLIFE CARE CENTER

SOUTH AFRICA

Just north of Johannesburg, South Africa's Tambotie Wildlife Care Center offers volunteers a chance to work with sick, injured, and orphaned wildlife, such as mongeese, servals, lion cubs, zebras, and giraffes. Participants help feed and care for the animals, clean their enclosures, and maintain the center's facilities. While a variety of species make their home in the center, many others are just passing through for treatment and rehabilitation before being returned to the wild.

CONTACT: African Conservation Experience, Unit 1, Manor Farm, Churchend Ln, Charfield, Gloucester, GL12 8LJ, UK; Tel: 08455200888; Web: www.conservationafrica.net; Email: Contact form on website.

LOCATION: North of Johannesburg, South Africa.

CATEGORY: Rehabilitation.

COST: US$3,255 for 2 weeks; extended stays available for additional fee. Fee includes round-trip flight from London, accommodations, meals, project training and orientation, ground transfers, and in-country emergency support.

DATES & DURATION: Year-round; 2–12 weeks.

TO APPLY: Applications are accepted through the website (see Contact).

FIELD NOTES: Participants must be at least 18 years old. Positions are suitable for adult groups and solo travelers.

TUTUKA FAMILY CONSERVATION PROJECT

SOUTH AFRICA

The Tutuka Family Conservation Project is family friendly. Volunteers enjoy the beauty of the South African wilderness and its amazing animals, including elephants, buffalo, and even rhinos. Volunteer work varies seasonally, but participants generally help by doing field research; tracking migratory movements of various species; observing animal behavior; and studying the feeding patterns of lions, cheetahs, and leopards.

CONTACT: African Conservation Experience, Unit 1, Manor Farm, Churchend Ln, Charfield, Gloucester, GL12 8LJ, UK; Tel: 08455200888; Web: www.conservationafrica.net; Email: Contact form on website.

LOCATION: Limpopo Province, South Africa.

CATEGORY: Conservation.

COST: *Adults:* US$3,259 for 2 weeks; *children (8–16 years old):* US$2,405 for 2 weeks; extended stays available for additional fee. Fee includes round-trip flight from London, ground transfers, accommodations, meals, project training, and in-country emergency support.

DATES & DURATION: Varies; 2+ weeks.

TO APPLY: Applications are accepted through the website (see Contact).

FIELD NOTES: Volunteers must be at least 8 years old. Positions are suitable for families, groups, and solo travelers.

VERVET MONKEY SANCTUARY

SOUTH AFRICA

Every year, thousands of vervet monkeys are captured and sold to laboratories for medical research, leaving younger monkeys unable to care for themselves. At South Africa's Vervet Monkey Sanctuary, volunteers help care for these orphaned monkeys, preparing their food, feeding them, cleaning their enclosures, and administering treatment for diseases and other conditions as needed. This exceptional program allows volunteers the opportunity to work alongside a world renowned primatologist. Lucky participants learn all aspects of primate care, including the role of surrogate parenthood to orphaned babies and how to reintroduce juvenile monkeys into the wild.

CONTACT: *Africa Office:* Enkosini Eco Experience, PO Box 1197, Lydenburg 1120, South Africa; Tel: 27824426773; *US Office:* Enkosini Eco Experience, PO Box 15355, Seattle, WA 98115; Tel: 2066042664; Fax: 3103590269; Web: www.enkosini ecoexperience.com; Email: info@enko sini.com and enkosini@yahoo.com (send email to both addresses).

LOCATION: Tzaneen, South Africa.

CATEGORY: Conservation and rehabilitation.

COST: US$1,195–$4,995 for 4–24 weeks. Fee includes accommodations, meals, ground transfers, training, and support.

DATES & DURATION: Year-round; 4–24 weeks. Arrivals and departures are scheduled on Mondays and Tuesdays to coincide with weekly town trips.

TO APPLY: Applications are accepted directly by Enkosini; contact one of the offices (see Contact).

FIELD NOTES: Training is provided onsite. This program is popular and accepts only 10 to 15 volunteers at a time; volunteers are encouraged to apply well in advance. Participants should expect to get dirty. All volunteers must also get a chest X-ray or skin test for tuberculosis before having any contact with the monkeys (completed in advance or upon arrival at the Tzaneen Medical Clinic). Positions are suitable for adult groups and solo travelers.

WHALE AND DOLPHIN PROJECT

SOUTH AFRICA

Working along South Africa's Pletten-berg Bay, volunteers team up with local conservationists to protect the region's amazing marine wildlife, including humpbacks, killer whales, southern right whales, bottlenose and common dolphins, and even great white sharks. Participants help researchers identify, tag, and monitor these incredible species while patrolling the bay area to ensure the safety of the animals. Volunteers may also work on public education programs.

CONTACT: *Africa Office:* Enkosini Eco Experience, PO Box 1197, Lydenburg 1120, South Africa; Tel: 27824426773; *US Office:* Enkosini Eco Experience, PO Box 15355, Seattle, WA 98115; Tel: 2066042664; Fax: 3103590269; Web: www.enkosini ecoexperience.com; Email: info@enko sini.com and enkosini@yahoo.com (send email to both addresses).

LOCATION: Plettenberg Bay, South Africa.

CATEGORY: Conservation.

COST: US$900–$6,000 for 1–12 weeks. Fee includes accommodations, meals, and living expenses.

DATES & DURATION: Year-round; 1–12 weeks. Programs begin on Sundays, Mondays, or Tuesdays.

TO APPLY: Applications are accepted directly by Enkosini; contact one of the offices (see Contact).

FIELD NOTES: Participants must be at least 18 years old. Volunteers who stay more than 4 weeks may participate in the certified marine guiding course. Positions are suitable for adult groups and solo travelers.

ZINGELA PREDATOR CONSERVATION PROJECT

SOUTH AFRICA

Volunteers in the Zingela Predator Conservation Project will find themselves trekking through the South African bushland, documenting the beneficial effect that big-game predators have on the ecosystems of nature reserves and other parks. Participants locate, track, and observe the behavior and hunting habits of cheetahs, leopards, hyenas, and other species. Using GPS equipment, volunteers determine the species' home ranges, movement patterns, and kill sites. Participants travel on foot and in vehicles during their research term.

CONTACT: African Conservation Experience, Unit 1, Manor Farm, Churchend Ln, Charfield, Gloucester, GL12 8LJ, UK; Tel: 08455200888; Web: www.conserva tionafrica.net; Email: Contact form on website.

LOCATION: Limpopo Province, South Africa.

CATEGORY: Research.

COST: US$3,200–$7,400 for 2–12 weeks. Fee includes round-trip flight from London, transfers, meals, accommodations,

all project-related costs, and emergency support.

DATES & DURATION: Year-round; 2–12 weeks.

TO APPLY: Applications are accepted by mail and through the website (see Contact).

FIELD NOTES: This trip is suitable for families with older children, groups, and solo travelers. Couples can be accommodated. Upon request, volunteers can be booked with others in their own age range.

ZULULAND ENDANGERED SPECIES

SOUTH AFRICA

Exploring three incredible wildlife reserves in South Africa, volunteers of the Zululand Endangered Species project help scientists monitor local endangered species, such as the cheetah, leopard, and black rhino. Volunteers track and monitor a variety of species to determine the population status, behavioral patterns, and ecological data of these amazing animals.

CONTACT: *Africa Office:* Enkosini Eco Experience, PO Box 1197, Lydenburg 1120, South Africa; Tel: 27824426773; *US Office:* Enkosini Eco Experience, PO Box 15355, Seattle, WA 98115; Tel: 2066042664; Fax: 3103590269; Web: www.enkosini ecoexperience.com; Email: info@enko sini.com and enkosini@yahoo.com (send email to both addresses).

LOCATION: Kwa-Zulu Natal, South Africa.

CATEGORY: Preservation.

COST: US$1,300–$2,000 for 2–4 weeks. Fee includes accommodations, meals, and living expenses while in the field.

DATES & DURATION: Year-round; 2–4 weeks. Arrivals and departures are scheduled on Tuesdays and Fridays to coincide with weekly town trips.

TO APPLY: Applications are accepted directly by Enkosini; contact one of the offices (see Contact).

FIELD NOTES: Participants must be at least 18 years of age. All training, including advanced instruction in radio telemetry and GPS tracking, is provided on-site. Participants are required to sign an indemnity form acknowledging and accepting the consequences of working with wild animals. Positions are suitable for adult groups and solo travelers.

TANZANIA AFRICAN WILDLIFE CONSERVATION PROGRAM

TANZANIA

Set in the breathtaking Kilombero Valley, the Tanzania African Wildlife Conservation Program offers volunteers the chance to see lions, hippos, elephants, and leopards in their natural environment. Volunteers participate in biodiversity surveys and help record animal distribution patterns. Trekking through the savanna and nearby mountains, participants study both large and small mammals with the help of sand traps and cameras.

CONTACT: The Society for Environmental Exploration (operating as Frontier),

50-52 Rivington St, London, EC2A 3QP, UK; Tel: 4402076132422; Fax: 4402076132992; Web: www.frontier.ac. uk/gap_year_projects/Tanzania/Tan zania_African_Wildlife_Conservation_ Adventure; Email: info@frontier.ac.uk.

LOCATION: Kilombero Valley, Tanzania.

CATEGORY: Conservation.

COST: US$1,947–$4,742 for 3–20 weeks. Fee includes accommodations, meals, ground transfers, airport drop-off, orientation and training, equipment and materials, and in-country emergency support. A free safari is provided for volunteers who commit to 10+ weeks.

DATES & DURATION: Varies; 3–20 weeks. Programs begin monthly on the first Monday.

TO APPLY: Applications are accepted through the website (see Contact).

FIELD NOTES: The work is intense and challenging; volunteers must be at least moderately fit. Positions are suitable for adult groups and solo travelers.

TANZANIA MARINE CONSERVATION AND DIVING PROGRAM

TANZANIA

Diving off Tanzania's Mafia Island, participants in the Tanzania Marine Conservation and Diving Program encounter a rich, unspoiled marine environment. The shorelines host an array of tropical fish species, rays, turtles, and other marine life, and the deep offshore waters are home to sharks and dolphins. Volunteers locate and map the region's coral reefs, protecting the area's diverse wildlife. Participants record observations of the feeding habits and behavioral patterns of a variety of marine creatures that will later aid in the protection of this unique ecosystem.

CONTACT: The Society for Environmental Exploration (operating as Frontier), 50-52 Rivington St, London, EC2A 3QP, UK; Tel: 4402076132422; Fax: 4402076132992; Web: www.frontier.ac.uk/gap_year_projects/Tanzania/Tanzania_Marine_Conservation_Diving; Email: info@frontier.ac.uk.

LOCATION: Mafia Island, Tanzania.

CATEGORY: Conservation.

COST: US$2,090–$5,867 for 3–20 weeks. Fee includes accommodations, meals, airport pickup and ground transfers, orientation and training, free dive training to PADI Advanced Open Water (for those staying for 4 weeks or more), group diving equipment, project materials, and in-country emergency support.

DATES & DURATION: Varies; 3–20 weeks. Programs begin monthly on the first Monday.

TO APPLY: Applications are accepted through the website (see Contact).

FIELD NOTES: Diving certification is required for participation and included in the price of the trip for volunteers committing to a 4-week or longer program. Participants can earn the internationally recognized BTEC Advanced Diploma or Advanced Certificate in tropical habitat conservation. Minimum age requirement is 18 years. Positions are suitable for adult groups and solo travelers.

ZANZIBAR ISLAND TURTLE PROJECT

TANZANIA

Working on the exotic shores of Zanzibar, in the village of Nungwi, volunteers with the Zanzibar Island Turtle Project help protect some of the world's most endangered species: the hawksbill, green, and loggerhead sea turtles. At a community-run reserve, participants feed the turtles in captivity and help guide tours. Volunteers also work in the wild, patrolling nesting sites and cleaning debris from the local beaches. Depending on the time of service, participants may get to help with the release of the hatchlings.

CONTACT: Global Vision International, 252 Newbury St, #4, Boston, MA 02116; Tel: 8886536028; Fax: 6176742109; Web:

LOCATION: Zanzibar, Tanzania.

CATEGORY: Conservation.

COST: US$1,200–$5,500 for 1–12 weeks. Fee includes accommodations, meals, ground transfers, training, and in-country emergency support.

DATES & DURATION: Year-round; 1–12 weeks. Programs start every other Saturday.

TO APPLY: Applications are accepted online and by fax or mail. Contact the office (see Contact).

FIELD NOTES: Training is provided on-site. This trip is suitable for families with older children, groups, and solo travelers.

www.gviusa.com/projects/africa/tanzania/volunteer-turtle/home; Email: info@gviworld.com.

JANE GOODALL INSTITUTE

UGANDA

Working at the world-renowned Jane Goodall Institute in Uganda, volunteers promote conservation to the local public, focusing on the importance of protecting the endangered chimpanzee. Participants rotate among locations: Entebbe, Lake Edward, and Budongo Forest service points.

CONTACT: Global Vision International, 252 Newbury St, #4, Boston, MA 02116; Tel: 8886536028; Fax: 6176742109; Web: www.gviusa.com/projects/Africa/Uganda/volunteer-jane-goodhall-institute-uganda/home; Email: info@gviworld.com.

LOCATION: Uganda.

CATEGORY: Conservation.

COST: US$3,250 for 24 weeks. Fee

includes accommodations, meals, ground transfers, project training, and in-country emergency support.

DATES & DURATION: Programs begin February and mid-September; 24 weeks.

TO APPLY: Applications are accepted online and by fax or mail. Contact the office (see Contact).

FIELD NOTES: This very popular program takes only one volunteer at a time; volunteers must apply well in advance of their desired start date. Position is suitable for adults traveling solo.

ANTELOPE PARK LION BREEDING AND REHABILITATION PROJECT

ZIMBABWE

Lion populations are on the decline, drawing the attention of conservation programs. Volunteers working at Zimbabwe's private reserve Antelope Park Lion Breeding and Rehabilitation Project help with studies of lion behavior and rehabilitation. Participants truly get up close and personal with the lions, bottle-feeding cubs, cleaning enclosures, and helping with feedings. Lucky volunteers may also work with orphaned elephants.

CONTACT: African Impact, PO Box 1218, Gweru, Zimbabwe, Africa; Tel: 263425710 (ZIM); 8772532899 (USA); 08005200926 (UK); 27710814990 (SA); Fax: 263425710; Web: www.africanimpact.com/volun

teers/lion-rehabilitation-zimbabwe;
Email: info@africanimpact.com.

LOCATION: Antelope Park, Zimbabwe.

CATEGORY: Conservation.

COST: US$1,800–$4,490 for 2–6 weeks. Fee includes all transfer to and from airport (Bulawayo or Harare International), orientation, food and lodging (3 meals per day; unlimited coffee, tea, and juice), and weekly laundry.

DATES & DURATION: Year-round; 2–6 weeks.

TO APPLY: Applications are accepted through the website (see Contact).

FIELD NOTES: Visitors can also explore the area on horseback (lessons are

provided) or on an elephant. Participants must be at least 17 years old. Positions are suitable for families with older children, groups, and solo travelers.

EUROPE

Croatia, Czech Republic, Greece, Iceland, Ireland,
Italy, Poland, Portugal, Russia, Scotland, Slovakia

GRIFFON VULTURE PROJECT

CROATIA

Volunteers at the Griffon Vulture Project join researchers in their effort to protect this endangered bird. Volunteers prepare food, placing it in known feeding areas. Participants also assist with cleaning and monitoring the resident griffons, and help with rescue efforts of birds that have accidentally fallen from their cliff nesting sites into the sea.

CONTACT: Eco Volunteer Organization, c/o The Great Canadian Travel Company Ltd, 158 Fort St, Winnipeg, MB, Canada R3C 1C9; Tel: 2049490199 or 8006613830; Web: www.ecovolunteer.org; Email: eco volunteer@gctc-mst.com.

LOCATION: Cres, Croatia.

CATEGORY: Conservation.

COST: US$188–$286 for 1 week; additional fee for extra weeks. Fee includes accommodations and training.

DATES & DURATION: March through October; 1-week minimum.

TO APPLY: Applications are accepted online by contacting the office (see Contact).

FIELD NOTES: Participants must be at least 18 years of age. Although no special skills are required, volunteers must be able to swim and be on their feet for long periods at a time. A working knowledge of English is requested. Positions are suitable for adult groups and solo travelers.

MOUNTAIN WATERS PROJECT

CZECH REPUBLIC

Situated in northern Bohemia, the Mountain Waters Project gathers environmental data. Participants collect water samples from rain and fog gauges and take temperature, pH, conductivity, and oxygen readings from more than 30 streams and reservoirs in the area. Participants also help catch, examine, and reintroduce fish and other aquatic organisms into the area's waters as part of the greater effort to rehabilitate the mountain ecosystem.

CONTACT: Earthwatch Institute, 3 Clock Tower Pl, Suite 100, Box 75, Maynard, MA 01754; Tel: 9784610081 or 8007760188; Fax: 9784612332; Web: www.earthwatch .org/europe/exped/krecek.html; Email: expeditions@earthwatch.org.

LOCATION: Prague, Czech Republic.
CATEGORY: Rehabilitation.
COST: US$2,750 for 15 days. Fee includes accommodations, meals, ground transfers, and training.
DATES & DURATION: Varies; 15 days.
TO APPLY: Applications are accepted online and by fax or mail. Contact the office (see Contact).
FIELD NOTES: This project requires a moderate level of physical fitness; volunteers walk for long periods, hiking through dense forests. A maximum of eight volunteers can participate at a time, and volunteers must be at least 18 years of age. Positions are suitable for adult groups and solo travelers; couples can be accommodated.

DOLPHIN CONSERVATION PROJECT

GREECE

Participants in the Dolphin Conservation Project work alongside marine biologists in the Ionian Sea. Volunteers contribute to a research study of the behavioral patterns, ecology, and conservation status of the area's dolphin population. Participants learn and contribute to all aspects of fieldwork, including observation techniques and photo identification procedures. When windy conditions prevail, volunteers remain at base until it is deemed safe to return to the waters. While on base, volunteers take part in the digital cataloging of species and attend any lectures currently being offered.

CONTACT: Global Vision International, 252 Newbury St, #4, Boston, MA 02116; Tel: 8886536028; Fax: 6176742109; Web: www.gviusa.com/projects/Europe/Greece/dolphin-conservation-greece/home; Email: info@gviworld.com.

LOCATION: Greece.

CATEGORY: Conservation.

COST: US$850–$1,000 for 1 week. Fee includes accommodations, meals, ground transfers, orientation, training, and in-country emergency support.

DATES & DURATION: April through September; 1+ weeks.

TO APPLY: Applications are accepted online and by fax or mail. Contact the office (see Contact).

FIELD NOTES: Participants must be at least 18 years old. Volunteers must be in good physical condition and have the ability to speak English. This project uses inflatable boats for observation needs, and sun exposure is at a maximum. Positions are suitable for adult groups and solo travelers.

TURTLE CONSERVATION PROJECT

GREECE

At the Turtle Conservation Project in Greece's pristine Lakonikos Bay, volunteers work hands on with one of the Mediterranean's most endangered species: the loggerhead turtle. Participants conduct nest surveys, patrol nest sites, excavate and relocate nests, and create public awareness campaigns.

CONTACT: Global Vision International, 252 Newbury St, #4, Boston, MA 02116; Tel: 8886536028; Fax: 6176742109; Web: www.gviusa.com/projects/Europe/ Greece/volunteer-turtle-conservation -project-greece/home; Email: info@gvi world.com.

LOCATION: Mavrovouni, Greece.

CATEGORY: Conservation.

COST: US$1,600–$5,500 for 2–12 weeks. Fee includes accommodations, meals, ground transfers, training, and in-country emergency support.

DATES & DURATION: June through September; 2–12 weeks.

TO APPLY: Applications are accepted online and by fax or mail. Contact the office (see Contact).

FIELD NOTES: A maximum of eight volunteers can participate at a time. No specific qualifications are required, but the work is very demanding. Training is provided on-site. Positions are suitable for adult groups and solo travelers.

ICELANDIC GLACIER PROJECT

ICELAND

Volunteers of the Icelandic Glacier Project experience glaciers first-hand by working with a dedicated staff to unearth the reasons for glacier outburst floods. Participant responsibilities include sampling and measuring both sediment and glacial ice, and collecting and documenting a variety of data to help scientists understand the evolution of the Icelandic landscape.

CONTACT: Earthwatch Institute, 3 Clock Tower Pl, Suite 100, Box 75, Maynard, MA 01754; Tel: 9784610081 or 8007760188; Fax: 9784612332; Web: www.earthwatch.org/europe/exped/russell_iceland.html; Email: expeditions@earthwatch.org.

LOCATION: Southeastern Iceland.

CATEGORY: Research.

COST: US$2,450 for 8 days. Fee includes accommodations, meals, ground transfers, orientation, training, and in-country emergency support.

DATES & DURATION: July through August; 8 days.

TO APPLY: Applications are accepted online and by fax or mail. Contact the office (see Contact).

FIELD NOTES: A maximum of 12 volunteers are accepted at a time. Participants must be at least 18 years old; 16- to 17-year-olds may participate if accompanied by a parent or guardian. Positions are suitable for adult groups and solo travelers.

IRISH SEAL SANCTUARY

IRELAND

As Ireland's only seal rescue rehabilitation facility, the Irish Seal Sanctuary helps protect a vast array of marine species. At this site, volunteers help with the conservation efforts for the world's first protected species, the gray seal. Duties include rehabilitating housed seals, preparing food, force-feeding sick or injured seals, cleaning enclosures, keeping records, collecting sick seals from around the country, and ultimately releasing rehabilitated seals back into the wild.

CONTACT: Irish Seal Sanctuary, Tobergregan, Garristown, County Dublin, Ireland; Tel: 00353018354370; Web: www.irishsealsanctuary.ie.

LOCATION: Dublin, Ireland.

CATEGORY: Conservation.

COST: Free for service. Food, accommodations, and daily transportation to and from sanctuary are provided. Volunteers are responsible for travel to and from the site.

DATES & DURATION: Year-round; 3–10 months. To qualify, volunteers must commit to 3 months.

TO APPLY: Applications are accepted online by contacting the office (see Contact).

FIELD NOTES: Participants need a command of the English language and must be at least 18 years of age. A valid driver's license is also required. Training is provided on-site. Positions are suitable for adult groups and solo travelers.

DOLPHIN PROJECT

ITALY

Dolphin Project volunteers help conduct research in the Thyrrhenian Sea near the volcanic island of Ischia. Participants assist in underwater camera monitoring, behavioral data collection, photo identification, and acoustic recording of dolphin echolocation. Volunteers may also get to see fin and sperm whales because the area is a well-known feeding site.

CONTACT: Eco Volunteer Organization, c/o The Great Canadian Travel Company Ltd, 158 Fort St, Winnipeg, MB, Canada R3C 1C9; Tel: 2049490199 or 8006613830; Web: www.ecovolunteer.org; Email: eco volunteer@gctc-mst.com.

LOCATION: Italy.

CATEGORY: Conservation.

COST: US$1,046–$1,185 for 1 week, depending on season. Fee includes accommodations, meals, drinks, and training.

DATES & DURATION: June through October; 1–19 weeks. Programs begin Mondays.

TO APPLY: Applications are accepted online by contacting the office (see Contact).

FIELD NOTES: A maximum of six volunteers can be accommodated at a time. Volunteers must be at least 18 years old, but younger children may participate on personal request and staff approval. Positions are best suited for families with older children, small groups, and solo travelers. Volunteers need to be comfortable both on watercraft and for long hours in the hot sun.

LIGURIAN SEA DOLPHIN AND WHALE PROJECT

ITALY

Participants of the Ligurian Sea Dolphin and Whale Project live on a sailboat while conducting research and studying the needs of several cetacean species, including dolphins and whales. Volunteers participate in photo identification and remote-tracking procedures. Participants also work in distance sampling, behavioral sampling, and acoustic recording, all while learning the basic principles of sailing.

CONTACT: Global Vision International, 252 Newbury St, #4, Boston, MA 02116; Tel: 8886536028; Fax: 6176742109; Web: www.gviusa.com; Email: info@gvi world.com.

LOCATION: Ligurian Sea, Italy.

CATEGORY: Conservation.

COST: US$1,000–$1,250 per week, depending on season, for 1–12 weeks. Last-minute placements are sometimes available at a discounted rate.

DATES & DURATION: May through October; 1–12 weeks.

TO APPLY: Applications are accepted online and by fax or mail. Contact the office (see Contact).

FIELD NOTES: Maximum of 11 volunteers are taken at a time. Participants must be at least 18 years old, comfortable in hot weather, and English speaking. Positions are suitable for adult groups and solo travelers.

BEAVER PROJECT

POLAND

Beaver Project volunteers help monitor beaver behavior, evaluate new beaver release sites, and analyze the effects of beaver reintroduction on the environment. Duties include searching for beaver, observing and recording their activity in mountain streams, and helping solve issues that arise from human–beaver conflict.

CONTACT: Eco Volunteer Organization, c/o The Great Canadian Travel Company Ltd, 158 Fort St, Winnipeg, MB, Canada R3C 1C9; Tel: 2049490199 or 8006613830; Web: www.ecovolunteer.org; Email: eco volunteer@gctc-mst.com.

LOCATION: Bieszczady Mountains, Poland.

CATEGORY: Research.

COST: US$1,000–$1,856 for 1–2 weeks; US$800 per extra week. Fee includes accommodations, meals, ground transfers, and training.

DATES & DURATION: April through June; September through November; 1-week minimum.

TO APPLY: Applications are accepted online by contacting the office (see Contact).

FIELD NOTES: Volunteers must be at least 18 years of age and speak English to participate. A moderate level of physical fitness is required. Positions are suitable for adult groups and solo travelers.

FASCINATING CREATURES OF THE DEEP PROGRAM

PORTUGAL

Situated in the mid-Atlantic, the Azores Archipelago is a group of nine magnificent islands. Volunteers of the Fascinating Creatures of the Deep Program assist scientists and staff with identifying and cataloging different baleen whale species, including blue, fin, sei, humpback and minke; sperm whales; as well as bottlenose and Risso's dolphins. Participants also help tag loggerhead turtles and collect environmental data.

CONTACT: Biosphere Expeditions, PO Box 917750, Longwood, FL 32791; Tel: 8004075761; Fax: 8004075766; Web: www.biosphere-expeditions.org; Email: northamerica@biosphere-expeditions.org.

LOCATION: Horta, Faial, Azores.

CATEGORY: Conservation.

COST: US$1,570 for 9 nights. Fee includes accommodations, meals, and training.

DATES & DURATION: April through May; 9 nights.

TO APPLY: Applications are accepted online and by fax or mail. Contact the office (see Contact).

FIELD NOTES: This project is boat based, but nights are spent onshore. No special skills or fitness levels are required. Everyone is welcome, and there are no minimum or maximum age limits. Positions are suitable for families, groups, and solo travelers.

IBERIAN WOLF PROJECT

PORTUGAL

Volunteers in the Iberian Wolf Project work in the Wolf Recovery Center in the historic town of Mafra. Tasks include monitoring, feeding, and taking care of captive wolves that no longer have the ability to live in the wild.

CONTACT: Eco Volunteer Organization, c/o The Great Canadian Travel Company Ltd, 158 Fort St, Winnipeg, MB, Canada R3C 1C9; Tel: 2049490199 or 8006613830; Web: www.ecovolunteer.org; Email: ecovolunteer@gctc-mst.com.

LOCATION: Mafra, Portugal.

CATEGORY: Conservation.

COST: US$25–$55 per night. Fee includes accommodations and training.

DATES & DURATION: Year-round. To qualify, volunteers must commit to 15 days; longer stays are available, if desired. Arrivals are available Tuesdays, Wednesdays, and Thursdays only.

TO APPLY: Applications are accepted online by contacting the office (see Contact).

FIELD NOTES: Participants must be at least 18 years of age and in good physical health. Positions are suitable for adult groups and solo travelers.

BROWN BEAR PROJECT

RUSSIA

Participants in the Brown Bear Project work with Russian scientists to rescue orphaned bear cubs and release them back into the wild. Volunteers have the option of working either at the cub rescue facility, preparing food and feeding cubs; or in the field, radio-tracking cubs that have already been released.

CONTACT: Eco Volunteer Organization, c/o The Great Canadian Travel Company Ltd, 158 Fort St, Winnipeg, MB, Canada R3C 1C9; Tel: 2049490199 or 8006613830; Web: www.ecovolunteer.org; Email: ecovolunteer@gctc-mst.com.

LOCATION: Southwestern Valday Hills, Russia.

CATEGORY: Conservation.

COST: US$450 for 1 week. Fee includes accommodations, meals, and training.

DATES & DURATION: February through October. To qualify, volunteers must commit to a 1-month stay.

TO APPLY: Applications are accepted online by contacting the office (see Contact).

FIELD NOTES: Participants must be between 18 and 45 years old. Participants must be physically fit and speak English. Previous experience in animal handling is preferred but not required for direct interaction with the cubs. Positions are suitable for adult groups and solo travelers.

MOUNTAIN GHOSTS PROJECT

RUSSIA

Volunteering for the Mountain Ghosts Project requires trekking through the mountains of central Asia to track and study the snow leopard and its prey species—the Argali sheep and the Altai ibex. Researchers are interested in the predator's distribution and kill patterns. Lucky participants may even encounter marmots and some of the region's diverse bird species. Volunteers work on foot and by vehicle in their search for this unique species. Participants record any sightings and signs, such as tracks, kill sites, and scat. Variable weather conditions can make this eco-adventure as demanding as it is rewarding.

CONTACT: Biosphere Expeditions, PO Box 917750, Longwood, FL 32791; Tel: 8004075761; Fax: 8004075766; Web: www.biosphere-expeditions.org; Email: northamerica@biosphere-expeditions.org.

LOCATION: Altai Republic, Russia.

CATEGORY: Conservation.

COST: US$2,690 for 12 nights. Fee includes accommodations, meals, project orientation, training, and in-country emergency support.

DATES & DURATION: Varies; 12 nights.

TO APPLY: Applications are accepted online and by fax or mail. Contact the office (see Contact).

FIELD NOTES: All field training is provided on-site. No specific skills are required to participate, but volunteers should be aware that this trip requires long treks through mountainous terrain. Participants should, therefore, be physically fit. Positions are suitable for adult groups and solo travelers.

WOLVES OF RUSSIA

RUSSIA

Participants in the Wolves of Russia project study the local migration routes and travel patterns of wolves, and monitor their interactions with other species in the southwestern Valday Hills. Volunteers work in the field, searching for trails, identifying resting and meeting places, and looking for prey remains.

CONTACT: Eco Volunteer Organization, c/o The Great Canadian Travel Company Ltd, 158 Fort St, Winnipeg, MB, Canada R3C 1C9; Tel: 2049490199 or 8006613830; Web: www.ecovolunteer.org; Email: ecovolunteer@gctc-mst.com.

LOCATION: Valday Hills, Russia.

CATEGORY: Conservation.

COST: US$822 for 2 weeks. Fee includes accommodations, meals, and training. Ground transfers available for extra fee.

DATES & DURATION: Year-round; 8+ weeks. From March to September, shorter participation is available (2–4 weeks).

TO APPLY: Applications are accepted online by contacting the office (see Contact).

FIELD NOTES: Participants must be in good physical condition and be able to walk great distances. Although a maximum age limit of 50 is suggested, older applicants may apply if they feel capable. A working knowledge of the English language is required. Positions are suitable for families with older children, groups, and solo travelers.

SCOTTISH WILDLIFE RESCUE

SCOTLAND

The Scottish Wildlife Rescue project is dedicated to saving and rehabilitating the animals of Scotland. Scientists and volunteers help injured animals return to the wild. Volunteers can expect to work with birds and mammals and to be involved with hand rearing, cleaning, feeding, and other general duties.

CONTACT: Hessilhead Wildlife Rescue Trust, Hessilhead, Gateside, Beith Ayrshire KA15 1HT, UK; Tel: 441505502415; Web: www.greenvolunteers.com/scottishwildlife.html; Email: hessilhead@hessilhead.netlineuk.net.

LOCATION: West-central Scotland.

CATEGORY: Rehabilitation.

COST: Free for service. Basic accommodations are provided. Volunteers are responsible for their own food.

DATES & DURATION: March through October. To qualify, volunteers must commit to 2–3 weeks.

TO APPLY: Applications are accepted by email or mail. Contact the office (see Contact).

FIELD NOTES: Participants must be at least 18 years old. Long-term positions are available. Positions are suitable for adult groups and solo travelers.

WHALE AND DOLPHIN PROJECT OF THE HEBRIDES

SCOTLAND

The unspoiled Hebrides are home to an array of marine life, including whales, dolphins, and porpoises. Surrounded by the striking scenery of the northern Scotland coast, volunteers in the Whale and Dolphin Project of the Hebrides record cetacean populations and acoustic behaviors. Volunteers photograph dolphins and whales for identification purposes, and collect environmental data.

CONTACT: Earthwatch Institute, 3 Clock Tower Pl, Suite 100, Box 75, Maynard, MA 01754; Tel: 9784610081 or 8007760188; Fax: 9784612332; Web: www.earthwatch.org; Email: expeditions@earthwatch.org.

LOCATION: Argyll Island Atlantic area, Scotland.

CATEGORY: Conservation.

COST: US$2,350–$2,550 for 9–12 days. Fee includes accommodations, meals, ground transfers, project training, and in-country emergency support.

DATES & DURATION: August through September; 9–12 days.

TO APPLY: Applications are accepted online and by fax or mail. Contact the office (see Contact).

FIELD NOTES: Participants live on a boat, and physical activity is moderate. Participants must be at least 18 years old. Positions are suitable for adult groups and solo travelers.

WHALE AND DOLPHIN PROJECT OF MORAY FIRTH

SCOTLAND

The warm Atlantic and the cold Arctic meet in Scotland's Moray Firth, attracting an abundance of wildlife. Volunteers in the Whale and Dolphin Project of Moray Firth spot, identify, and observe whales and dolphins in the southern Moray Firth. Participants may be asked to assist with live rescue efforts when whales or dolphins become stranded. Visitors get to see large groups of wintering sea ducks, saw bills, and puffins as well as many other seabird species.

CONTACT: Earthwatch Institute, 3 Clock Tower Pl, Suite 100, Box 75, Maynard, MA 01754; Tel: 9784610081 or 8007760188; Fax: 9784612332; Web: www.earthwatch .org/europe/exped/robinson.html; Email: expeditions@earthwatch.org.

LOCATION: Banff, Scotland.

CATEGORY: Conservation.

COST: US$2,450 for 11 days. Fee includes accommodations, meals, ground transfers, project training, and in-country emergency support.

DATES & DURATION: June through September; 11 days.

TO APPLY: Applications are accepted online and by fax or mail. Contact the office (see Contact).

FIELD NOTES: Volunteers can expect a moderate activity level. Only five participants can be accommodated at a time. Participants must be at least 18 years old. Positions are suitable for adult groups and solo travelers.

WHITE WILDERNESS PROGRAM

SLOVAKIA

Participants in the White Wilderness Program trek through the Tatra Mountains of Slovakia to monitor wild wolf and lynx populations. Volunteers learn to record signs of wolf and lynx presence, collect samples for genetic analysis, and survey prey species, all in the greater effort to create and maintain a suitable habitat in which these and other species can once again thrive.

CONTACT: Biosphere Expeditions, PO Box 917750, Longwood, FL 32791; Tel: 8004075761; Fax: 8004075766; Web: www.biosphere-expeditions.org; Email: northamerica@biosphere-expeditions.org.
LOCATION: Tatra Mountains, Slovakia.

CATEGORY: Conservation.

COST: US$1,570 for 6 nights. Fee includes accommodations, meals, training, equipment, and support.

DATES & DURATION: Varies; 6 nights.

TO APPLY: Applications are accepted online and by fax or mail. Contact the office (see Contact).

FIELD NOTES: A maximum of 10 volunteers at a time. Training is provided on-site. No special skills or fitness levels are required. Participants must, however, be able to trek long distances in mountainous terrain. Everyone is welcome, and there are no minimum or maximum age limits. This trip is suitable for families with older children, groups, and solo travelers.

ASIA

Borneo, Cambodia, China, India, Indonesia, Laos,
Mongolia, Oman, Sri Lanka, Thailand

BORNEO RAIN FOREST AND ORANGUTAN PROGRAM

BORNEO

Once covered by dense mangrove forests, Borneo, the world's third-largest island, was left largely unexplored. Now, due to deforestation, less than half of that forest remains, but scientists continue to discover new species of flora and fauna. Volunteers in the Borneo Rain Forest and Orangutan Program help researchers better understand the island's ecosystem by completing biodiversity surveys and living among some of the world's most fascinating creatures: pygmy elephants, proboscis monkeys, and even orangutans. Because Borneo is also home to some spectacular coral reefs, participants have the chance to dive, snorkel, and explore these sites as well.

CONTACT: The Society for Environmental Exploration (operating as Frontier), 50-52 Rivington St, London, EC2A 3QP, UK; Tel: 4402076132422; Fax: 4402076132992; Web: www.frontier.ac.uk/gap_year_projects/Borneo/Borneo_Rainforest_and_Orangutan_Adventure; Email: info@frontier.ac.uk.

LOCATION: Borneo.

CATEGORY: Conservation.

COST: US$1,842 for 15 days. Fee includes accommodations, meals, project equipment, training, orientation, and in-country emergency support.

DATES & DURATION: Varies; 15 days.

TO APPLY: Applications are accepted through the website (see Contact).

FIELD NOTES: Outside of the official project, travelers can participate in a number of other activities, such as canopy tours and river rafting, which can both be booked by the provider. For jungle trekking, participants must be in moderate physical shape and able to endure high temperatures and humidity. Positions are suitable for adult groups and solo travelers.

CAMBODIA TROPICAL WILDLIFE CONSERVATION AND ADVENTURE PROGRAM

CAMBODIA

Deep in the wild, dense Cambodian jungle, volunteers for the Cambodia Tropical Wildlife Conservation and Adventure Program have the chance to catch a glimpse of some of the world's most endangered species, such as sun bears, tigers, Asian elephants, and gibbons. Conducting biodiversity surveys, participants help local conservationists better understand the jungle ecosystem and improve their efforts to protect the area's remarkable wildlife. Because much of the area remains unexplored, lucky participants may even encounter yet-undiscovered species.

CONTACT: The Society for Environmental Exploration (operating as Frontier),

50-52 Rivington St, London, EC2A 3QP, UK; Tel: 4402076132422; Fax: 4402076132992; Web: www.frontier .ac.uk/gap_year_projects/Cambodia/ Cambodia_Tropical_Wildlife_ Conservation_Adventure_Project; Email: info@frontier.ac.uk.

LOCATION: Cambodia.

CATEGORY: Conservation.

COST: US$1,500–$4,200 for 3–20 weeks. Fee includes accommodations, meals, ground transfers, training, and in-country emergency support.

DATES & DURATION: Varies; 3–20 weeks.

Programs begin monthly on the first Monday.

TO APPLY: Applications are accepted through the website (see Contact).

FIELD NOTES: Participants stay in tented camps. Camp food is basic, consisting mainly of rice, beans, vegetables, and noodles. This trip also requires a great deal of hiking, so volunteers should be relatively fit. All participants assist with daily camp duties, including cooking, removing rubbish, purifying water, and collecting firewood. Positions are suitable for adult groups and solo travelers.

PANDA BREEDING CENTER

CHINA

Now endangered, the giant panda needs our help more than ever. At the Panda Breeding Center in Chengdu, China, participants help feed adult pandas, take care of cubs, clean enclosures, and maintain the facilities. Volunteers help center scientists collect observational data that may ultimately help with the survival rate of the wild panda. In addition, participants may assist with medical procedures and breeding efforts.

CONTACT: The Society for Environmental Exploration (operating as Frontier), 50-52 Rivington St, London, EC2A 3QP, UK; Tel: 4402076132422; Fax: 4402076132992; Web: www.frontier.ac.uk/gap_year_projects/China/China_Panda_Breeding_Centre; Email: info@frontier.ac.uk.

LOCATION: Bifengxia, China.

CATEGORY: Conservation.

COST: US$2,200 for 4 weeks; extended stays available for additional fee. Fee includes accommodations, meals, airport pickup and drop-off, ground transfers, local orientation, project training, and in-country emergency support.

DATES & DURATION: Varies; 4 weeks. Programs begin monthly on Mondays.

TO APPLY: Applications are accepted through the website (see Contact).

FIELD NOTES: Volunteers stay at a local hotel. Meals are chosen from a set menu. Positions are suitable for adult groups and solo travelers.

CROCODILE CONSERVATION PROGRAM

INDIA

Originally designed as a breeding center for India's crocodiles, the Crocodile Conservation Program is now home to many of the country's most endangered species, including 14 species of crocodiles, 12 types of turtles and tortoises, monitor lizards, pythons, iguanas, and even king cobras. On-site, volunteers help feed the animals, clean their enclosures, and assist in research projects. Participants also help with public education programs about the center and its continued importance.

CONTACT: Twin Work & Volunteer Abroad, 2nd Floor, 67-71 Lewisham, London, SE13 5JX, UK; Tel: 08008048380; Fax: 08707775206; Web: www.workand volunteer.com/programme/?pgid=83; Email: Contact form on website.

LOCATION: Outside Chennai, India.

CATEGORY: Conservation.

COST: US$900–$2,010 for 4–16 weeks. Fee includes accommodations, breakfast and dinner, ground transfers, training, and support.

DATES & DURATION: Year-round; 4–16 weeks. Programs begin monthly on the second Monday.

TO APPLY: Applications are accepted through the website (see Contact).

FIELD NOTES: Participants must be at least 18 years old. There are no specific skills required. The program offers a free weekend trip after 2 weeks of service. Positions are suitable for adult groups and solo travelers.

ORANGUTAN PROJECT

INDONESIA

With no natural immunity to parasites and bacteria, orangutans must—just like us—take medicine to stay healthy. Scientists have recently discovered that orangutans eat certain plants not just for their nutritional value but for their curative properties. The problem is, scientists don't know which plants these amazing creatures use as medicine. To that end, volunteers on the Orangutan Project work deep in the Indonesian rain forest, collecting behavioral data and fecal samples to analyze back at base. Other tasks include nest counting, organizing orangutan food-stuffs, and even following orangutans through the forest.

CONTACT: Eco Volunteer Organization, c/o The Great Canadian Travel Company Ltd, 158 Fort St, Winnipeg, MB, Canada R3C 1C9; Tel: 2049490199 or 8006613830; Web: www.ecovolunteer.org; Email: ecovolunteer@gctc-mst.com.

LOCATION: North Sumatra.

CATEGORY: Conservation.

COST: US$1,289 for 14 days. Fee includes basic accommodations, meals, ground transfers, training, and in-country support.

DATES & DURATION: Year-round (except December and January); 14 days. Programs begin monthly on the first Monday.

TO APPLY: Applications are accepted through the website (see Contact).

FIELD NOTES: Participants aged 18 to 50 are welcome to apply. Those over 50 who would like to participate are urged to contact the office for approval. Participants stay in basic cabins with squat toilets. Positions are suitable for adult groups and solo travelers.

ORANGUTANS OF SUMATRA

INDONESIA

Orangutans, like humans, sometimes need to take medicine. But they don't need just any medicine—they need the *right* medicine. Volunteers in the Orangutans of Sumatra project travel to lush forests to help biologists better understand what plants work best for what orangutan ailments so that this information can be taught to apes at the rehabilitation center, allowing them to care for themselves in the wild. As part of the research team, volunteers track the great apes through the jungle. Once the animals are located, participants observe and record all behaviors. Volunteers receive full scientific training before the start of their program.

CONTACT: Global Vision International, 252 Newbury St, #4, Boston, MA 02116; Tel: 8886536028; Fax: 6176742109; Web: www.gviusa.com/projects/asia/indonesia/volunteer-orangutan-sumatra/home; Email: info@gviworld.com.

LOCATION: Sumatra.

CATEGORY: Conservation.

COST: US$1,289 for 2 weeks. Fee includes accommodations, meals, ground transfers, project orientation and training, and in-country emergency support.

DATES & DURATION: Varies; 2 weeks.

TO APPLY: Applications are accepted online and by fax and mail. Contact the office (see Contact).

FIELD NOTES: Volunteers live in very basic

huts and camp in the jungle for many consecutive nights. A maximum of six volunteers can participate at a time. There is no hot water, and only traditional squat toilets are available. Positions are suitable for adult groups and solo travelers.

BAN HAD KAI PROJECT

LAOS

Ban Had Kai Project volunteers not only have the opportunity to explore the dense jungles of Laos—hiking through the forest in search of the Asian elephant—but also help develop the local ecotourism industry, teaching would-be tour guides basic English-language skills. Living in the small farming village of Ban Had Kai, participants also help educate schoolchildren, work in hospitality training, and promote ecotourism programs.

CONTACT: Openmind Projects, 856/9 Moo.15, Prajark Rd, A. Muang, Nongkhai, 43000 Thailand; Tel: 6642413678; Fax: 6642413678; Web: www.openmindprojects.org; Email: Contact form on website.

LOCATION: Phu Khao Khouay, Laos.

CATEGORY: Conservation.

COST: US$1,000–$3,000 for 1–20 weeks; US$100 per extra week. Fee includes accommodations, meals, extensive project training, and in-country emergency support.

DATES & DURATION: Year-round.

TO APPLY: Applications are through the website (see Contact).

FIELD NOTES: No specific skills are required. Accommodations are with a host family in a basic village house or in the jungle. Participants may also travel to nearby Vientiane, where supermarkets, restaurants, banks, Internet cafés, a post office, and telephones are available. Positions are suitable for adult groups and solo travelers.

BAN NA PROJECT

LAOS

Working to improve the local eco-tourism industry, participants in the Ban Na Project teach English to aspiring tour guides in Ban Na, a remote village in the Laotian jungle. Volunteers also have the chance to track wild elephants and can stay overnight at the village's elephant observation tower. Participating volunteers may also be called on to take part in eco-related hospitality training and promotional programs.

CONTACT: Openmind Projects, 856/9 Moo.15, Prajark Rd, A. Muang, Nongkhai, 43000 Thailand; Tel: 6642413678; Fax: 6642413678; Web: www.openmind projects.org; Email: Contact form on website.

LOCATION: Phu Khao Khouay, Laos.

CATEGORY: Conservation.

COST: US$1,000–$3,000 for 1–20 weeks; US$100 per extra week. Fee includes accommodations, meals, extensive project training, and in-country emergency support. Volunteers are responsible for travel to and from the site.

DATES & DURATION: Year-round.

TO APPLY: Applications are accepted through the website (see Contact).

FIELD NOTES: Accommodations are with a host family in a basic village house or in the jungle in an elephant watchtower. Volunteers may also travel to Vientiane, where supermarkets, restaurants, banks, Internet cafés, a post office, and telephones are available. Positions are suitable for adult groups and solo travelers.

WILDLIFE OF THE MONGOLIAN STEPPE

MONGOLIA

Volunteers in the Wildlife of the Mongolian Steppe program hike through the breathtaking desert-steppe environment of Mongolia to study the ecology and biodiversity of this unique habitat. Working alongside a dedicated team of researchers, participants collect behavioral data on such rare creatures as the lesser kestrel, hedgehogs, Pallas's cats, and corsac foxes. Participants can expect to encounter the Argali sheep, Siberian ibex, and cinereous vulture.

CONTACT: Earthwatch Institute, 3 Clock Tower Pl, Suite 100, Box 75, Maynard, MA 01754; Tel: 9784610081 or 8007760188; Fax: 9784612332; Web: www.earthwatch .org/exped/reading.html; Email: expedi tions@earthwatch.org.

LOCATION: Mongolia.

CATEGORY: Conservation.

COST: US$3,000 for 14 days. Fee includes accommodations, meals, ground transfers, training, and in-country emergency support.

DATES & DURATION: Varies; 14 days.

TO APPLY: Applications are accepted online and by fax or mail. Contact the office (see Contact).

FIELD NOTES: In their spare time, volunteers may wish to explore the Natural History Museum or the Zanabazar Museum of Fine Arts, located in the capital city of Ulaanbaatar. Participants must be in good physical shape because the trip requires both hiking and camping. Accommodations vary but include traditional Mongolian *gers* and tents. A cook is on staff to prepare meals, but volunteers assist with daily camp duties. Camps include basic solar showers, solar lights, and outhouses. Positions are suitable for adult groups and solo travelers.

ELUSIVE AND UNKNOWN CAT PROJECT

OMAN

Working with a dedicated team of scientists, volunteers for the Elusive and Unknown Cat Project travel to the desert mountains of Oman to study the Arabian leopard. Participants help record leopard sightings and collect data on the distribution of leopards and their prey throughout the region. Volunteers also help document interspecies interactions among the leopard, wolf, and striped hyena.

CONTACT: Biosphere Expeditions, PO Box 917750, Longwood, FL 32791; Tel: 8004075761; Fax: 8004075766; Web: www .biosphere-expeditions.org; Email: northamerica@biosphere-expeditions.org.

LOCATION: Dhofar, Oman.

CATEGORY: Conservation.

COST: US$1,950 for 12 nights. Fee includes accommodations, meals, ground transfers, project orientation, training, and support.

DATES & DURATION: Varies; 12 nights.

TO APPLY: Applications are accepted online and by fax or mail. Contact the office (see Contact).

FIELD NOTES: There are no specific skills or age requirements that need to be met for participation in this project, but volunteers must be able to walk great lengths and over mountainous terrain. Positions are suitable for adult groups and solo travelers.

ELEPHANT ORPHANAGE

SRI LANKA

Located in Kegalle, the Elephant Orphanage provides a safe haven for juvenile elephants that are lost or abandoned. Volunteers are welcome to take part in a hands-on experience to ensure that this majestic species has a continued existence. Participants assist with daily elephant bathing duties, cleaning and maintaining enclosures, and hand-feeding of the extremely young. The Elephant Orphanage is home to many young elephants that are lost or abandoned by their mothers. Here the elephants are fed, nursed, and taken care of by professional handlers and volunteers. This project is a rare opportunity for those interested in working with elephants.

CONTACT: Global Crossroad, 4425 West Airport Fwy, Suite 210, Irving, TX 75062; Tel: 9722524191 or 2256144695; Fax: 9728527999; Web: www.globalcrossroad .com/srilanka/elephant_conservation .php; Email: info@globalcrossroad.com.

LOCATION: Kegalle, Sri Lanka.

CATEGORY: Rehabilitation.

COST: US$650–$963 for 1–3 weeks; extended stays are available for an additional fee. Fee includes accommodations and three meals per day. Airport pickup and transfers are additional.

DATES & DURATION: Year-round. Programs are offered weekly on the first and third Mondays. Volunteers commit to a 25- to 35-hour workweek.

TO APPLY: Applications are accepted online and by fax and mail. A nonrefundable US$350 deposit is required upon booking.

FIELD NOTES: No special skills are required to participate. Positions are suitable for adult groups and solo travelers.

SRI LANKA LEOPARD CONSERVATION PROGRAM

SRI LANKA

With the local leopard population on the decline, conservationists in Sri Lanka are stepping up their efforts to protect this amazing creature. But before they can help, scientists need to know more about the leopard in its native habitat. To that end, volunteers with the Sri Lanka Leopard Conservation Program collect behavioral data and track leopard movement through the jungle.

CONTACT: The Society for Environmental Exploration (operating as Frontier), 50-52 Rivington St, London, EC2A 3QP, UK; Tel: 4402076132422; Fax: 4402076132992; Web: www.frontier.ac.uk/gap_year_projects/Sri%20Lanka/Sri_Lanka_Leopard_Conservation; Email: info@frontier.ac.uk.
LOCATION: Sri Lanka.

CATEGORY: Conservation.
COST: US$1,990 for 4 weeks; US$423 per extra week; extended stays available on request. Fee includes accommodations, meals, local orientation, comprehensive project training, equipment and materials, and in-country emergency support.
DATES & DURATION: Varies; 2–4 weeks. Programs begin on the first and third Mondays.
TO APPLY: Applications are accepted through the website (see Contact).
FIELD NOTES: Volunteers stay in basic rooms at the field lodge and may share their rooms with two to eight other participants. Meals largely consist of rice, beans, vegetables, and noodles. Positions are suitable for adult groups and solo travelers.

ELEPHANT ECO-CENTER PROGRAM

THAILAND

While Thailand's wild elephants are severely endangered, many domesticated elephants can still be seen on the country's city streets, performing with their handlers, or *mahouts*. To rescue these elephants, the Elephant Eco-Center Program adopts the elephants *with* their mahouts, getting them both off the streets and into a safe environment. At the center, volunteers help the mahouts exercise, bathe, and feed the elephants, and maintain and clean the facilities.

CONTACT: The Society for Environmental Exploration (operating as Frontier), 50-52 Rivington St, London, EC2A 3QP, UK; Tel: 4402076132422; Fax: 4402076132992; Web: www.frontier.ac.uk/gap_year_projects/Thailand/Thailand_Elephant_Eco-Centre; Email: info@frontier.ac.uk.

LOCATION: Thailand.

CATEGORY: Conservation.

COST: US$2,000 for 4 weeks; US$350 per extra week. Fee includes accommodations, meals, ground transfers, project training, and support.

DATES & DURATION: Year-round; 2–4 weeks.

TO APPLY: Applications are accepted through the website (see Contact).

FIELD NOTES: Participants stay in traditional shared huts. In a nearby village, volunteers have access to Internet cafés, shops, banks, and restaurants. Positions are suitable for adult groups and solo travelers.

ELEPHANT PROGRAM

THAILAND

Working in the Elephant Program, associated with a rehabilitation center in southern Thailand, volunteers help care for elephants rescued from exploitation and abuse. Participants wash, feed, and bathe the elephants, and clean their enclosures and the center. Volunteers take the elephants on daily walks and swim trips in an effort to create a more natural setting for animals who have spent entirely too much of their lives living in captive conditions.

CONTACT: Eco Volunteer Organization, c/o The Great Canadian Travel Company Ltd, 158 Fort St, Winnipeg, MB, Canada R3C 1C9; Tel: 2049490199 or 8006613830; Web: www.ecovolunteer.org; Email: ecovolunteer@gctc-mst.com.

LOCATION: Southern Thailand.

CATEGORY: Rehabilitation.

COST: US$550 for 1 week; US$320 per extra week. Fee includes accommodations, meals, training, and in-country support.

DATES & DURATION: Year-round; 1 week.

TO APPLY: Applications are accepted through the website (see Contact).

FIELD NOTES: Participants must be at least 18 years of age and in good physical condition. Volunteers stay in basic bungalows. Rooms are suitable for two to four people, and there is no hot running water. Volunteers are expected to help with house duties and are responsible for cooking their own breakfast from the supplies provided. Positions are suitable for adult groups and solo travelers.

GIBBON REHABILITATION PROJECT

THAILAND

Located in Phuket, Thailand, the Gibbon Rehabilitation Project works to rehabilitate sick, injured, and orphaned white-handed gibbons. Volunteers assist in the daily care of this unique species. Food preparation, cleaning of enclosures, mapping, and trail maintenance are all tasks performed by volunteers. Participants also work with public education initiatives focused on the threats that the gibbon currently faces, such as poaching and deforestation.

CONTACT: Twin Work & Volunteer Abroad, 2nd Floor, 67-71 Lewisham, London, SE13 5JX, UK; Tel: 08008048380; Fax: 08707775206; Web: www.workand volunteer.com/programme/?pgid=90; Email: Contact form on website.

LOCATION: Phuket, Thailand.

CATEGORY: Rehabilitation.

COST: US$700 for 3 weeks; US$80 per extra week. Fee includes accommodations, ground transfers, training, and in-country support.

DATES & DURATION: Year-round; 3–24 weeks. Programs begin on Mondays.

TO APPLY: Applications are accepted through the website (see Contact).

FIELD NOTES: Volunteers should expect to work 6 days a week, 8 hours per day. Volunteers entering the program are required to have a series of inoculations, including hepatitis A and B, tuberculosis, diphtheria, rabies, pertussis, tetanus, and Japanese encephalitis, before the start of the program. Positions are suitable for adult groups and solo travelers.

INDIGENOUS WILDLIFE RESCUE PROGRAM

THAILAND

Located on temple grounds in southern Thailand, the Indigenous Wildlife Rescue Program houses more than 300 animals that have been previously abused or exploited. On-site, volunteers encounter the Malayan sun bear, slow loris, civet, and three different types of gibbons—white-handed, golden-cheeked, and siamang. Participants help prepare food, clean animal enclosures, and even construct new habitats for future residents at this ever-expanding wildlife center.

CONTACT: Eco Volunteer Organization, c/o The Great Canadian Travel Company Ltd, 158 Fort St, Winnipeg, MB, Canada R3C 1C9; Tel: 2049490199 or 8006613830; Web: www.ecovolunteer.org; Email: ecovolunteer@gctc-mst.com.

LOCATION: Southern Thailand.

CATEGORY: Rehabilitation.

COST: US$784 for 2 weeks. Fee includes accommodations, meals, training, and support.

DATES & DURATION: Year-round; 2 weeks.

TO APPLY: Applications are accepted through the website (see Contact).

FIELD NOTES: Participants must be at least 18 years old, in good physical condition, and able to work independently. Participants stay in basic bungalows, where there is no hot water. Before working with the primates, volunteers must be properly vaccinated. For a current list of required vaccinations, contact the office (see Contact). Positions are suitable for adult groups and solo travelers.

KAENG KRACHAN NATIONAL PARK

THAILAND

Commercial poaching inside of Thailand's Kaeng Krachan National Park is taking its toll on the area's wildlife and ecosystem. The World Wildlife Fund (WWF) has joined other conservation organizations in an effort to reduce this destruction and to educate local populations about wildlife and habitat management. Kaeng Krachan is home to many species, including wild elephants, gaurs, bears, tigers, leopards, gibbons, languars, over 400 species of birds, and the nearly extinct Siamese crocodile. Volunteers track and observe species in the park while teaching rangers the English skills necessary to be successful tour guides. Participants may also work at the refugee school in the nearby village of Karen.

CONTACT: Openmind Projects, 856/9 Moo.15, Prajark Rd, A. Muang, Nongkhai, 43000 Thailand; Tel: 6642413678; Fax: 6642413678; Web: www.openmind projects.org; Email: Contact form on website.

LOCATION: Thailand.

CATEGORY: Conservation.

COST: US$1,000–$3,000 for 1–20 weeks; US$100 per extra week. Fee includes accommodations, meals, extensive project training, and in-country emergency support. Volunteers are responsible for travel to and from the site.

DATES & DURATION: Year-round.

TO APPLY: Applications are accepted through the website (see Contact).

FIELD NOTES: Volunteers stay in basic bungalows located in the park headquarters or at the ranger station inside the jungle. Separate bedrooms are provided. Participants assist staff with cooking and household duties. Volunteers should wear long shorts, neutral-colored shirts, and hiking shoes and socks to protect against insects and leeches. Positions are suitable for adult groups and solo travelers.

KHAO PHANOM BENCHA NATIONAL PARK

THAILAND

Working in Thailand's idyllic Khao Phanom Bencha National Park, volunteers help train park rangers and local residents in tourism-related English. Participants also help construct hiking paths and maintain the park's visitors center. Volunteers may assist with the development of trekking and tour packages, and help staff create other recreational opportunities that can be enjoyed within the park's boundaries. Participants may also enjoy on-site bird watching and cave touring.

CONTACT: Openmind Projects, 856/9 Moo.15, Prajark Rd, A. Muang, Nongkhai, 43000 Thailand; Tel: 6642413678; Fax: 6642413678; Web: www.openmindproj ects.org; Email: Contact form on website.

LOCATION: North Krabi Province, Thailand.

CATEGORY: Conservation.

COST: US$1,000–$3,090 for 1–20 weeks; US$100 per extra week. Fee includes accommodations, meals, extensive project training, and in-country emergency support. Volunteers are responsible for travel to and from the site.

DATES & DURATION: Year-round.

TO APPLY: Applications are accepted through the website (see Contact).

FIELD NOTES: Volunteers stay in basic bungalows located within the park grounds. Bottled water is provided. There are no specific skills needed for participation. Positions are suitable for adult groups and solo travelers.

KHLONG LAN NATIONAL PARK

THAILAND

Volunteers at Thailand's Khlong Lan National Park conduct biodiversity surveys and educate local residents on the importance of conservation. Participants also assist the staff with interpretive programs provided to visitors and help create and design tour packages for future ecotourists.

CONTACT: Openmind Projects, 856/9 Moo.15, Prajark Rd, A. Muang, Nongkhai, 43000 Thailand; Tel: 6642413678; Fax: 6642413678; Web: www.openmind projects.org; Email: Contact form on website.

LOCATION: Kamphaeng Phet Province, Thailand.

CATEGORY: Conservation.

COST: US$1,000–$3,090 for 1–20 weeks; US$100 per extra week. Fee includes accommodations, meals, extensive project training, and in-country emergency support. Volunteers are responsible for travel to and from the site.

DATES & DURATION: Year-round.

TO APPLY: Applications are accepted through the website (see Contact).

FIELD NOTES: In their downtime, volunteers can enjoy a variety of eco-adventures, including bird- and butterfly-watching, rafting, canoeing, and cave touring. Volunteers stay in basic bungalows located on park grounds. Meals are served at the national park restaurant. Positions are suitable for families, groups, and solo travelers.

KUI BURI NATIONAL PARK

THAILAND

Home to elephants, tigers, tapirs, and many different bird species, Thailand's Kui Buri National Park is an established wildlife haven. Trekking through the park's jungle landscape, participants have the chance to track and spot elephants along the trails. Volunteers also help teach park rangers and village women the English skills necessary to be successful ecotour guides.

CONTACT: Openmind Projects, 856/9 Moo.15, Prajark Rd, A. Muang, Nongkhai, 43000 Thailand; Tel: 6642413678; Fax: 6642413678; Web: www.openmindprojects.org; Email: Contact form on website.

LOCATION: South of Bangkok, Thailand.

CATEGORY: Conservation.

COST: US$1,000–$3,090 for 1–20 weeks; US$100 per extra week. Fee includes accommodations, meals, extensive project training, and in-country emergency support. Volunteers are responsible for travel to and from the site.

DATES & DURATION: Year-round.

TO APPLY: Applications are accepted through the website (see Contact).

FIELD NOTES: Participants stay at basic bungalows located either in the park headquarters or at the ranger station in the jungle. Volunteers are provided food at the headquarters, where staff and volunteers cook together. House duties are everyone's responsibility, and volunteers need to participate. When the staff goes to the nearby town, participants are welcome to join. Supermarkets, Internet cafés, and public telephones are all available there. Volunteers should wear neutral-colored, knee-length shorts; shirts with sleeves; and hiking shoes and socks to protect against insects and leeches. Long days and nights are spent trekking through the jungle in search of wild elephants, so a moderate level of physical fitness is required. Positions are suitable for adult groups and solo travelers.

MAE WONG NATIONAL PARK

THAILAND

Working in the rugged, mountainous terrain of Mae Wong National Park, volunteers help survey the local flora and fauna and develop ecotourism packages for future visitors. Participants also instruct park rangers in tourism-related English. Lucky volunteers have the chance to catch a glimpse of the park's diverse species, including over 450 different types of birds, Asiatic jackals, wild pigs, and civets.

CONTACT: Openmind Projects, 856/9 Moo.15, Prajark Rd, A. Muang, Nongkhai, 43000 Thailand; Tel: 6642413678; Fax: 6642413678; Web: www.openmind projects.org; Email: Contact form on website.

LOCATION: Kamphaeng Phet Province, Thailand.

CATEGORY: Conservation.

COST: US$1,000–$3,090 for 1–20 weeks; US$100 per extra week. Fee includes accommodations, meals, extensive project training, and in-country emergency support. Volunteers are responsible for travel to and from the site.

DATES & DURATION: Year-round.

TO APPLY: Applications are accepted through the website (see Contact).

FIELD NOTES: During their spare time, volunteers can enjoy hiking on the nature trails, which provide an unsurpassed view of Mae Wong's strikingly beautiful waterfalls. On-site, volunteers can enjoy an array of activities, including canoeing, trekking, bird-watching, and swimming in the hot springs. Participants stay in basic bungalows located on park grounds. Meals are served at the national park restaurant. Cellular telephones and Internet service are available. Positions are suitable for adult groups and solo travelers.

MOO KOH PHI PHI NATIONAL PARK

THAILAND

Home to the famous Phi Phi Islands Archipelago, Moo Koh Phi Phi National Park attracts an impressive 84,000 visitors every year. The park's success, however, has come at a price. With the increase in tourism, boats are constantly shuttling travelers from one island to another. Boat traffic, unfortunately, is potentially damaging to the park's plentiful coral reefs. To help protect this underwater habitat, volunteers work with park staff in efforts to develop eco-programs that offset this destruction. Volunteers assist staff in the development of eco-tour and activity packages as well as the development of the park's new visitors center.

CONTACT: Openmind Projects, 856/9 Moo.15, Prajark Rd, A. Muang, Nongkhai, 43000 Thailand; Tel: 6642413678; Fax: 6642413678; Web: www.openmind projects.org; Email: Contact form on website.

LOCATION: West of Krabi Province, Thailand.

CATEGORY: Conservation.

COST: US$1,000–$3,090 for 1–20 weeks; US$100 per extra week. Fee includes accommodations, meals, extensive project training, and in-country emergency support. Volunteers are responsible for travel to and from the site.

DATES & DURATION: Year-round.

TO APPLY: Applications are accepted through the website (see Contact).

FIELD NOTES: Volunteers stay in basic bungalows located on park grounds. The park features a 100-million-year-old shell cemetery, where volunteers can see fossilized shells. Positions are suitable for adult groups and solo travelers.

PANG SIDA NATIONAL PARK

THAILAND

Working in Thailand's Pang Sida National Park, volunteers help educate park rangers in tourism-related English and on environmental and conservation issues. While there, participants have the unique opportunity to see the Siamese crocodile, a species previously thought to be extinct that now makes its home at the park's breeding center. Volunteers may also get to see tigers, leopards, guars, and over 400 different species of butterflies.

CONTACT: Openmind Projects, 856/9 Moo.15, Prajark Rd, A. Muang, Nongkhai, 43000 Thailand; Tel: 6642413678; Fax: 6642413678; Web: www.openmind projects.org; Email: Contact form on website.

LOCATION: Sa Kaew Province, Thailand.

CATEGORY: Conservation.

COST: US$1,000–$3,090 for 1–20 weeks; US$100 per extra week. Fee includes accommodations, meals, extensive project training, and in-country emergency support. Volunteers are responsible for travel to and from the site.

DATES & DURATION: Year-round.

TO APPLY: Applications are accepted through the website (see Contact).

FIELD NOTES: Volunteers stay in bungalows located within the park. Positions are suitable for adult groups and solo travelers.

PHU WUA WILDLIFE RESERVE

THAILAND

At Thailand's Phu Wua Wildlife Reserve, located near the Mekong River, volunteers not only help teach local villagers English but have a wildlife adventure as well. Participants track wild elephants, work at the local primary school, and develop ecotourism packages for future visitors. Participants also learn how to survive in a jungle environment and conduct surveys of the area's flora.

CONTACT: Openmind Projects, 856/9 Moo.15, Prajark Rd, A. Muang, Nongkhai, 43000 Thailand; Tel: 6642413678; Fax: 6642413678; Web: www.openmind projects.org; Email: Contact form on website.

LOCATION: Nongkhai Isan, Thailand.

CATEGORY: Conservation.

COST: US$1,000–$3,090 for 1–20 weeks; US$100 per extra week. Fee includes accommodations, meals, extensive project training, and in-country emergency support. Volunteers are responsible for travel to and from the site.

DATES & DURATION: Year-round.

TO APPLY: Applications are accepted through the website (see Contact).

FIELD NOTES: Accommodations are basic: mattress, linen, fan, mosquito net, toilets, and cold showers. Separate bedrooms are provided. Several convenience stores are located in the village for snacks, drinks, and toiletries. Dress is casual. Knee-length shorts and sleeveless tops are recommended. Positions are suitable for adult groups and solo travelers.

PRIMATE PROJECT

THAILAND

Originally founded as a rehabilitation center for abused gibbons, the sanctuary at Thailand's Khao Phra Thaew National Park now offers a permanent home for many local primates. While volunteers for the Primate Project have found that most of these rescued monkeys can never be reintroduced into the wild, the rescued gibbons still need our support. To that end, project participants help prepare food for the monkeys and apes, clean enclosures, and maintain the center's facilities.

CONTACT: Eco Volunteer Organization, c/o The Great Canadian Travel Company Ltd, 158 Fort St, Winnipeg, MB, Canada R3C 1C9; Tel: 2049490199 or 8006613830; Web: www.ecovolunteer.org; Email: ecovolunteer@gctc-mst.com.

LOCATION: Khao Phra Thaew National Park, Thailand.

CATEGORY: Rehabilitation.

COST: US$1,090 for 3 weeks; extended stays are available upon request for an additional fee.

DATES & DURATION: Year-round; 3 weeks.

TO APPLY: Applications are accepted through the website (see Contact).

FIELD NOTES: Volunteers must be at least 18 years of age and in good physical shape. Participants work 6 days per week, 8 hours per day. Before working with the monkeys, volunteers must be properly vaccinated; for a current list of required vaccinations, please contact the office (see Contact). Participants, however, are not allowed to handle the gibbons at any time. Positions are suitable for adult groups and solo travelers.

TAI MUANG NATIONAL MARINE PARK

THAILAND

Thailand's Tai Muang National Marine Park offers volunteers a diverse range of eco-adventures. At the park's conservation center, volunteers help conservationists breed giant clams, four species of sea turtles, and more than 30 different types of fish. Volunteers may also help survey the park's diverse marine wildlife, diving deep underwater to collect samples and record distribution data. Back at Tai Muang beach, the country's longest beach, visitors find the endangered leatherback turtle at its last remaining nesting site in Thailand.

CONTACT: Openmind Projects, 856/9 Moo.15, Prajark Rd, A. Muang, Nongkhai, 43000 Thailand; Tel: 6642413678; Fax: 6642413678; Web: www.openmind projects.org; Email: Contact form on website.

LOCATION: Tai Muang, Thailand.

CATEGORY: Conservation.

COST: US$1,000–$3,090 for 1–24 weeks; US$100 per extra week. Fee includes accommodations, meals, extensive project training, and in-country emergency support. Volunteers are responsible for travel to and from the site.

DATES & DURATION: Year-round.

TO APPLY: Applications are accepted through the website (see Contact).

FIELD NOTES: Volunteers stay either in basic bungalows or in simple rooms at the conservation center. No specific skills are required. Meals are provided at the national park restaurant. Diving certification is required for those participating in the underwater survey program. Positions are suitable for adult groups and solo travelers.

THAN BOK KHORANI NATIONAL PARK

THAILAND

Established in 1998, Thailand's Than Bok Khorani National Park boasts a diverse range of ecological sights. From the tall limestone towers of the park's mainland to the lush rain forests of its 23 islands, there's something here for every would-be adventurer. At this site, volunteers survey terrestrial and aquatic wildlife to improve conservationists' understanding of the park's ecosystem. Participants also teach English to park rangers and help with interpreting information.

CONTACT: Openmind Projects, 856/9 Moo.15, Prajark Rd, A. Muang, Nongkhai, 43000 Thailand; Tel: 6642413678; Fax: 6642413678; Web: www.openmind projects.org; Email: Contact form on website.

LOCATION: Au Luek District, Thailand.

CATEGORY: Conservation.

COST: US$1,000–$3,090 for 1–20 weeks; US$100 per extra week. Fee includes accommodations, meals, extensive project training, and in-country emergency support. Volunteers are responsible for travel to and from the site.

DATES & DURATION: Year-round.

TO APPLY: Applications are accepted through the website (see Contact).

FIELD NOTES: Accommodations are basic rooms. Bottled water is provided. Knee-length shorts and sleeveless shirts are acceptable. This trip is suitable for families with older children, groups, and solo travelers.

AUSTRALIA

Australia, Fiji, New Zealand

AUSTRALASIA ETHICAL CONSERVATION EXPERIENCE

AUSTRALIA AND NEW ZEALAND

With various projects in both Australia and New Zealand to choose from, volunteers of the Australasia Ethical Conservation Experience can enjoy the beauty of the wilderness while helping to protect the region's endangered species. Some participants may work on conservation efforts already under way to preserve the habitats of both the koala and the kangaroo. Other participants may help researchers survey the local flora and fauna. Whether in Australia or New Zealand, volunteers also get to experience the relaxed culture of the local populations. Volunteer services may include tree planting, erosion control, seed collection, track construction, flora and fauna surveys, habitat restoration, endangered species protection, weed control, fence and trail construction, and environmental monitoring. Project locations include national and state parks, along with coastal reserves.

CONTACT: The Society for Environmental Exploration (operating as Frontier), 50-52 Rivington St, London, EC2A 3QP, UK; Tel: 4402076132422; Fax: 4402076132992; Web: www.frontier .ac.uk/gap_year_projects/Australia/ Australasia_Ethical_Conservation_ Experiences; Email: info@frontier.ac.uk.

LOCATION: Adelaide, Alice Springs, Bathurst, Bendigo, Brisbane, Broome, Cairns, Canberra, Darwin, Geelong, Gladstone, Hobart, Launceston, Mackay, Melbourne, New Castle, Perth, Port

Macquarie, Sydney, Townsville, and Wollongong in Australia and New Zealand.

CATEGORY: Conservation.

COST: US$1,533 for 4 weeks. Fee includes ground transfers, accommodations, three meals per day, local orientation, project training, and in-country emergency support.

DATES & DURATION: Monthly (4 weeks); programs begins on the first Friday of the month (Saturday in Auckland).

TO APPLY: Applications are accepted online and by fax and mail. Contact the office (see Contact).

FIELD NOTES: Work hours are Monday through Friday from 8 a.m. to 4 p.m. Positions are suitable for families, groups, and solo travelers.

CONSERVATION AUSTRALIA PROGRAM

AUSTRALIA

Working with a team of 6 to 10 other volunteers, participants in the Conservation Australia Program have a variety of conservation projects to choose from throughout Australia. Some volunteers may help construct fences and walking trails, while others may plant trees or conduct biodiversity surveys. Participants may even have the chance to help protect areas with endangered species. Program participants committing to more than 1 week of service have the chance to work on a variety of projects in several locations throughout Australia.

CONTACT: Twin Work & Volunteer Abroad, 2nd Floor, 67-71 Lewisham, London, SE13 5JX, UK; Tel: 08008048380; Fax: 08707775206; Web: www.workand

volunteer.com/programme/?pgid=79; Email: Contact form on website.

LOCATION: Adelaide, Bathurst, Bendigo, Broome, Canberra, Darwin, Geelong, Hobart, Launceston, Melbourne, Newcastle, Perth, and Sydney in Australia.

CATEGORY: Conservation.

COST: US$400–$900 for 1–6 weeks; from US$150 per extra week up to 24 weeks, visa permitting. Fee includes accommodations and meals.

DATES & DURATION: Year-round; 1–24 weeks. Projects begin on Fridays.

TO APPLY: Applicants are accepted through the website (see Contact).

FIELD NOTES: This project is open to volunteers ages 18 to 70. Participants must be physically fit, but there are no specific skills needed to join the program. Positions are suitable for adult groups and solo travelers.

WALLABY RESCUE

AUSTRALIA

Volunteers in the Wallaby Rescue program work in scenic Queensland, Australia, rescuing and rehabilitating baby wallabies, or "joeys," whose mothers have been killed for meat or in traffic accidents. Lucky participants have the opportunity to work hands-on with these adorable creatures, feeding them and cleaning their enclosures. Volunteers should be prepared to feed and hand-rear newborn wallabies.

CONTACT: The Society for Environmental Exploration (operating as Frontier), 50-52 Rivington St, London, EC2A 3QP, UK; Tel: 4402076132422; Fax: 4402076132992; Web: www.frontier.ac.uk/gap_year_projects/

Australia/Australia_Wallaby_Rescue;
Email: info@frontier.ac.uk.

LOCATION: Queensland, Australia.

CATEGORY: Conservation and rehabilitation.

COST: US$1,401 for 4 weeks. Fee includes airport pickup and drop-off, project orientation, accommodations, meals, ground transfers, project equipment, and in-country emergency support.

DATES & DURATION: Year-round; 4 weeks.

TO APPLY: Applications are accepted online and by fax or mail. Contact the office (see Contact).

FIELD NOTES: Off-site, the Australian outback offers its own sights and pleasures. Visitors can see kangaroos and koalas in the wild, or simply relax in one of the most laid-back environments on earth. Participants must be at least 18 years old. Participants should be reasonably fit and able to work in the early morning. Positions are suitable for adult groups and solo travelers.

FIJI MARINE CONSERVATION AND DIVING PROJECT

FIJI

Volunteers in the Fiji Marine Conservation and Diving Project explore the pristine coral reefs off of Fiji's Gau Island, helping marine biologists map sea-grass beds and regional mangrove fringes. On land, participants are involved with public outreach programs concerning the importance of this amazing marine environment. Volunteers also help locate and protect sea turtle nesting sites on the island.

CONTACT: The Society for Environmental Exploration (operating as Frontier), 50-52 Rivington St, London, EC2A 3QP, UK; Tel: 4402076132422; Fax: 4402076132992; Web: www.frontier.ac.uk/gap_year_projects/Fiji/Fiji_Marine_Conservation_Diving; Email: info@frontier.ac.uk.

LOCATION: Gau Island, Fiji.

CATEGORY: Conservation.

COST: US$2,359–$5,560 for 4–20 weeks. Fee includes accommodations and meals, local orientation, comprehensive project training, project equipment, camp diving equipment, research materials, and 24-hour in-country and international HQ emergency support. Airport pickup and internal ground transfers are available only for volunteers who commit to at least 10 weeks.

DATES & DURATION: January, February, April, May, July, August, October, and November: 4–6 weeks. January, April, July, and October: 8–20 weeks. Programs begin monthly on first Monday.

TO APPLY: Applications are accepted online and by fax and mail. Contact the office (see Contact).

FIELD NOTES: All volunteers must be certified for scuba diving. The minimum standard required to participate is a PADI Advanced Open Water/BSAC Diver. Because Frontier is a registered PADI Educational Facility, professional diving officers are available to train and qualify volunteers in the field at no additional cost. Positions are suitable for adult groups and solo travelers.

TURTLE PROJECT OF VANUATU ISLAND

FIJI

Recently dubbed "the happiest place on earth," Vanuatu offers visitors gorgeous ocean views and incredible wildlife, including sea turtles. Volunteers with the Turtle Project of Vanuatu Island help tag turtles, clean their nesting sites, and patrol the local beaches.

CONTACT: Global Vision International, 252 Newbury St, #4, Boston, MA 02116; Tel: 8886536028; Fax: 6176742109; Web: www.gviusa.com/projects/oceania/vanuatu/volunteer-turtles-vanuatu/home; Email: info@gviworld.com.

LOCATION: Vanuatu Island.

CATEGORY: Conservation.

COST: US$2,320–$3,790 for 4–8 weeks; extended stays available for additional fee. Fee includes accommodations, meals, ground transfers, orientation, project training, equipment, and in-country emergency support.

DATES & DURATION: September through January; 4–8 weeks.

TO APPLY: Applications are accepted online and by fax or mail. Contact the office (see Contact).

FIELD NOTES: During the trip, volunteers can also visit Yassur, one of the world's most active volcanoes, and go diving to explore the wreck of the SS *Coolidge*, a World War II–era cruise ship. A maximum of seven volunteers at a time. Participants who wish to go scuba diving must be certified. Volunteers must be at least 18 years old. Positions are suitable for adult groups and solo travelers.

BOUNDARY STREAM MAINLAND ISLAND PROJECT

NEW ZEALAND

In the lowland forests of northeastern New Zealand's Boundary Stream Scenic Reserve, volunteers in the Mainland Island Project help researchers monitor the North Island brown kiwi, kākā, kōkako, New Zealand falcon, and kererū. Volunteers also train as guides for future ecotourism tours. Depending on their previous wilderness experience, participants may also help maintain trails and control pests, such as possums and rats, in the greater effort of supporting this ecosystem for its wildlife inhabitants.

CONTACT: Department of Conservation, Hawke's Bay Area Office, PO Box 644, Napier, 4140; Tel: 6468343111; Fax: 6468344869; Web: www.doc.govt.nz/conservation/land-and-freshwater/land/mainland-islands-a-z/boundary-stream/you-can-help; Email: napier-ao@doc.govt.nz.

LOCATION: East Coast, Hawke's Bay Region, New Zealand.

CATEGORY: Education and preservation.

COST: Free for service. Accommodations, meals, and training are provided.

DATES & DURATION: Year-round. To qualify, volunteers must commit to 3 weeks.

TO APPLY: Contact the volunteer program supervisor at the Department of Conservation's Hawke's Bay Area Office (see Contact).

FIELD NOTES: Participants should be in good physical shape and be familiar with using maps and compasses. Volunteers should also be able to work both independently and in teams. Positions are suitable for families, groups, and solo travelers. Children under 16 years of age must be under the supervision of a parent or guardian.

CONSERVATION NEW ZEALAND PROGRAM

NEW ZEALAND

Volunteers enjoy the beauty of New Zealand while lending a hand in the Conservation New Zealand Program, which focuses on protecting local environments. Participants plant trees, protect endangered species, construct trail and fencing, and survey flora and fauna.

CONTACT: Twin Work & Volunteer Abroad, 2nd Floor, 67-71 Lewisham, London, SE13 5JX, UK; Tel: 08008048380; Fax: 08707775206; Web: www.workand volunteer.com/programme/?pgid=81; Email: Contact form on website.

LOCATION: Greater Auckland area, New Zealand.

CATEGORY: Conservation.

COST: US$400–$950 for 1–6 weeks; US$150 per extra week up to 24 weeks, visa permitting. Fee includes accommodations and meals.

DATES & DURATION: Year-round; 1–24 weeks. Projects begin on Saturday.

TO APPLY: Applicants are accepted through the website (see Contact).

FIELD NOTES: Specific volunteer projects vary by location and conservation priorities at the time of service. Participants ages 18 to 70 are welcome to apply. Volunteers must be reasonably fit. Positions are suitable for adult groups and solo travelers.

HEN AND CHICKENS ISLANDS WEEDING PROJECT

NEW ZEALAND

Working in the isolated nature reserve at New Zealand's Hen and Chickens Islands, participants in the Hen and Chickens Islands Weeding Project not only can enjoy breathtaking views of the sparkling waters and see a variety of plant and animal species—such as tuatara, lizards, saddleback, kākā, and kō kako—but also can help preserve this rich environment by weeding invasive species. The islands' inhabitants have all but disappeared from the mainland; thus, volunteers have a one-of-a-kind experience, especially because the islands are closed to the general public.

CONTACT: Department of Conservation, Whangarei Area Office, PO Box 147, Whangarei 0140; Tel: 6494703304; Fax: 6494703361; Web: www.doc.govt.nz/getting-involved/in-your-community/volunteer-programme/volunteer-programme-by-region/northland/hen-and-chickens-islands-weeding; Email: whangareiao@doc.govt.nz.

LOCATION: North Auckland Peninsula, New Zealand.

CATEGORY: Restoration.

COST: Free in exchange for service. Tents, air mattress, food, cooking and eating utensils, and transportation to and from the islands are provided. The volunteer is responsible for all other needs.

DATES & DURATION: Varies on an annual basis; 10 days. Specific dates available on website (see Contact) in August.

TO APPLY: Contact Monica Valdes at mvaldes@doc.govt.nz or Lynnie Gibson at lgibson@doc.govt.nz from the Department of Conservation.

FIELD NOTES: Participants must be very physically fit and able to maneuver themselves over steep rocky terrain. Volunteers work and live in close proximity with a small group of other participants. Access to this isolated location is by boat only. Positions are suitable for adult groups and solo travelers.

INDEX

J. Clark Salyer National Wildlife Refuge (North Dakota, USA), 102
jackals
Africa, 220
See also specific jackals
Jackson National Fish Hatchery (Wyoming, USA), 141
jaguarondi, 129
jaguars
Jaguar Project (Brazil), 160
South America, 161, 177, 178, 184, 187, 193
Tracking Brazil's Elusive Jaguar, 165
Jane Goodall Institute (Uganda), 253–54
John F. Kennedy Space Center, 42
Jones Hole National Fish Hatchery (Utah, USA), 133
Jordan River National Fish Hatchery (Michigan, USA), 70

Kaeng Krachan National Park (Thailand), 295
kākās, 315, 317
kangaroos, 309
Kansas (USA), 55–56
Kanuti National Wildlife Refuge (Alaska, USA), 7
Kariega Game Reserve (South Africa), 233
Kemp's Ridley sea turtles, 125
Kenai National Wildlife Refuge (Alaska, USA), 8
Kenya, 203–8
Kenya Forest Wildlife Project, 205
Kenya Great Rift Valley Conservation Project, 206
kererūs, 315
Kern National Wildlife Refuge (California, USA), 24
Kgaswane Mountain Reserve (South Africa), 227
Khao Phanom Bencha National Park (Thailand), 296
Khao Phra Thaew National Park (Thailand), 303
Khlong Lan National Park (Thailand), 297
Kilauea Point National Wildlife Refuge (Hawaii, USA), 45
killer whales, 13, 247
Kilombero Valley (Tanzania), 250
king cobras, 282
kit foxes, 132
koalas, 309
Kodiak brown bears, 9
Kodiak National Wildlife Refuge (Alaska, USA), 9
kōkakos, 315, 317
Kokanee salmon, 133
Kooskia National Fish Hatchery (Idaho, USA), 49
Kootenai National Wildlife Refuge (Idaho, USA), 50
Koyukuk National Wildlife Refuge (Alaska, USA), 10
Kui Buri National Park (Thailand), 298

Lacassine National Wildlife Refuge (Louisiana, USA), 64
Laguna Atascosa National Wildlife Refuge (Texas, USA), 124
Lake Andes National Wildlife Refuge (South Dakota, USA), 117
Lake Edward (Uganda), 253
lake trout, 70
Lake Woodruff National Wildlife Refuge (Florida, USA), 40
Lakonikos Bay (Greece), 262
Langosta Beach (Costa Rica), 180
languars, 295
Laos, 285–86
large mouth bass, 108
Las Baulas National Park (Costa Rica), 180
laughing gulls, 63, 128
Laysan albatross, 45
leatherback turtles
Asia, 304
Leatherbacks of Panama Project, 190–91
North America, 43
South America, 175, 179, 180, 189
lemurs
Africa, 212
Lemurs of Madagascar, 210
North America, 44
leopards
Africa, 200, 213, 219, 220, 223, 232, 235, 239, 248, 249, 250
Asia, 295, 301
Namibia Leopard and Cheetah Conservation Program, 218
North America, 34
Sri Lanka Leopard Conservation Program, 290
See also specific leopards
lesser kestrels, 287
lesser sandhill cranes
North America, 89
See also sandhill cranes
Ligurian Sea Dolphin and Whale Project (Italy), 266
lions
Africa, 206, 219, 220, 223, 229, 232, 233, 235, 241, 244, 250
Antelope Park Lion Breeding and Rehabilitation Project (Zimbabwe), 254–55
Lion Adventure Program (South Africa), 234
North America, 34, 127
Little Pend Oreille National Wildlife Refuge (Washington, USA), 139
Liwonde National Park (Malawi), 213
lizards
Australia, 317
See also specific lizards

PHOTO CREDITS

Pages 3, 4: Donna Dewhurst/USFWS
Page 5: Art Sowls/USFWS
Page 6: Craig Koppie/USFWS
Page 7: Mike Boylan/USFWS
Page 8: Jon R. Nickles/USFWS
Page 9: Dave Menke/USFWS
Page 10: Karen Laubenstein/USFWS
Page 11: Lisa Haggblom/USFWS
Page 12: Kevin Bell/USFWS
Page 13: Glen Smart/USFWS
Page 14: USFWS
Page 16: Donna Dewhurst/USFWS
Page 17: USFWS
Page 18: Gary Stolz/USFWS
Page 19: Dave Menke/USFWS
Page 20: Gary Stolz/USFWS
Page 21: Ken Stansell/USFWS
Page 22: Phil Million/USFWS
Page 23, 24: Dave Menke/USFWS
Page 26: Beth Jackson/USFWS
Page 27: Lee Karney/USFWS
Page 28: USFWS
Page 30: Dave Menke/USFWS
Page 31: Tim Bowman/USFWS
Page 32: Eric Engbretson/USFWS
Page 33: Gary Stolz/USFWS
Page 34: John and Karen Hollingsworth/USFWS
Page 35: Lee Karney/USFWS
Page 36: Doug Perrine/USFWS
Page 37: Jim Reid/USFWS
Page 39, 42: George Gentry/USFWS
Page 43: Michael Lusk/USFW
Page 44: John and Karen Hollingsworth/USFWS
Page 45: Michael Lusk/USFWS
Page 46: USFWS
Page 47: Lee Karney/USFWS
Page 48: Dave Menke/USFWS

Page 50: Jim Leupold/USFWS
Page 52: USFWS
Page 53: Dave Menke/USFWS
Page 55: Ronald Laubenstein/USFWS
Page 56: Jim Leupold/USFWS
Page 58: Dick Bailey/USFWS
Page 60: John and Karen Hollingsworth/USFWS
Page 62: Ryan Haggerty/USFWS
Page 63: Donna Dewhurst/USFWS
Page 64: Gary Stolz/USFWS
Page 67: USFWS
Page 68: Gene Nieminen/USFWS
Page 71: USFWS
Page 72: Steve Maslowski/USFWS
Page 73: Bill West/USFWS
Page 77: Eugene Hester/USFWS
Page 78: Jim Leupold/USFWS
Page 79: USFWS
Page 80: Ryan Haggerty/USFWS
Page 83: Beth Jackson/USFWS
Page 84: USFWS
Page 85: Gary Zahm/USFWS
Page 86: Elaine Rhode/USFWS
Page 87: Ryan Haggerty/USFWS
Page 89: William Vinge/USFWS
Page 93: Gene Nieminen/USFWS
Page 95: Curtis Carley/USFWS
Page 96: John and Karen Hollingsworth/USFWS
Page 97: Tim McCabe/USFWS
Page 98: Tim Bowman/USFWS
Page 99: John Foster/USFWS
Page 101: USFWS
Page 102: Lee Karney/USFWS
Page 103: Ashton Graham/USFWS
Page 104: Jim Leupold/USFWS
Page 106: Gary Stolz/USFWS
Page 107: Dr. Thomas Barnes/USFWS

Page 111: Lee Karney/USFWS
Page 118: Donna Dewhurst/USFWS
Page 121: Allen Montgomery/USFWS
Page 127: Ken Stansell/USFWS
Page 129: John and Karen Hollingsworth/USFWS
Page 132: B. Peterson/USFWS
Page 142: Robert Karges II/USFWS
Page 145: USFWS
Page 152: OAR/NURP
Page 154: Dr. James McVey/NOAA
Page 157: Gary Stolz/USFWS
Page 158: NOAA/NGS/Sean Linehan
Page 159: NOAA
Page 160: Gary Stolz/USFWS
Page 165: John and Karen Hollingsworth/USFWS
Page 166: OAR/NURP/NOAA
Page 168: Gary Stolz/USFWS
Page 174: NOAA/Florida Keys National Marine Sanctuary
Page 177: Dr. Dwayne Meadows/NOAA/NMFS/OPR
Page 180: NPS/NOAA
Page 185: Rosalind Cohen/NODC/NOAA
Page 189: Dr. Dwayne Meadows/NOAA/NMFS/OPR
Page 190: NPS/NOAA
Page 195: James McVey/NOAA
Pages 199, 200, 202: Wildlife Pictures Online
Page 204: NOAA/Commander Grady Tuell
Pages 205, 206: Wildlife Pictures Online
Page 207: pdphoto.org
Page 208: NOAA/Commander Grady Tuell
Page 209: Wildlife Pictures Online
Page 210: pdphoto.org
Page 211: Dr. Aleksey Zuyev/NOAA
Page 213: Wildlife Pictures Online
Page 214: Dr. Dwayne Meadows/NOAA/NMFS/OPR
Page 215: NOAA
Pages 216, 217, 218, 219, 221: Wildlife Pictures Online

Page 222: Dr. James P. McVey/NOAA
Page 223: Wildlife Pictures Online
Page 224: animalpicturesarchive.com
Page 226: Wildlife Pictures Online
Page 228: NOAA/Lieutenant Philip Hall
Pages 229, 230, 231, 232, 233, 234, 325, 236: Wildlife Pictures Online
Page 237: Michael Van Woert/NOAA Nesdis, ORA
Page 238: NOAA/Lieutenant Philip Hall
Pages 239, 240: Wildlife Pictures Online
Pages 241, 242, 243: pdphoto.org
Page 244, 245, 246: Wildlife Pictures Online
Page 247: NOAA
Pages 248, 249, 250: Wildlife Pictures Online
Page 251: OAR/NURP/NOAA
Page 253: NOAA
Page 255: Wildlife Pictures Online
Page 261: James O'Clock/NOAA
Page 263: USFWS
Page 264: Liz Labunski/USFWS
Page 265: Frank Ruopoli/NOAA
Page 267: Steve Hillebrand/USFWS
Page 268: Dan Shapiro/NOAA
Page 270: Karen Laubenstein/USFWS
Page 274: USFWS
Page 275: Anne Morkill/USFWS
Page 281: USFWS
Page 286: Wildlife Pictures Online
Page 303: junglewalk.com
Page 304: NOAA/Florida Keys National Marine Sanctuary
Page 305: Dr. James McVey/NOAA
Page 310: NOAA/National Geophysical Data Center
Page 311: easystockphotos.com
Page 312: David Burdick/NOAA

All other photos are in the public domain.